THE SERVANT
ECONOMY

Also by Jeff Faux

New Hope for the Inner City
The Star-Spangled Hustle (with A. Blaustein)
Rebuilding America (with G. Alperovitz)
Reclaiming Prosperity (with T. Schafer)
The Party's Not Over
The Global Class War

THE SERVANT ECONOMY

Where America's Elite Is Sending the Middle Class

Jeff Faux

John Wiley & Sons, Inc.

To my wife, Marge,
helpmate and soul mate

Published by John Wiley & Sons, Inc., Hoboken, New Jersey
Published simultaneously in Canada

For general information about our other products and services, please contact our Customer Care Department within the United States at (800) 762-2974, outside the United States at (317) 572-3993 or fax (317) 572-4002.

Wiley also publishes its books in a variety of electronic formats and by print-on-demand. Some content that appears in standard print versions of this book may not be available in other formats. For more information about Wiley products, visit us at www.wiley.com.

Library of Congress Cataloging-in-Publication Data:
Faux, Geoffrey P.
   The servant economy: where America's elite is sending the middle class/Jeff Faux.
      pages cm
   Includes bibliographical references and index.
   ISBN 978-0-470-18239-0 (cloth);   ISBN 978-1-118-22011-5 (ebk);
   ISBN 978-1-118-23386-3 (ebk);   ISBN 978-1-118-25848-4 (ebk)
  1. United States–Economic policy–2009   2. United States–Economic
conditions–2009   3. Middle class–United States–Economic conditions.   I. Title.

  HC106.84.F38 2012

  330.973–dc23

                             2012013719

Printed in the United States of America

10 9 8 7 6 5 4 3 2 1

Contents

Part I

The Pursuit of Folly

The future ain't what it used to be.

—Yogi Berra

1

The Politics of Hope

Historians who look back to our time will surely conclude that our problem was not that we didn't know where we were headed, it was that we didn't act on what we knew.

Even before the financial crash of 2008–2009 and the Great Recession that followed, there was ample warning. Whether you were a journalist who produced the news, a politician who made the news, or a citizen who read or watched the news, it was hard not be aware that for the past thirty years, the following had been happening:

- Most Americans had experienced stagnant real incomes, shrinking financial security, and fraying social safety nets.
- The nation had been buying more from the rest of the world than it had been selling and was borrowing to finance the difference.
- Despite the erosion of U.S. economic power, the governing class—Democrats and Republicans alike—insisted on maintaining its global hegemony, whatever the cost.

Sweeping historical analogies between the present-day United States and the decline and fall of earlier empires, once the subject of rarified university seminars, had been seeping into public consciousness for the previous three decades. Yale historian Paul

3

Kennedy's best-selling book, *The Rise and Fall of the Great Powers*, revived grand theories of the natural life cycles of empires that had been proposed earlier in the twentieth century by German philosopher Oswald Spengler and British historian Arnold Toynbee. Looking at the erosion of U.S. leadership in technology and trade competitiveness, Kennedy suggested that the United States might be headed for the same fate as past superpowers that had collapsed because their political ambitions had expanded beyond their economic bases.[1] His book spawned an academic cottage industry that fondled the historical analogies: Were we Rome in the fourth century? Spain in the sixteenth century? England at the beginning of the twentieth century?

Kennedy's book also spawned an even larger industry of politicians, pundits, and academics who flatly rejected the notion that anyone could hear the bells of history tolling the end of America's time in the sun. Indeed, the neoconservative academic Francis Fukuyama responded that the bell was tolling for history itself: the United States had already achieved the best possible society in an imperfect world. Fukuyama later backed off, but his thesis remains the operating assumption of the U.S. governing class.

Still, throughout the giddy years of the successive stock market and real estate booms, Kennedy's analysis touched an undercurrent of economic anxiety among traditionally optimistic middle-class Americans, who were increasingly aware that more of their shoes, underwear, televisions, automobiles, and computers were being made in China, Korea, and Mexico. A stream of books, news articles, and websites pumped out the accumulating statistics of working Americans' financial stress. Plots about lousy jobs, layoffs, and maxed-out credit cards popped up in TV sitcoms, Hollywood movies, and popular music. In his 1992 campaign for president Bill Clinton observed in television advertisements that Americans were "working harder for less." Fifteen years later, at the peak of the financial bubble, the numbers showed that they still were.

The United States remains rich in industrious and adaptable people, stable political institutions, a widespread commitment to material progress, and more than its share of the planet's natural assets, but it is no longer rich enough to continue to finance America's three principal national dreams:

1. The dream of the business elite for subsidized, unregulated capitalism
2. The dream of the political elite for global hegemony
3. The dream of the people for a steadily rising standard of living

We can certainly continue to have one out of three, and perhaps even two out of three. But, three out of three? No.

Nevertheless, the end-of-empire story has limited appeal for the U.S. governing class: the politicians, the media pundits, and the policy managers who move through revolving doors to and from investment banks, global corporations, universities, think tanks, and high-level government jobs.[2] Of course they admitted that the country had problems; indeed, it was their job to solve them. But the suggestion that the United States might no longer be able to have it *all* was not very useful for ambitious leaders whose careers depended on their ability to project self-confidence. Nor was it useful for their wealthy patrons who valued the prices of the futures in their global portfolios more than the future of their country.

Acknowledging these limits is dangerous territory for them. If the market is no longer delivering the prosperity promised the citizen in the American dream, then the political system bears more responsibility than our leaders want to admit for the relentless redistribution of income and wealth from the bottom and the middle of the pyramid to the top. Most dangerous of all, such an acknowledgment encourages discussion about who our political representatives actually represent. The Democrats are no more eager to have this conversation than the Republicans are.

Ronald Reagan's election, like Franklin Roosevelt's half a century earlier, profoundly changed the way that Americans think collectively about the future.

The stock market crash of 1929 and the Great Depression that followed thoroughly discredited the system of unregulated financial speculation that had driven the country and the world to its economic knees. In response, the New Deal not only expanded the role of government in managing the market and protecting the public from the hard edges of laissez-faire, it also established a presumption of collective responsibility for the future. The New Deal restored the earlier idea of internal development as a conscious national enterprise, which had been lost in the late nineteenth century when industrialization morphed into finance capitalism and the westward expansion morphed into the thirst for overseas empire.

Roosevelt understood that investment is *the* future-shaping act. The government financed dams, rural electrification, schools, roads and bridges, agricultural research, parks, and conservation and urban renewal projects and connected these infrastructure needs of the future to the immediate need to create jobs. Social Security, unemployment compensation, and other social insurance programs reflected a political ethos of taking shared responsibility for tomorrow. The United States would remain a private market economy, but be guided by shared public goals.

The age of Roosevelt lasted almost fifty years as the framework by which the governing class managed the nation's economy, under Republicans as well as Democrats. Dwight Eisenhower and Richard Nixon actually expanded Democratic initiatives for federal investment in housing, highways, education, environmental protection, and the alleviation of poverty. The exploration of space was perhaps the most vivid example of the national commitment to the future regardless of which party was in power. Both Republican administrations strengthened the capacity of the federal government to anticipate and plan ahead just as the Democratic administrations did.

All that ended with the age of Reagan, in which we still live. By demonizing, downsizing, and demoralizing civilian government—calling it the problem and not the solution—Reagan and his successors destroyed not only its capacity to plan but also its capacity to react to signals of trouble ahead. With the market in charge, no one is responsible. "You're doing a heck of a job, Brownie," George W. Bush said to Michael Brown, the bumbling head of the Federal Emergency Management Agency who was supposed to be handling the flooding of New Orleans after Hurricane Katrina in 2005. Bush's mindless remark reflected the casual, amateurish way in which the governing class had come to treat public service.

The Democrats ridiculed Reagan, but the next generation of liberals, the "neoliberals," followed his lead. Bill Clinton, who deregulated trade, privatized government, and lifted the New Deal protections against destructive Wall Street speculation, declared during his State of the Union Address in 1996: "The era of big government is over."

The smart Clinton, fast on his ideological feet, rode to reelection defending Social Security, Medicare, and environmental protection from the bumbling Republicans. But Reagan's strategic instinct had been intellectually sounder. Having captured the *context* of politics, it was only a matter of time before conservatives would take over the *content* as well. The future fell into their hands. With each turn of the global economic screw, the country looked farther to the right, and the Republican Party pushed beyond Reaganomics to the populist nihilism of the Tea Party.

The dismantling of the New Deal also profoundly affected the way in which the private corporate sector treated the future. Time itself became increasingly monetized as deregulation dramatically shortened the horizons of U.S. business. Banks and investment houses were once again free to use the nation's money to chase short-term speculative profits. The idea that had emerged after World War II—that corporations were social institutions, responsible to their employees, suppliers, surrounding communities, and other stakeholders—not just the owners of the corporation's stock—faded. Management was now judged solely by the quarterly bottom line it delivered to the shareholders of record, who would most likely be different by the next quarter. Leveraged buyouts became the dominant business model: companies were bought with other people's money, stripped of their assets, and sold off in pieces.

American conservatism had traditionally been a severe philosophy, built on the assumption of a dog-eat-dog competition in which most people will be losers. Reagan returned the portrait of Calvin Coolidge to the White House, along with Coolidge's laissez-faire faith. But Reagan understood that after Roosevelt, most Americans were not ready to abandon their fate to the cold dictates of the free market. So the economics of the dour Coolidge had to be repackaged. Enter the politics of hope.

In the watershed election of 1980, Jimmy Carter, who came on like an Old Testament prophet demanding sacrifice and hard work, was the perfect foil for Reagan, the upbeat, piety-with-a-wink materialist who promised Hollywood happy endings. The next generation of Democrats got the point. Clinton was the man from Hope. Barack Obama's book proclaimed himself fit to be president because he had the "audacity" to have hope.

Hope is not a strategy. In the absence of a collective effort to shape the future, the individual must now guess where the unpredictable market—the labor market, the stock market, the real estate market—is headed. Prognostication has replaced planning, and everyone goes to the fortune-teller who predicts money, love, and long life.

Personal optimism is a well-recognized American trait. "Wait till next year," "Tomorrow is another day," "If at first you don't succeed, try, try again," and a thousand similar phrases resonate in our cultural surround sound from the cradle to the grave. As Nellie Forbush, the heroine of the 1949 Broadway musical *South Pacific*, sang, this is the land of "cock-eyed optimists." Foreign visitors are commonly surprised that when they attempt to answer truthfully the ritual greeting "How are you?," the average American reacts with surprise and some distaste. The expected answer is "Great," "Fine," or "Wonderful, how are *you* doing?" Recently, the Republican governor of South Carolina—a state with an unemployment rate of more than 11 percent—instructed state employees to greet everyone with "It's a great day in South Carolina. How can I help you?" When the French writer Simone de Beauvoir described her visit to the United States, she reported seeing a sign in a drugstore that read NOT TO GRIN IS A SIN.[3]

Nevertheless, millions of us suffer clinical depression, and we are by far the world's largest consumers of antidepressants. Every week or so, another one of us goes berserk and murders coworkers, family members, or perfect strangers. But these people are considered so marginal and insignificant that we cannot bring ourselves to limit their freedom of access to guns. In global surveys of happiness, however defined, the United States ranks nowhere near the top in any of them.[4]

Yet, no matter how many of its people might be leading internal lives of quiet desperation, outwardly the United States is still the land of the happy face.

Faith in the future has been an enormous national asset. It inspired immigrants to cross the sea in stinking ships and pioneers to cross the continent in rickety wagons. Optimism built the great industrial and financial enterprises that made the country the world's preeminent power. It motivated people to invest against all odds in restaurants, hi-tech start-ups, and initial public offerings that were issued by companies they'd never heard of and labeled "junk bonds." Optimism nurtured George Washington at Valley Forge and Abraham Lincoln in the darkest days of the Civil War. It was Roosevelt's trump card against the Depression. It stiffened the resolve of labor leader Eugene Debs in an Atlanta prison and Martin Luther King Jr. in a Birmingham jail. It sustained the suffragist when prison guards pumped a force-feeding tube down her throat.

Optimism has also had its liabilities, collective blind spots of complacency that ultimately produced recessions, depressions, and financial collapses; the dead and maimed of Vietnam, Iraq, and Afghanistan; and bodies floating in the streets of New Orleans.

Continuing your patterns of behavior in the face of evidence that you will end up badly is a well-known psychological construct. Cognitive dissonance, in which people feel discomfort when they hold conflicting ideas simultaneously, can sometimes be a variant of this. Denial of what is objectively apparent is another. Psychologists have catalogued numerous ways in which people would rather hunker down in their present dysfunctional jobs, relationships, or lifestyles that are leading to personal disaster than risk the discomfort and uncertainty that come with taking responsibility for their futures. The enabling wife or husband of an alcoholic or the cheating spouse is a stock character in our popular melodramas.

In her book, *Never Saw It Coming: Cultural Challenges to Envisioning the Worst*, sociologist Karen Cerulo reported that although most people can conjure up a detailed picture of what they'd like their futures to be, they have trouble specifying negative scenarios.

When subjects are asked what the best thing is that could happen to them, their answers are precise: get married, win the lottery, be a professional basketball player. But when they are asked what is the worst thing that can happen to them, their vision clouds up: "Maybe death?"

Despite the fact that one out of two American marriages ends in divorce, Cerulo reported, 64 percent of married Americans say they are "very happy," and another 33 percent say they are "pretty happy." Only 2 percent of newlyweds have a prenuptial agreement to make divorce easier if something goes wrong.

This individual predilection for projecting a rose-colored future, what Cerulo called "positive asymmetry," can become a collective blind spot, "obscured or blurred by a variety of routine and patterned sociocultural practice—practice that despite a single individual's intention can veil the worst and make it difficult to define."[5]

There also seems to be a gap between what we think might happen to the world around us and what we think might happen to ourselves personally. This helps to explain the appeal, in the midst of our personal optimism, of the dark view of the future in our entertainment culture. For a society that constantly promotes optimism, we are surprisingly addicted to depictions of dystopian futures. Movies like *Soylent Green*, *Blade Runner*, *Children of War*, and books like *1984*, *Brave New World*, *Fahrenheit 451*, and *The Handmaid's Tale* speak to our fears of where society is headed and provide the details that are so hard for us to imagine.

Because these projections of our fears are fictitious, we can seal ourselves off from the truly frightening implication that we might bear some responsibility for our collective future. Thus, for example, the evidence of global warming often gets stuck in a catch-22. The science tends to be dry and abstract for most people, but attempts to make the consequences of climate change vivid with depictions of floods, droughts, and other large-scale catastrophes seem like a familiar tale from dystopian science fiction and are easily dismissed.

Novelist Benjamin Kunkel noted that most of these apocalyptic narratives reinforce the soothing notion that individual survival is compatible with social collapse. The heroes and heroines resolve their entrapment in the nightmare future society by escaping, not by political resistance. Kunkel observed that this type of story "tends to reflect the default creed of neo-liberalism, according to which kindness may flourish in private life but the outside world remains now and forever a scene of vicious but inevitable competition."[6] Survival depends on the individual's own talent and virtue.

Social critic Barbara Ehrenreich wrote her book *Bright-Sided: How Positive Thinking Is Undermining America* after her encounter with the demand that she exercise cheerful denial as a response to her cancer. It led her to examine how the positive-thinking industry has gone from publishing self-improvement books and training salespeople to smile even when they don't feel like it to a loosely constructed system of social engineering that distracts and discourages Americans from dealing with what is happening to their society.[7]

Thus, when the economy crashes, the unemployed are instructed to look to themselves for survival. Along with handing out the pink slips, corporate personnel departments provide motivational speakers for those being tossed out on the street. The message is to not waste energy on anger at the company, the economy, or the country's leaders. Instead, concentrate on the more practical task of beating the hundreds of others who are lined up to apply for a handful of jobs. It has never been easier to find work, wrote the upbeat pundit Thomas Friedman of the *New York Times*, "for those prepared for this world—to invent a job or find a customer. Anyone with the spark of an idea can start a company overnight, using a credit card, while accessing brains, brawn and customers anywhere."[8]

Behind Friedman's cheery optimism is the widely shared assumption that the United States is the world's foremost land of upward mobility. The distribution of income and wealth may be more unequal here, goes the story, but it is more than made up for by the opportunity for the poor to rise up the social ladder, and, yes, for the rich to fall down. Therefore, the story continues, the notion of economic class has much less meaning in the United States than it has in countries at similar levels of development where the welfare state and high taxation crush incentives to better oneself.

There is perhaps no single assumption about the United States that is so widely shared by its citizens, its leaders, and much of the rest of the world. And it is perhaps the principal reason why high levels of inequality and the persistence of abject poverty are so tolerated by the U.S. electorate as an unfortunate but necessary price to pay for our meritocracy.

Yet, what evidence we have suggests that this assumption of greater mobility is not true. Virtually every credible recent study comparing economic mobility among advanced nations shows that the incidence of children moving out of the income class of their parents is greater in western Europe and Canada than it is in the United States. One 2006 review of over fifty such studies covering nine countries found Canada, Norway, Finland, and Denmark were the most mobile; Sweden, Germany, and France were in the middle. The United States and Britain were the countries where moving out of one's class was least likely. Mobility, as it turns out, is correlated with more equality and less poverty.[9]

Given the persistent myth of their country's superior social mobility, and the assumption that it is a product of greater economic freedom, it comes as no surprise that so many Americans say that politics is irrelevant to their lives. Voter turnout is famously low. For many who do go to the polls, which candidate actually wins the election is a matter of indifference; their voting is a social rather than a political act, and elections themselves are like sporting contests or reality shows. That the popularity of a candidate almost always surges after he or she wins an election reinforces the point. Shouting protesters make good visuals for the nightly news, but they represent a tiny share of the electorate. Most Americans go through their lives without participating in a political demonstration.

"Where is the outrage?" asked the bloggers, columnists, and political activists as the economy dragged into the third year of high rates of joblessness, heartbreaking foreclosures, and grim prospects. Pollsters also had many answers: The people were ignorant of economics. They were confused by Fox News and the right-wing media. They did not trust government. All of these were true.

But the polls also revealed something else: a gap between people's perception of the nation's economic fate and their own. The same polls that reported that Americans were pessimistic about the country's future and believed that the next generation would be poorer also showed that they were optimistic about their own prospects.

What one might call the "Lake Wobegon effect" is strikingly persistent. In June 2010, for example, 71 percent of Americans reported that they were doing better than average. Their neighbors and coworkers might be in for a rough time, but they and their children would be fine. When asked by Pew Charitable Trust pollsters about the next forty years, 56 percent thought that the U.S. economy would be weaker, but 64 percent were optimistic about the prospects for themselves and their children. In a 2011 Hart poll for Citibank, 16 percent of respondents described themselves as "well off" at present, while 50 percent said they would be well-off within five to ten years. In the fall of 2011, after three years of high joblessness, a New York Times–CBS News poll reported that 54 percent of the unemployed were confident that they would soon find stable long-term employment; in the same poll, 64 percent of respondents said they expected to make more money in their next job than they made in their previous job, compared to 22 percent who disagreed. A 2011 poll by the Sun Financial Group reported that 60 percent of Americans were hopeful about the future, only 2 percentage points below the level reported just before the 2008 crash. Pew's poll reported that by a margin of 63 to 31, most respondents agreed with the statement that "although there may be bad times every now and then, America will always continue to be prosperous and make economic progress."[10]

The public's attitude reflects the message of the country's governing class. For all of the public laments about the various crises in competitiveness, indebtedness, education, and political civility, the bottom-line message from the top is: have patience. Markets will eventually recover, and nudged on by a few marginal changes in policy or a change of the party in control of Congress or the White House, you and your family will soon be back on your rightful track to perpetual prosperity.

The overwhelming evidence, however, is to the contrary. The economic problem at least 80 percent of Americans now face is not simply a severe business cycle, it is a profound and historic decline in their economic and political bargaining power. Since, as this book will also argue, the governing class is constitutionally unwilling to make the necessary concessions to restore that bargaining power, a substantial drop in living standards over the next dozen decades is predictable.

In her 1984 book, *The March of Folly: From Troy to Vietnam*, historian Barbara Tuchman described the way in which countries throughout history have come to grief because their leaders refused to act on the evidence that they were pursuing policies that would eventually lead to ruin.

Folly is not stupidity. To qualify as one of Tuchman's examples, a policy had to have been clearly seen as a mistake "in its own time," not just in hindsight. The decisions were not based simply on current information that turned out wrong, nor were they well-intentioned errors whose consequences could not have been foretold. The rulers in her stories had ample warning that the policy path they were taking their people down was "wooden-headed," a metaphor Tuchman took from the legend of the Trojan horse, the prototypical story of political self-deception.

"Wooden-headedness," she wrote, "consists in assessing a situation in terms of preconceived fixed notions while ignoring or rejecting any contrary signs. It is acting according to wish while not allowing oneself to be deflated by the facts."[11]

As examples, Tuchman presented the Renaissance popes who lost half of Christendom for the Catholic Church; the Aztec king Montezuma, who gave away his empire to the Spanish conquistador Hernando Cortez; King George III of England, who provoked the American Revolution; King Philip of Spain, who destroyed his navy in an effort to invade Britain; the World War I German general staff's U-boat campaign against U.S. ships; Napoleon and Hitler, who each foolishly invaded Russia; the Japanese bombing of Pearl Harbor; and the three U.S. presidents who committed their nation to the Vietnam War.

The future is, of course, unknowable, and prediction is always a matter of probabilities. History, like life, is marked by unexpected turns. Black swans, to use author Nassim Nicholas Taleb's metaphor for the unforeseen, fly in undetected by our best radar. But major dislocating events that could not have been foretold are rarer than we commonly acknowledge.

It's true that plenty of forecasted disasters never occurred. An old joke has it that economists have predicted five out of the last three recessions. So judgment is required. But before you can make a judgment, you have to pay attention. Paddling into a strong current and accelerating toward the sound of a waterfall does not guarantee that you and your canoe will crack up, but if you ignore the evidence, that is certainly the most likely outcome.

Denying the evidence in front of your nose leads to what Max Bazerman, a business school professor, and Michael Watkins, a business consultant, have usefully called "predictable surprises." Bazerman and Watkins identified a variety of individual traits—"positive illusions, egocentrism, discounting the future, omission bias [e.g., first do no harm], the desire to maintain the status quo, and inattention to data that is not vivid"—that seem to be hardwired in individuals. Other predictable surprises are common organizational failures such as mismatched incentives, information overload, secrecy, and loss of collective memory.[12]

In the cases cited by both Tuchman and Bazerman and Watkins, kings, popes, presidents, and corporate CEOs were surrounded by circles of advisers who made persuasive arguments in favor of ignoring the evidence. The present cost of changing course was just too great. Typically, the costs would be paid by those at the top, and advocating a level of change to match the level of the danger ahead was too risky for one's career. It was better, these men thought, to trust that the future cost of not changing course would be mitigated by the exceptional virtue, strength, and destiny of those in charge. History and common sense did not apply to them; they were "exceptional."

The widespread belief among Americans that our country is "exceptional" is not unique. All countries, like all human beings, are exceptional in the sense of being different from one another. When you peel away the unworldliness of the most sophisticated Britons, Russians, Chinese, or Brazilians, you find a patriotic devotion to their native culture. It is the rare mother who does not think that her child is exceptional in a way that translates into "better." Similarly, it is common for citizens to think that their particular culture is better in some sense than others.

But the assumption of two-hundred-plus years of success intoxicates, and it will take a while to sober up. In 2011, the third year of the global recession, the PEW Research Center polled public attitudes in the United States, Germany, Britain, France, and Spain. Only in the United States did a majority agree with the statement "Our people are not perfect, but our culture is superior to others'." Even the notoriously proud French were only half as convinced of their exceptional culture as Americans were.[13]

It is therefore not surprising that members of the U.S. governing class assume that their rise to the top of the global hierarchy is the result of their nation's—and therefore its leaders'—inherent superiority. The assumption of exceptionalism relieves our governing class from having to learn the lessons of history. Every episode of our country's expansion—from the ethnic cleansing of Native Americans to the invasion of Iraq—has been accompanied by the confidence that success was certain because of our moral virtue. When a journalist asked President Kennedy how he expected to conquer Vietnam when the French army—which included the world-class soldiers of the Foreign Legion—had failed, Kennedy replied that "that was the French. They were fighting for a colony, for an ignoble cause. We're fighting for freedom, to free them from the Communists, from China, for their independence." He forgot, noted Tuchman, that like the French, the Americans were white.[14]

As then Secretary of State Madeleine Albright proclaimed on the *Today* show on February 19, 1998, "If we have to use force, it is because we are America. We are the indispensable nation. We stand tall, and we see further into the future."

History, as the adage says, is written by the victors. George Orwell famously stated, "He who controls the present controls the past. He who controls the past controls the future."[15] This is a point we normally think of as referring to the ability of conquerors to justify and immortalize their victories. But it also applies to the way the "winning" generations think about past losers. From the perspective of the former, the price, however steep, paid by the latter were clearly worth it. We in the succeeding generations take for granted that the pain and suffering of those who went before us justifies our happiness.

Scolding those who worry about the country's prospects, John Podhoretz, editor of *Commentary Magazine*, told a conservative business audience in the fall of 2011 that the country's past is ample proof of its future success. "The amazing durability of the American system over 235 years is the primary reason for optimism about the American future."[16]

But what do we mean when we speak of "America's" future? Having expropriated the term "America" from the rest of the Western Hemisphere, we, of course, mean the United States. But the way we think and talk about this United States of America confuses the variety of possible meanings and obscures the differences in the time frames in which the somewhat abstract nation-state and the people that inhabit it live.

The United States as a country will obviously survive most any conceivable economic hard times. It will continue to be a—but not the only—military super power for as far into the future as we can see. As long as we intervene in the political life of others we will experience sporadic 9/11-type attacks, but there will be no threat of occupation by any outside force, including China, for perhaps hundreds of years.

Given its level of development and size, even as its relative rankings decline, the United States will continue to have one of the world's largest economies. The disconnect between the interests of the nation's citizens and its economic elite will accelerate the decline, but the process will occur over decades. It took more than three centuries for Rome to fall, and a century for the British to drop to the second tier of world powers. In any practical sense, the United States is immortal.

Although not quite as secure, the largest concentrations of wealth held by Americans also have a sort of immortality that is the special privilege bestowed on the corporation by the state. Individual corporations can die from bad luck and incompetence or a reorganization of investors' portfolios. But adequately managed, the wealth moves from one protected corporate nest to another—deathless as long as its special status is indulged by society.

"In the long run," John Maynard Keynes famously said, "we are all dead." But living off large privileged stores of capital, most members of the governing classes are protected on the downside from the natural capitalist cycles of boom and bust. Recessions, even depressions and other economic calamities, are not typically life-threatening. As the crash of 2008 taught us once more, money may be lost, CEOs may be forced to retire early, and some assets might have to be sold, but those who drove the economy off the cliff did not end up sleeping on park benches. Three years later, Wall Street profits and bonuses were at or exceeding precrash levels.

The interpretation of the past, upon which much of the optimism for the future is based, also blurs the difference between the life of *America* and the lives of *Americans*. Ordinary citizens live in shorter, more fragile time frames. The damage from being out of work for six months, losing your house and/or your marriage, not being able to afford an operation, or having to drop out of college is never made up over a lifetime. The call for patience and shared sacrifice for the future has costs for the governed that those who govern typically never face.

Thus, a *Forbes* magazine writer takes a group of Americans to task for their creeping pessimism "We are longer-lived and with access to more knowledge and experiences than any king or pope who has come before, nevermind the lives of the countless billions whose ordinary tragedies are collectively called 'history.' This much luck should make us hug ourselves with delight."

Furthermore, he argues, "Having slipped catastrophes like the 1914–1945 worldwide conflicts (with 100 million dead), or the nuclear threat of the 44 cold war years that followed, there are also reasonable grounds to believe we can work out our problems. The daily advances in science and technology lend hope that on balance things can be even better."[17]

Unfortunately for them, the nineteen-year-olds whose futures were blown to pieces at Verdun, Iwo Jima, or Khe Sanh; the young immigrant women incinerated in the Triangle Shirtwaist Factory fire; and the kidnapped slaves from Africa worked to death on cotton plantations did not "slip the catastrophes" of history. We cannot ask them if their sacrifices were worth it. If we could, it is unlikely that most of them would have volunteered to die or suffer in order to produce our world. People will sacrifice—though not nearly as much as our mythology teaches—for their living children or grandchildren, but hardly ever for descendants unborn, and never for someone else's unborn progeny. Not only were we not very much on the minds of earlier generations, it is also unlikely that they would have thought it fair that their sacrifices were redeemed by our shop-till-you-drop life-style. Most Americans today are certainly not ready to sacrifice so that the strangers who will be alive fifty years from now will be richer than they are.

There is obviously no way to indemnify the dead. And if one believes that sometimes, at least, sacrifices must be made for the collective good, there obviously are ways of sharing the costs and the benefits in the times of both present and future generations.

The age of Reagan greatly strengthened the class solidarity of our financial elites and therefore their ability to offload the costs of their folly onto the rest of us. Whether the folly was an unnecessary war, the bursting of a financial bubble, or an environmental disaster, our culture of optimism has been generous and forgiving to those at the top. The governing class prefers not to dwell on its past mistakes; rather, it urges us to move on to a better tomorrow. Lieutenant William Calley got a life sentence for the massacre at My Lai. Private Lynndie England was sent to prison for mistreating captured Iraqi soldiers at Abu Ghraib. Defense secretary Robert McNamara and deputy defense secretary Paul Wolfowitz both moved on to the presidency of the World Bank.

The United States of America has had its share of fools at its helm. It has also had its share of farsighted leaders who shaped the nation's future. The Constitution—with its separation of powers, its Bill of Rights to protect us from tyranny, and the rest of the amendments to correct and reform—provided the framework within which democratic politics could evolve. The great public accomplishments that have expanded the freedom of Americans to pursue their private destinies include the Louisiana Purchase; the public school system; the national investment in canals, roads, railroads, and aviation; Lincoln's defense of the Union; the Homestead Act; women's suffrage, Social Security, the G.I. Bill, and the Civil Rights Act.

Today, these outcomes are treated as inevitable consequences of the country's exceptional virtues: our pluck, our luck, and (to some) our role as an instrument of God's plan. But success was not preordained, and in the context of the time in which each of these struggles was fought, the outcome could have gone the other way. Looking back half a century, the defeat of Germany in World War II appears inevitable. But on the eve of the invasion of Normandy, General Eisenhower drafted two messages: one announcing that the Allies had attained a foothold on the French coast, and one announcing that they had been driven back into the English Channel.[18]

Tuchman, the chronicler of folly, greatly admired the U.S. Founding Fathers for the institutions they designed and their political skill in bringing them to life. "Never before or since has so much careful and reasonable thinking been invested in the formation of a governmental system," she wrote. "For two centuries that American arrangement has always managed to right itself under pressure without discarding the system and trying another after every crisis, as have Italy and Germany, France and Spain."[19]

She also recognized that the Founding Fathers' success rested on some unique conditions that buffered the United States from the dangers of her European parents. "Social systems can survive a good deal of folly when circumstances are historically favorable, or when bungling is cushioned by large resources or absorbed by sheer size as in the United States during its period of expansion. Today, when there are no more cushions, folly is less affordable."[20]

2

A Brief History of
America's Cushion

B arbara Tuchman's admiration for the architects of our republic was well-placed. They designed the world's most successful political charter. It's true that they made some big errors; their compromise on slavery, for instance, had to be corrected by the deadliest war in our history. But however qualified, the basic assumptions of equality in the Declaration of Independence and of democracy in the Constitution built a foundation that shaped more than two centuries of economic growth, creating a huge cushion that protected the middle class from the various follies of their political leaders.

The explanation of how that cushion was created is an ideological battleground: Free markets versus government investments. Anglo-Saxon culture versus immigrant energies. Genius inventors versus our ability to exploit others' inventions. Great managers versus industrious workers. Religious values versus secular materialism. Democratic institutions versus private undemocratic corporations. And so on.

There was, of course, not just one factor or even one set of factors. In a review of the question of why some nations are rich and others poor, economist Jeff Madrick wisely observes that economic growth "is not a simple box into which one places inputs, such as capital and inventions, and out of which emanate rising incomes."[1] It is an organic process in which humans, their ideology, and their natural environment interact over time in ways that even the most sophisticated social science model cannot capture.

Whatever you think best explains the rise of the United States from a collection of small colonies clinging to a thin strip of territory on the east coast of North America to the world's economic and military superpower, it is clear that the geography itself was an essential ingredient: the Atlantic Ocean to the east and almost three million square miles of sparsely inhabited land to the west, which included a disproportionate share of the world's most productive agricultural land.

The vast "moat" of the Atlantic, which in those days required several months to cross, permitted the thirteen colonies to break free from the crippling rule of Britain in a way that an even more oppressed Ireland, for example, could not. Although the British army was able to sack and burn Washington in 1812, the difficulty of transporting and supplying armies across the Atlantic was just too great for England to sustain the military effort to bring the colonies back to heel. After that, the saltwater buffer permitted the United States to expand without interference from Europe's stronger powers. Had an ocean not separated France from the Louisiana Territory, it is unlikely that Napoleon Bonaparte would have sold that tract of land to Thomas Jefferson. The crafty emperor knew that sooner or later the Americans would seize it by force. The Atlantic was too big a hurdle for his armies, however formidable they might be in Europe.

The water to the east protected the infant nation from threats from Europe. The land to the west protected the colonial elite from domestic class conflict. Plentiful cheap land was both a source of growth and a release valve for the political pressures that inevitably built up in a growing population of ambitious immigrants with no ethnic loyalty to the ruling elites.

The territory to the west became the cornerstone of the U.S. social contract. It provided land for farmers, investment opportunities for capitalists, and relatively high wages for workers. The land was cheap, but agricultural labor was a scarce resource. Thus, relative to their European cousins, American workers had more natural bargaining power with their bosses, and so their wages were higher.

In 1751, when the thirteen colonies still had only a tenuous foothold on the Atlantic coast, Benjamin Franklin described the important relationship between land and working-class incomes: "So vast is the territory of North America that it will require many ages to settle it fully; and till it is fully settled, labor will never be cheap here, where no man continues long a laborer for others and a journeyman to a trade, but goes among those new settlers, and sets up for himself."[2]

The abundance of land as a safety valve against the building up of social tensions was cited by many early observers as the reason for the absence of radicalism among American workers. In Europe, wrote the nineteenth-century French economist Michel Chevalier, a coalition of workers demanding higher pay had to threaten revolution. "But, in America, on the contrary, such a coalition means, raise our wages or we go to the West."[3]

Once they had driven the French from Canada, the British became preoccupied with wars elsewhere. They were reluctant to finance military campaigns against the Native Americans west of the Allegheny Mountains. British resistance to expansion beyond the Appalachian mountain range was a major source of discontent among the colonial elites. After independence, the leaders of the new nation quickly pushed out the indigenous population so that white settlers could develop the wilderness that stretched to the Mississippi River. With the Louisiana Purchase in 1803, the new nation doubled in size.

America's distance from Europe rationalized the protectionism that characterized U.S. trade policy for a century and a half. Both Alexander Hamilton and Thomas Jefferson, who represented opposite ideological poles among the Founding Fathers, supported protection from foreign imports. Both saw the need to expand indigenous industries in order to reduce dependence on Europe. The second bill that George Washington signed as president was to establish high tariffs, which became the federal government's chief source of revenue.

Henry Clay famously labeled high tariffs and public investment in canals, roads, and other infrastructure the "American system" of development. Later, Southern plantation owners, who wanted to trade their agricultural produce for cheaper goods from Europe, dissented. The conflict over trade became a major economic cause of the Civil War. The protectionists—led by Abraham Lincoln—won. Tariff rates rose and fell over the years, but government regulation of trade through tariffs remained a bedrock of U.S. economic policy until the end of World War II.

The Native Americans were, of course, no match against the white man's numbers, technology, or rationalizations that he had a sacred mission to civilize and Christianize the benighted heathens. The expansion to the Pacific coast was also accommodated by another piece of good luck: the military weakness of our North American neighbors.

By the mid-nineteenth century, the United States and Germany were the two most dynamic economies in the world. But German expansion was constrained and ultimately halted by the surrounding nation-states, whereas U.S. growth did not depend on taking over areas that were thickly settled and developed by ethnic groups with long histories as independent peoples. Had the Mexicans created a stronger nation-state after their own independence in 1821, they might still govern what are now California, Nevada, Utah, Arizona, New Mexico, and parts of Colorado and Wyoming. In the 1860s, had either Mexico or Canada, relative to the United States, been as strong as Britain and France were relative to Germany, they might have taken advantage of our Civil War to annex chunks of territory that now appear to have been destined to become U.S. states.

The result of this U.S. growth was the world's largest internal market facilitated by a single language, enforceable laws, and a rough social contract that could accommodate the market's growth without being seriously derailed by the social tensions generated by the relentless creative destruction of capitalism.

Social tensions certainly existed. With the introduction of the steamship, immigration accelerated, and the cities of the Northeast filled up with large numbers of non-English-speaking poor. In 1845, the country's population was roughly twenty million people. Throughout the next ten years, approximately three million immigrants arrived. Most were stuffed into vastly overcrowded city slums, where they and their children suffered brutal working conditions and a life of squalor and disease.

Howard Zinn, who told the story of the United States from the perspective of the poor and the working class, wrote, "In Philadelphia, working-class families lived fifty-five to a tenement, usually one room per family, with no garbage removal, no toilets, no fresh air or water. . . . In New York . . . filthy water drained into yards and alleys, into the cellars where the poorest of the poor lived, bringing with it a typhoid epidemic in 1837, typhus in 1842. In the cholera epidemic of 1832, the rich fled the city; the poor stayed and died."[4]

It would take a generation of assimilation—learning the language, the laws, and the culture—before most families could move out of the slums. Meanwhile, westward expansion was blocked by the insistence of the Southern aristocracy that slavery be allowed in the new states being created west of the Mississippi River.

Thus, in the two decades prior to the Civil War, the cities were simmering with working-class resentment. Virtually all of the major cities saw demonstrations, strikes, and riots. In 1857, after a speculative bubble driven by corruption, fraud, and stock market manipulation, the unregulated economy collapsed in a deep recession. Approximately two hundred thousand people in New York alone were unemployed. A substantial number of Europeans who had crossed the Atlantic managed to return home. Many more might have gone back, but they had exhausted their resources in paying for their one-way passage to America and could not make enough money to return. The Atlantic acted like a giant fish trap; once the immigrants had swum into it, it was very hard to swim out again.[5]

The Civil War destroyed the political obstacle to westward settlement. In 1862, with the Southerners no longer represented in Congress, Abraham Lincoln signed both the Pacific Railroad Act, which subsidized the construction of railroad and telegraph lines, and the Homestead Act, which gave virtually free land to those who would settle the new territories. The Union victory fully opened up the west, which relieved the political heat in the eastern cities.

The Homestead Act, said one senator, "will postpone for centuries, if it will not forever, all serious conflict between capital and labor in the older Free States, withdrawing their surplus population to create in greater abundance the means of subsistence."[6] In the thirty years after the Pacific Railroad Act, the U.S. railroad network expanded from 30,000 to 170,000 miles, which dramatically reduced the cost of transporting goods and stimulated the creation of the U.S. steel and other manufacturing industries behind a wall of protective tariffs.[7]

The post–Civil War westward expansion that once again kept new Americans moving after they landed on the East Coast helped create a culture of restless mobility. America became the land of the "second chance." Economic failure or social disgrace was not permanent if you could move west. If you ran out of luck in one town, you could just move to another. If that didn't pan out, there was another town beyond that. In the United States, you could keep going in the hope that you would finally find a place where you fit in.

All working people could not escape their woes by moving west, and many failed as homesteaders. But the western frontier blossomed in the public's mind as well as on the visible horizon. The late-nineteenth-century historian Frederick Jackson Turner famously maintained that the settling of the western frontier defined the American character: self-sufficient, practical, independent, and democratic. Later scholars have challenged his views as overly romantic and culturally myopic, but the settlement of the West remains an iconic episode in our collective consciousness. In an electrifying speech before the 1984 National Democratic Convention, Governor Mario Cuomo of New York, a son of Italian immigrants who never lived west of the Hudson River, reminded the nation that the "wagon train" had been a collective enterprise.

"The Republicans," said Cuomo, "believe that the wagon train will not make it to the frontier unless some of the old, some of the young, some of the weak are left behind by the side of the trail. The strong, they tell us, 'will inherit the land.' . . . We Democrats believe that we can make it all the way with the whole family intact, and we have more than once. Ever since Franklin Roosevelt lifted himself from his wheelchair to lift this nation from its knees— wagon train after wagon train—to new frontiers of education, housing, peace; the whole family aboard, constantly reaching out to extend and enlarge that family; lifting them up into the wagon on the way; blacks and Hispanics, and people of every ethnic group, and native Americans—all those struggling to build their families and claim some small share of America."[8]

● ● ●

Jefferson's assumption that the United States could grow and prosper as a land of small independent farmers would, in his day, have seemed a good bet. The 1790 census showed that 95 percent of Americans lived in rural areas. In 1860, on the eve of the Civil War, the country was still 80 percent rural. By 1910, a majority of Americans lived in cities.

In 1890, the U.S. Census Bureau announced that the frontier was closed. There were fewer places "out there" to which the ambitious and discontent could escape. Moreover, the rapid industrialization of the cities and the mechanization of agriculture reduced the potential for independent self-sufficient farming to relieve social tensions. The next fifty years saw a tempestuous and often violent search for some new social contract between labor and capital that fit the urban experience.

The post–Civil War expansion of railroads, the telegraph, and telephone communication created vast profit opportunities for businesses that could now reach larger markets. Wealth went to those who could centralize production, marketing, and finance. Corporations burst across political jurisdictions, well beyond the power of local customs and state regulation to protect workers and communities. As corporations and banks became continental, they increasingly used the federal government to promote their economic interests. The 1886 U.S. Supreme Court decision *Santa Clara County v. Southern Pacific Railroad Co.* bestowed on corporations the same protections that individual citizens have under the Fourteenth Amendment; this resulted in a serious weakening of the capacity of the states to regulate business.

The engine of economic growth was now the factory and the bank. The assembly line spread, dividing industrial work into smaller and smaller operations that required less training or special skills than did the economy of artisans and craftsmen who made products from start to finish. Employers wanted workers who were disciplined and literate (by 1900 thirty of the forty-five states required children up to age fourteen to attend school), although not necessarily talented. At the same time, the bargaining power of the working class as a whole weakened. With the large influx of immigrant labor, workers were no longer in short supply. And the concentration of economic and political power in the owners of gigantic corporations strangled the early efforts at organizing trade unions to bargain collectively. Workers' wages now lagged behind their productivity as investors commandeered more of the surplus.

The effects of the concentration of economic power extended to the farm. The monopoly power of the railroads and the large grain trusts kept farmers in perpetual debt. Improvements in storage and shipping allowed speculators to manipulate commodity prices, which depressed farm incomes. Much of the promise of the Homestead Act withered in the face of fraud, corruption, and land speculation that gradually concentrated the ownership of the most productive agricultural land in corporate hands. In the South, slavery was replaced by the exploitative sharecropper system. African Americans went from chattel slavery to debt slavery.

The United States had birthed a modern economic elite and a resulting dynamic that would, to various degrees and with marginally changing players, become the dominant force in American life for more than a century. By the end of the nineteenth century, the distribution of income, wealth, and political power was more unequal than it had been at the start of the Civil War. The quality of life of much of the working class, natives as well as immigrants, was brutal and harsh. In 1880, one out of six children under sixteen was a worker. In 1890, the superrich, a sliver of 0.031 percent of the population, possessed 9 to 14 percent of the nation's personal wealth.

The turn of the twentieth century was an era of violent strikes and lockouts in mines, railroads, steel mills, and textile factories. The police, and sometimes the army, were used to suppress efforts to bargain collectively. Reformers passed laws to appease the growing demand for economic justice. But corporate lawyers and fixers quickly turned them into instruments to further the power of the powerful. The Fourteenth Amendment had been added to the constitution to protect African Americans. But despite the oppression of Southern Blacks between 1890 and 1910, only 19 cases that were brought to the Supreme Court alleging a violation of Fourteenth Amendment protections involved racial violence; another 288 cases were complaints by businesses of alleged violations by their workers of corporations' so-called civil rights. The Sherman Anti-Trust Act, promoted as a regulation of the great monopolies, was primarily used instead to break trade unions on the grounds that they represented a "restraint of trade."[9]

Anarchist and socialist ideas spread among the working class. *Looking Backward*, Edward Bellamy's novel about a utopian socialist United States of the future, became one of the best-selling books of all time. As agitation grew, the Democratic Party, which like the Republicans had been a reliable client of the robber barons, was forced to take up some of the populist cause. The election of 1896, in which William Jennings Bryan opposed William McKinley, was a decisive political moment. It was the first modern election campaign in the sense that it involved massive business mobilization for McKinley. Huge amounts of money were made available for political propaganda and the buying of votes. Bosses threatened to close down plants if workers elected Bryan.

While the dream of a prosperous middle class remained mostly a dream, the U.S. governing elite had found a taste for ascendant military clout. The election of 1896 paved the way for the modern use of war to pump up the cushion of American living standards without having to address the vast inequality of income, wealth, and power.

U.S. foreign economic policy was initially aimed at curbing the economic imperialism of its European rivals, who were conquering colonies to secure monopoly markets for their goods and privileged access to raw materials. The United States, with a more limited military reach, promoted an open-door policy for markets like China, arguing that all Western powers should have equal access to the underdeveloped world—while maintaining a high tariff to protect its own home markets. The partitioning of China into economic spheres of influence by the European powers convinced the U.S. political class that the country needed its own imperial system. In 1898, the U.S. State Department officially observed, "It seems to be conceded that every year we shall be confronted with an increasing surplus of manufactured goods for sale in foreign markets if American operatives and artisans are to be kept employed the year round. The enlargement of foreign consumption of the products of our mills and workshops has, therefore, become a serious problem of statesmanship as well as commerce."[10]

Imperialism became a unifying theme for U.S. politics, diverting class conflict into jingoist patriotism. "In strict confidence," Theodore Roosevelt wrote to a friend in 1897, "I should welcome almost any war, for I think this country needs one."[11]

Big business was the great beneficiary, but small business, populist farmers, and the nascent labor movement came aboard as well. Crushed by Wall Street's control of the dominant Republican Party after the election of 1896, labor's next best hope was faster growth through the exploitation of foreign markets. Increasing the size of the pie seemed to be the best way to increase the size of labor's small slices.

The expansion of overseas markets was not free trade. High tariff walls against imports remained. The objective was exactly the opposite: a mercantilist policy aimed at selling more to the rest of the world than the United States was buying. It worked. Between 1851 and 1875, the United States had run a trade deficit in twenty-two out of twenty-five years, but for the next twenty-five years, the nation had a surplus every year but three. And after the turn of the century, the surplus lasted for more than thirty consecutive years.

Backed by corporate interests, the media fanned the nationalist flames. An editorial in the *Washington Post* on the eve of the Spanish-American War proclaimed:

> A new consciousness seems to have come upon us—the consciousness of strength—and with it a new appetite, the yearning to show our strength. . . . Ambition, interest, land hunger, pride, the mere joy of fighting, whatever it may be, we are animated by a new sensation. We are face to face with a strange destiny. The taste of Empire is in the mouth of the people even as the taste of blood in the jungle.[12]

Between 1893 and the eve of World War I, the U.S. government annexed Hawaii after overthrowing its government, began a thirty-year off-and-on occupation of Cuba, annexed Puerto Rico and the Philippines as territories, and brought all of Central America under the control of U.S. commercial interests.

At home, despite the exploitation and suffering, the Industrial Revolution raised average living standards. The statistics we have for those early years are not precise, but the most reliable estimates indicate that between 1870 and 1929, real wages for unskilled labor in manufacturing rose a little more than 0.5 percent a year.[13] Given the huge supply of immigrant labor, this understates the general progress of native-born working people. Real wages for skilled workers probably went up about twice as fast.

The wages, of course, went only to those who were working. The same decades were punctuated with seventeen separate economic downturns. Several were deep enough and long enough to classify as depressions. The unemployment rates reach high double digits in a society with no safety net.

Neither was there much improvement in the distribution of income and wealth. In fact, from 1890 to 1914, the society became more unequal. When the Democrats finally came back to the White House, the Republican-dominated Supreme Court declared even the modest effort of the Wilson administration to regulate child labor unconstitutional.

World War I and the good economic times associated with it kept the demand for a new social contract at bay. Nationalistic politics created a sense of common interest between American capitalists and American workers. It was enough to isolate the populist forces. By 1915, U.S. loans to Britain and France to purchase war materials from the United States generated an economic boom, and the distribution of income actually improved.

After the war, inequality rose once more, and a recession in 1920–1921 generated protests and strikes. A massive political campaign against "subversives" led by the attorney general, Mitchell Palmer, associated unions with foreign radicalism, so these strikes were suppressed by the police and soldiers. The economy as a whole recovered and blossomed into a decade of fast economic growth, fueled at the beginning by an expanding domestic auto industry, trade protection (the Fordney-McCumber Act of 1922, which raised tariffs even more than the more famous Smoot-Hawley Act eight years later), and at the end by real estate and financial speculation.

Cheap land for agriculture was running out, but the land brought forth a new gift that would enable the United States to dominate the next stage of global industrialization. The transition from a nation of farmers to a nation of urban workers was lubricated with oil. In the nineteenth century, the British Empire ran on coal from the rich seams of Yorkshire, South Wales, and Lancashire. The twentieth century for the United

States was fueled by the oil from Pennsylvania, Texas, and the American Southwest. In 1914, at the beginning of World War I, the United States produced as much as 65 percent of the entire world's oil supply.[14]

Oil profoundly reshaped the United States—economically, politically, and socially. The automobile and the public construction of roads allowed everyone to experience the physical sensation of freedom and individual independence from the rest of society. Only a few people could ever have lived the life of the pioneer. Even those who did go west were tied to family, community, and the hard struggle to survive on the land that has been the lot of farmers for millennia. But having—or dreaming of having—a car of your own was the new psychological escape that helped to divert Americans from the social tensions of industrialization, corporatization, and urbanization.

The Roaring Twenties roared primarily at the top. In 1920, the richest 1 percent of families earned fifteen and a half times the disposable income of the bottom 93 percent. By 1929, they were earning thirty times as much and taking home 19 percent of the nation's personal income.[15]

The stock market crash of 1929 burst the bubble. It was hardly the first time in history that stock prices had collapsed and been followed by an economic depression. But by the 1930s, Americans had much less tolerance for hard times. They were more educated, they expected that their willingness to work would be matched by job availability, and they believed that the standard of living would steadily rise. Moreover, they were urban, so they could no longer hunker down on the land, growing their own food and getting by until markets and prices for their products improved. They now needed jobs to survive.

When the paychecks stopped, the bottom quickly fell out of people's lives. A little savings, and perhaps help from friends and family, might keep the rent paid and food on the table for a while. Next it was a choice of paying for food or paying the rent. Then there wasn't enough money for either.

World War I veterans marched on Washington to demand that their promised bonuses be paid now. Crowds forced evicting marshals and foreclosing sheriffs to back off. The hungry and jobless rioted from time to time, looting stores and smashing windows. Radicalism spread. Membership in the Communist Party rose.

American variants of socialist ideas were printed in pamphlets and newspapers and broadcast on the radio. Louisiana governor Huey Long, radio demagogue Father Charles Coughlin, and old-age pension advocate Dr. Francis Townsend all proposed radical wealth distribution and had large followings but soon turned against Roosevelt (for very different reasons) because of the New Deal. To others, both frightened conservatives and inspired radicals, the Soviet Union seemed to be the wave of the future.

The police and the National Guard kept things under control. A 20 to 25 percent unemployment rate meant that most people still had jobs, even though they paid less than they used to. The newspaper images—an evicted family huddled in the street, the bread lines, the farmer who was about to be evicted threatening the sheriff with a shotgun—reminded those who were still working of what might happen if they lost their jobs. Anger ran high, but so did fear.

A few businessmen were convicted in the most egregious cases of financial fraud, yet the business class remained Washington's most important constituency. Roosevelt's initial solution to the Depression was the National Recovery Act. This was an attempt to stop the fall in prices by establishing sectoral monopolies dominated by the National Association of Manufacturers and the Chamber of Commerce.

As the Depression dragged on, more Americans lost their patience. When sit-down strikes—spontaneous decisions by workers to take over the workplace—started to spread, the whiff of revolution drifted into the corporate suites. Despite its hatred for Roosevelt, the capitalist class grudgingly accepted his New Deal, a social contract that finally fit an industrialized urban society. The government now became an instrument for counterbalancing the inequalities of unregulated capitalism. Social Security cushioned the poverty of old age. Unemployment insurance and workers' compensation came to the aid of people who suffered job loss and work-related accidents. The right to join a union militated against the imbalance of power between boss and employee.

Underlying the New Deal was a shift in the basic theory of how capitalism works. The nineteenth-century conception of capitalism, held that wealth was created only through the efforts of competing individuals—primarily investors. A lopsided distribution of income and wealth was considered necessary to motivate people to compete.

Inequality was therefore thought to be fair: it reflected the incentives that would reward those with extraordinary talent, connections, perseverance, or luck for their contributions. Ordinary people had to be motivated as well—primarily through fear of hunger and poverty. High wages were a drag on capitalists' motivation to invest. It followed that the lower the wages, the higher the business investment and the faster the economic growth, which, it was claimed, would ultimately raise the standard of living for everyone.

This view of capitalism was shared by both hard-core robber barons, who believed that exploiting labor was the only way the system could prosper, and Marxists, who believed that the system was not reformable and had to be replaced. But it clearly did not describe the way a twentieth-century mass-market economy worked.

The boom of the 1920s had been driven by the spending of consumers, stimulated by advertising, and financed by the introduction of installment credit. When the Depression struck, sales dropped and business stopped investing. In response, employers cut wages, and therefore consumer spending, making things worse. Even Herbert Hoover—who, somewhat unfairly, was blamed for the Depression—understood that there was something fundamentally wrong in this response. In 1931, he signed the Davis-Bacon Act, which established the eight-hour workday in construction and required employers to maintain prevailing wage levels in government-financed projects.

British economist John Maynard Keynes provided the economic theory for what almost all businesspeople understood in practice: that they expanded their businesses not when workers received lower wages but when they saw customers coming in the door with money in their pockets. In 1914, Henry Ford, otherwise a brutal and repressive employer, doubled the basic wage he paid to his auto workers. When his horrified fellow capitalists complained, he reminded them that their workers had to earn enough to become customers for the products that they made. In the early 1920s, the head of the Moline Plow Company argued for government aid to farmers on the grounds that "You can't sell a plow to a busted customer."[16]

Thus, it gradually became apparent to those grappling to understand the Depression that in a mass-consumption economy, high wages are not a drag on profits; they are essential for keeping money in the pockets of the consumers. So, argued Keynes, in a recession, when businesses and consumers stop spending, increased government spending keeps the customers coming in the door and eventually reinvigorates investment. Keynes preferred to see the money spent on socially useful projects, but the most important thing is to *spend* the money—even, as he said half in jest, if it means burying cash in coal-slag heaps for people to dig out.

The new economics had an important implication for democracy. Prosperity began to be seen as being generated not just by the exceptionally talented manager, insightful investor, or genius inventor. It is the result of the interaction of all the actors in the economic drama—the majority of who are people of ordinary talent, connections, perseverance, and/or luck. All have their part to play as workers and consumers, and therefore all have a claim on the benefits of growth. Economic security—pooling risks through social insurance, subsidizing higher education, and collective bargaining—is as important as the freedom to buy low and sell high.

By providing a cushion for ordinary workers, the innovations of full employment, rising wages, unions, and government-sponsored safety nets also provided a protective cushion for the American capitalist class. After all, the implication of Keynes's proposition was that what is good for General Motors is good for America—even though the businessmen had to also accept its corollary that what is good for the United Auto Workers is good for General Motors.

Still, the nineteenth-century ideology died hard. Even Roosevelt did not fully understand Keynes's point. In 1937, with 13 percent of the labor force still unemployed, he tried to balance the budget by cutting government spending. The result was a recession within a depression, with the unemployment rate rising to 20 percent. Recovery came with U.S. government spending in the buildup to World War II. The war itself brought full employment, demonstrating Keynes's thesis that the government can spend an economy out of a depression. It also rescued FDR and the country from his act of economic folly.

Although travel time across the seas had shortened, the Atlantic and Pacific Oceans were still wide enough that we could fight a war in two arenas with little damage to our infrastructure and comparatively little sacrifice by the majority of our people.

The human cost of World War II for the United States—more than four hundred thousand dead nearly seven hundred thousand wounded, and the grief of their families—cannot be priced. But in terms of the economy, whatever sacrifices of rationing and minor scarcity were required of those on the home front was more than made up for by the creation of full employment after a decade of depression. The embarrassing fact that is usually left out of the paeans to the "greatest generation" of the World War II years is that for most Americans, the war meant jobs, rising wages, and economic opportunities.

Our country had experienced wartime prosperity before, but World War II was different. War mobilization in the framework of the New Deal created the political space to keep the economic cushion inflated far into the future. The post–World War II expansion of the middle class and its rising income and wealth was a three-legged stool. The first leg was the acceptance of Keynesian economics. The second was a permanently high level of military spending. The third was the global dominance of the dollar. Let us examine each of these in turn.

The wartime demonstration of Keynes's thesis gradually persuaded the governing class that the economy could be managed to even out business cycles and maximize growth. As economist Arthur Okun explained to Congress in 1970, recessions are actually preventable—they are more like airplane crashes than hurricanes. A resentful Richard Nixon believed that one reason he had lost the 1960 election to John Kennedy was that President Eisenhower had reacted too slowly to the economic downturn that had begun in 1959. The lesson was not lost; when Nixon finally became president, he famously quipped, "We are all Keynesians."[17]

Keynesian economics validated the New Deal, which framed the social contract between U.S. capital and labor for approximately fifty years. The leaders of the U.S. labor movement abandoned any dream of creating a socialist future in exchange for business acceptance of social insurance programs and collective bargaining rights. Social Security guaranteed a minimal level of income for the elderly regardless of how they had fared in the market. Workers' compensation buffered employees from the economic consequences of injury on the job, and unemployment insurance provided a way to ride out cyclical bouts of unemployment. The expansion of trade unions gave workers—not just unionized workers, but *all* workers—more bargaining power, spreading the benefits of rising labor productivity much more widely than ever before.

The rights and privileges of the investor class were maintained, at the price of a quite modest leveling of income and wealth. Corporate owners and top managers continued to get their disproportionate share of the revenue generated by an enterprise. Still, between 1947 and 1979, when the productivity of workers rose 106 percent, the compensation of nonsupervisory workers rose a respectable 75 percent. During the same three decades, the major indicators of income and wealth inequality declined. Large numbers of workers had job security, pension rights, and company-sponsored health care. Government programs of housing subsidies and aid to higher education gave millions of working-class Americans access to a middle-class lifestyle and created the expectation of a steady march toward a prosperous future for anyone willing and able to work.

The New Deal certainly did not end the struggle between workers and bosses for who gets what. Strikes, lockouts, and bitter labor disputes occurred, and owners chaffed at having to treat as equals at the bargaining table people whom they wouldn't allow in their country clubs. But by providing a single voice to represent workers' interests, unions helped smart managers to negotiate changes in procedures and work rules and make other improvements in efficiency. Capitalism was protected. The New Deal system unified the society against communism during the Cold War. "Abundance," observed sociologist Daniel Bell, "was the American surrogate for socialism."[18]

The expanding cushion for middle-class white Americans also enabled the country to finally address the racial divisions that had dogged it since its beginning. As whites moved up the job and economic ladder, it created space for African Americans and other minorities to move into jobs and even neighborhoods that had excluded them in the past. Martin Luther King Jr. and other civil rights leaders argued that poverty was a burden on the whole economy and that when black workers earned more they spent more, generating more income for everyone. The civil rights movement and President Johnson's War on Poverty program could not have achieved what they did without the expanding demand for workers and rising opportunities for everyone in the 1960s. There was back-lash, of course, against racial integration, especially of schools and housing. The right wing smeared the civil rights movement as a com-munist conspiracy, but the movement persevered and ultimately prevailed.

The Republicans who were elected during the post–World War II era were able to reduce our speed toward what seemed to be our social democratic future, but they could not alter the fact that we were headed in that direction. The voters were not interested in rolling back the New Deal, and they kept reelecting Democratic congresses in order to make sure it didn't happen. Thus, whenever the political pen-dulum swung back to the right, the result was a consolidation and reform of social democratic programs, not their elimination.

In fact, Eisenhower and Nixon expanded many policies that fit the framework of the New Deal, such as federal aid for housing and education, direct aid to the poor, and protection of the environment. To be sure, they were Republican variations: stressing more state and local control, bringing corporate management practices to govern-ment, and favoring Republican constituencies rather than Demo-cratic ones. But there was little doubt about the government's basic responsibilities.

The second aspect of post–World War II prosperity, the public toler-ance for high levels of military spending, occurred because Ameri-cans correctly identified the policy that ended the Depression: it wasn't just government spending, it was *military* spending.

World War II undercut the continental isolationism that had been the American public's—though not necessarily the American elite's—default ideology since the republic began. Those in charge of the coun-try after the defeat of Germany and Japan in 1945 were quite con-sciously determined not to give up the power and prestige that came with running the world's most important nation. The lesson of World War II, they insisted, was that prior U.S. isolationism had allowed fas-cism to flourish. Like it or not, the United States had to take responsi-bility for the world. And it certainly had the resources. According to historian Angus Maddison, in 1870 the United States accounted for

8 percent of the world's gross domestic product (GDP). By 1919, its share had risen to 19 percent. By the 1950s the United States produced more than 27 percent of the world's economic output.

The New Deal was popular, but not popular enough to avoid bitter political battles over every one of its programs—and not just with conservatives, but with the myriad domestic constituencies competing for the money. It was much easier to get a consensus among the elite and widespread support among the voters for military spending that would protect us from the threat of godless communism. The three great Cold War civilian investment programs—highways, public schools, and space exploration—were sold as part of our national defense.

The April 1950 National Security Council Report 68, which became the framework for U.S. Cold War strategy, reminded the foreign policy elite of the importance of U.S. economic power: "One of the most significant lessons of our World War II experience was that the American economy, when it operates at a level approaching full efficiency, can provide enormous resources for purposes other than civilian consumption while simultaneously providing a high standard of living."[19] For Paul Nitze, the principal author, "purposes other than civilian consumption" meant the defense budget.

This "military Keynesianism" was the perfect economic engine to fuel the ambitions of U.S. policy makers. Inasmuch as a large part of the budget of the military-industrial complex was secret, even from government auditors, decisions were hidden under a cloak of national security. Military spending was no less politically motivated than civilian spending was. Bases and contracts were allocated to keep congressional support for the big Department of Defense budget. But the political decisions were much less accountable than those in the civilian sphere, because they were dominated by the iron triangle of the Pentagon, large corporate contractors, and chairmen of key congressional committees—the latter largely politicians whose safe districts allowed them to move steadily up the committee seniority ladder.

The juxtaposition of military power and private interest was nothing new. What made the post–World War II military business different was its permanent size, which provided a broad base of support for its budget and a complexity that allowed it to operate in secret. Thus, a vast new landscape of opportunity for investment and careers with upward mobility opened up for the postwar generation of working Americans. Generous contracts meant generous wages and support from both the local union and the chamber of commerce. The armed services, with its training and its educational benefits, became an avenue of upward mobility for African Americans and poor whites.

The national security agencies became an increasing source of funding for academics and journalists. The Department of Defense created a new model, the nongovernmental think tank, where smart people could come up with new ideas (or rationalizations for old ones).

The military budget had often supported the incubation of new civilian technologies. Thus, for example, the modern assembly line and the steel ship were developed for the Union armed forces in the Civil War. And at the end of World War I, the Secretary of the Navy, Franklin Roosevelt, organized the creation of a private Radio Corporation of America (RCA) in order to keep patents for long-distance radio in U.S. hands.

World War II intensified this big business–big government collaboration, which produced the jet engine, the computer, insecticide, the transistor, high-speed integrated circuits, and antibacterial drugs among the other innovations. By the 1960s the military budget was supporting about one-half of the country's research and development. A major partner in this process was Bell Labs, the research and development facility of the telephone giant AT&T. The combination of generous government contracts and AT&T's freedom from short-run competition gave Bell Labs scientists and engineers the resources and time to work on new ideas.[20]

The third legacy of World War II was the global supremacy of the U.S. dollar. The war had decimated the commercial and industrial rivals of the United States. So when the fighting stopped, the question was not whether we could compete; a Made in the USA label made virtually anything automatically sellable anywhere in the world. Rather, it was whether our foreign customers, whose economies were wrecked, could afford to buy. The main answer to this dilemma was the Marshall Plan, in which the U.S. government provided loans to bankrupted foreigners so they could purchase consumer and capital goods. Over eighteen months, the Marshall Plan transferred capital amounting to 2 percent of the U.S. GDP. It sparked the rebuilding of Western Europe as well as jobs and profits for Americans.

The Marshall Plan, however, was not a permanent solution to the larger problem that faced the capitalist world after World War II: the lack of a global banking system to accommodate international trade. For centuries, international trading accounts had been settled with payments in precious metals, principally gold. But the world's supply of gold depended on how much was produced rather than how much money the world needed to finance growth. As nations industrialized and expanded in the nineteenth century, gold production could not keep pace. The British pound sterling, the currency of the world's greatest creditor, was redeemable for gold and was therefore a substitute. So it functioned as the world's reserve currency; that is, along with gold, it could be used to support the value of other nation's money.

But World War I sapped Britain's economic strength and destroyed its capacity to play the role of world creditor. As a result, the world had no new source of credit when the private banking sector collapsed in the 1930s. In July 1944, confident that Germany would be defeated, the United States and Britain hosted a forty-four-nation conference at Bretton Woods, New Hampshire, to design a new international monetary system. Keynes, who in 1919 had predicted the disastrous consequences of the reparations imposed on Germany by the Treaty of Versailles after World War I, headed the British delegation. He argued for an international currency to settle global trading accounts.

The Americans would not agree. The dollar was now king, and Washington had little interest in giving up the power and international leverage that it would provide. The other nations, eager for dollar loans, lined up. The British, now hugely in hock to the United States for the loans it received during the war, capitulated. U.S. negotiators agreed to redeem dollars from foreign central banks at a fixed price of thirty-five dollars per ounce. Dollars were now as good as gold, and the world had a source of credit to grow on. The center of global financial power moved from London to New York.

The supremacy of the dollar gave the U.S. government a huge advantage in the Cold War. Until its collapse, the Soviet Union regularly produced far more gold than the United States did. But American diplomats did not have to depend on U.S. gold miners to bring cash to the table. Once the dollar was established as the world's currency, they just printed it.

The Russians could offer guns and rubles. The Americans could offer guns and dollars. It was no contest. Dollars provided access to the U.S. market and to most of the world's markets as well. Rubles could buy very little, even in the Soviet Union; the communist system kept most goods in the public sector, not in the market.

Just as the pound sterling did for British investors in its heyday, the dollar enabled U.S. investors to buy assets in other countries cheaply. This further extended American influence and culture and rationalized expanding the U.S. military to protect American economic interests. "Never forget," a German businessman remarked to this writer in the early 1980s, "when General Electric walks into the boardrooms here, the Sixth Fleet walks in behind it."

At home, the New Deal was the Good Deal: it benefited both the nation's citizens and its leaders. For the middle class it meant jobs, pay raises, and opportunities for their children. Trade unions were now partners—though junior partners, to be sure—to management and government. The industrial expansion had added millions to the membership rolls of the American Federation of Labor (AFL) and the Congress of Industrial Organizations (CIO).

In politics, trade unions were the most important source of support for social legislation that went way beyond the needs of just their members. They pushed for a minimum wage for all when virtually all union wages were well above the minimum, national health care when most union members had private health-care plans, workplace health and safety regulations when unionized members were most able to protect themselves, and the War on Poverty when most of their members were well above the poverty line. Unions were, as the saying went, "the people who brought you the weekend."

In the aftermath of John Kennedy's assassination in 1963, Lyndon Johnson ushered in the Great Society, the New Deal's second act. Within two years, Johnson had engineered Medicare, the Civil Rights Act, the Voting Rights Act, and the War on Poverty, which he confidently predicted would eliminate destitution in America within ten years. All of this would be painlessly and automatically financed by continual strong economic growth, because the progressive income tax brackets generated proportionally greater government revenues as people's incomes rose.

Although some of the traditional craft unions resisted opening themselves to minorities and women, the largest and most important were strong supporters of civil rights and antidiscrimination laws. On the historic 1965 protest march from Selma to Montgomery, Alabama, groups of white trade unionists marched under the banners of the United Auto Workers, the Machinists union, electrical workers, and others. There were no groups of executives representing General Motors, General Electric, or Goldman Sachs.

Despite the conflicts, the liberal vision of the future was widely accepted. As legal racial discrimination was abolished and the poor were helped out of poverty, full employment and a massive expansion of higher education would provide new opportunities for all Americans. The G.I. Bill had subsidized the working class's access to college. The National Education Defense Act of 1958, passed in response to the Soviet space triumph of Sputnik, gave their children access to graduate school. State universities became avenues of upward mobility for millions. In California, the top 12.5 percent of high school students were eligible to go to college. The top 30 percent could go to the next level of state universities. And everyone who could do the work could go to a community college. Tuition was free.

Conservatives groused about fiscal deficits. But almost every year the economy grew faster than the occasional deficit, and by 1974 the national debt had dropped from the World War II high of 114 percent to 25 percent of the national income. At the same time, the public sector's share of the economy rose from about 20 percent after World War II to 32 percent by the mid-1970s.

From 1947 to 1973, nonsupervisory U.S. workers (about 80 percent of the workforce) saw their average compensation, in terms of paychecks and benefits, increase about 75 percent (after adjusting for inflation)—2 percent per year. In the same period, the average household median income more than doubled, rising an average of

3 percent per year. The unemployment rate, which had ended the 1930s in double digits, averaged 4.6 percent. As their incomes were rising, Americans were actually working less; the average work week dropped from 44.7 hours in 1947 to 39.1 hours in 1978.[21]

The country became slightly more egalitarian as well as richer. Between those same years, the poorest 20 percent of Americans saw their incomes rise 117 percent. Income for the middle fifth rose 104 percent, and incomes for the richest rose 89 percent.

By the early 1970s, despite the political traumas of the assassinations, the war, and the Watergate scandal, virtually all Americans looked toward a personal future that was brighter and more promising than at any other time in our history. Young families were confident that by the time their children were ready to go to college, the cost of higher education everywhere would be close to zero and that they themselves would retire with free health care and generous pensions. African Americans, who had previously been excluded, could now imagine that they were at last on the road to full economic citizenship in society. The country truly seemed to be entering a golden age.

Optimism was in the political air. Policy intellectuals took seriously the question of how to manage permanent prosperity. In his book *The Affluent Society*, John Kenneth Galbraith argued that the problem of production had been solved; now the question was how to distribute its benefits. Economist Robert Theobold argued for putting the benefits of rising productivity into a reduced workweek so that citizens could have more leisure time to cultivate their lives outside the market. British economist E. F. Schumacher made the case for radically decentralizing economic power and production.

In 1964, a group of liberal academics and activists signed a memorandum to President Johnson outlining an economic vision called the Triple Revolution. They argued that with automation and computerization, society would need fewer and fewer workers. Rather than allowing the market to translate that process into joblessness and the pressure to lower wages, society should take it as an opportunity to end poverty, spread wealth more evenly, and increase public spending on health, education, and culture.

In 1930, John Maynard Keynes looked forward a hundred years and predicted that capitalism would evolve into a world in which "we shall once more value the ends above the means and prefer the good to the useful. We shall honor those who can teach us how to pluck the hour and the day virtuously and well, the delightful people who are capable of taking direct enjoyment in things, the lilies of the field who toil not, neither do they spin."[22]

As they looked to an ever more prosperous future, it appeared to more and more Americans that they might not have to wait a hundred years.

3

The Cushion Deflates

For the three decades immediately after World War II, U.S. wages and incomes rose three times as fast as they had in the previous seven decades. Then suddenly the paycheck prosperity came to a halt. After 1973, the average real wages for non-managers (adjusted for price changes) fell for several years, inched back up in 1979, and virtually stagnated for the next three decades. Having once risen 75 percent in twenty-six years (1947–1973), wages and benefits now rose less than 4 percent in the same amount of time (1979–2005).

Had the rate of increase in worker compensation remained the same, the average wage by 2009 would have been forty-two dollars per hour rather than twenty-two dollars per hour.

No one knows, of course, what the United States would be like if the trend had continued. But even with little change in the distribution of income and wealth, the general level of affluence that those wage levels imply would certainly have created the political space for universal access to first-class health care, education, and housing as well as leisure time for enjoyment and personal growth. We could very well have been in the midst of drawing the blueprint, if not the actual construction, of a future in which more of the best part of every citizen's life could be devoted to pursuits free of basic economic concerns.

Moreover, with the end of the Cold War ten years later, had the U.S. governing class turned its attention to domestic development in 1979, it might have broken out of the historical cycle of expansion and decline that had brought previous empires to ruin.

But it was not to be. The nation's elite ignored the signals that the conditions that had promoted widely shared American prosperity since the end of World War II were coming to an end. Just when the nation needed its leaders to take more responsibility for the future, the governing class took less, abandoning itself to an increasingly reactionary politics. The nation's economic future would no longer be a matter for democratic debate. Its fate would be left to a "free market" manipulated—ineptly, as it turned out—by plutocrats.

Americans were slow to see the deceleration of the material progress that they had come to assume was their birthright. This was partly because the decline occurred slowly. As the old story goes, if you place a frog in boiling water, it will jump out, but if you place a frog in room-temperature water and gradually bring the water to a boil, the frog will remain oblivious to its fate.

The stagnation of incomes and wages was also obscured because individuals continued to do better over their working lifetimes. After people enter the workforce, they get more experience, make more contacts, and work their way up in their occupations and/or companies. That upward progression remained after the 1970s, but the degree of workers' progress over time became less and less. By 2005, people were not earning any more than their counterparts in age and education had earned a quarter of a century ago.

By some measure, workers' real earnings were not just flat, they were falling. Economist Robert Frank calculated that in 1950, a worker earning the average wage had to work 42.5 hours a month in order to afford the average-priced house. By 1970, this "toil index" had dropped to 41.5 hours. By 2000, it was 67.4 hours.[1]

For a while, the average total household income continued to rise because families sent more members out to work, and thus the total family worked longer hours. Thirty years after wages started to flatten, the typical American household was working about 570 hours a year more than it had been working in 1979. The extra work came to more than fourteen weeks a year.[2] Even so, from 2000 to 2007, household incomes failed to rise between the peaks of a business cycle for the first time in the post–World War II era. The next year, they fell a record 3.5 percent.

By and large, economists were even slower than the American people to see the dramatic falloff in incomes. At first, they denied that it could be happening. When the statistics finally confirmed the trends, the conventional wisdom was that it could only be a temporary problem. They argued that the three oil price shocks of the 1970s had forced companies to cut costs, retool, and make other adjustments to the suddenly higher cost of oil. During this transition, worker productivity dropped. Inasmuch as conventional economic theory taught that wage growth depended on worker efficiency, it was natural that wages should falter. So the economists didn't worry. When the nation adjusted to the new higher price of oil, they thought, productivity would surely rise again.

In fact, it did. During the golden postwar years, worker productivity had increased 2.2 percent a year. In the 1970s, the rate dropped to about 1 percent. In 1980, productivity growth picked up again and averaged 2.1 percent until 2007, the year before the financial crash. Still, workers' inflation-adjusted average earnings remained flat.

Since the early 1980s, the conventional explanation for the discrepancy between productivity and wages did a complete turnabout. The problem was now said to be too much productivity rather than too little: automation and computerization were displacing old routine jobs. New jobs and skills were required, but the workers were not adapting. So, the story went, it was the workers' own fault for not keeping up or the fault of an education system that was not training them for the new skills they needed.

Economists still argue over the exact reasons for this dramatic gap between the rising value of what workers produce and the value of what they earn. The suspected reasons included trade deficits, the outsourcing of goods production, the decline of unions, the mysterious mismatch between the skills employers demanded and the skills workers had, the privatization of government services, the deregulation of the airlines and the utilities, increased immigration, and a winner-take-all business culture in which people at the top of their professions reaped more than their share of the rewards. After investigating the various culprits, economist Barry Bluestone, echoing the ending of the famous Agatha Christie mystery *Murder on the Orient Express*, quipped that "they all did it."[3]

The undisputed fact is that the productivity of American workers continues to increase year after year. What has changed since the 1970s is that most working Americans do not share in the benefits of the productivity gains.

U.S. goods could clearly not continue to dominate the global market as they did immediately after World War II. Sooner or later, the devastated economies of Europe and Japan would recover and generate tough competition for markets at home and abroad. Nor could the U.S. dollar continue forever to underwrite ever expanding global growth by being convertible to gold at thirty-five dollars an ounce. The demand for dollars grew with the booming global economy, and there was just so much gold at Fort Knox.

Competent governance of the United States would have consisted of planning an adjustment to the inevitable increase in competition for global markets. If the nation was not going to return to its historical protectionist policies, then it would have to increase the capacity of domestic production to compete. And if the dollar-to-gold connection would at some point have to be replaced in order for the world to have sufficient liquidity without an excessive burden on the United States, some new arrangement would have to be negotiated to succeed the Bretton Woods system. Given that the United States was still the world's economic superpower, leading the noncommunist world to a new system should not have been a strenuous political challenge.

But the demands of empire and the hubris of American exceptionalism blinded the U.S. elite to the early signs of the country's economic vulnerability. On the blithe assumption that nothing had changed, that the United States could continue to afford military adventure abroad and a perpetually rising good life for all at home, the march of folly resumed.

The widely accepted lesson of the Korean War had been "Never get into a land war in Asia." A decade later, we were once again sliding into a land war in Asia.

The rationale for the Vietnam War was the widely accepted "domino theory," the certainty that if we allowed the communists to take over the southern half of Vietnam, every country in Southeast Asia would fall to communism, with the line of collapsing dominoes reaching all the way to Australia and New Zealand to the east and India to the west.

As it turned out, the war in Vietnam did trigger a domino effect, but it was not the toppling of nations to communism. The Viet Cong turned out, as many opponents of the war had claimed, to be more interested in national independence than in being an instrument of anyone's foreign policy ambitions, including those of China or the Soviet Union. Rather, the war toppled the first dominoes of Americans' economic security.

The first dominoes were knocked over by the cost. As in most cases of historical folly, the war's promoters thought that the costs would be modest because the war would be short. The civilians in the administrations of Eisenhower, Kennedy, and Johnson thought they were in control, so that if their assumptions proved wrong, they could pull out. But as David Halberstam described in his classic history *The Best and The Brightest*, once the intervention began, the civilians, including the presidents, were no longer in charge.[4]

So there followed relentless pressure for more: more men, more hardware, more everything. Once the military men were activated, they dominated. Their particular power with Capitol Hill and with hawkish journalists, their identification in the public's mind with patriotism, and their particular certitude made them far more powerful players than the people who were raising doubts. Harry Truman had raised taxes to fund the Korean War. It made both the war and Truman unpopular, and it cost the Democrats the 1952 election. The lesson was not lost on either Lyndon Johnson or Richard Nixon.

The decision not to raise taxes to pay for the war was made with eyes wide open. Gardner Ackley, Johnson's chief economist, told him explicitly that with the economy already close to full capacity, taxes had to be raised to avoid inflation. But as Doris Kearns Goodwin wrote in her 1991 biography of LBJ, "the President was in no mood to listen to such warnings at the moment when the American people were enjoying all the favorable consequences of the boom. . . . While listening to Ackley's concerns, he flatly refused to consider a tax increase, sticking to his initial position that the American nation could afford guns and butter alike. This decision not to recommend a general tax increase in 1966 was the critical decision that set the economic system into a prolonged period of chaos, from which it has still not recovered."[5]

Among those who immediately saw the danger was Martin Luther King Jr. As King understood, the issue was not just money. The United States lacked the moral and political capital to fight the War on Poverty at home and a war on Asian peasants in Vietnam. "The bombs in Vietnam explode at home—they destroy the dream and possibility for a decent America," he said in 1967.[6] Vietnam was "taking the black young men who had been crippled by our society and sending them 8,000 miles away to guarantee liberties in Southeast Asia which they had not found in southwest Georgia and East Harlem."[7]

King was criticized by many liberals for endangering public support for domestic reform by linking it to foreign policy. But in the end he was right. The Vietnam War unbalanced the economy and required an aggressive jingoism that conflicted with the more humanitarian values required to support the War on Poverty.

The Great Society would, of course, have been difficult to maintain even without the war. The fallout over racial integration had an inevitable political cost to the Democrats for their leadership in trying to right the festering national injustice. When Lyndon Johnson signed the Civil Rights Act of 1964, he turned to his special assistant Bill Moyers and remarked that it meant the end of the Democratic Party in the South.

Still, had there been no war, the Democratic Party might have weathered the storm of Southern white reaction to the civil rights movement. Continued prosperity would have generated more money to ease the transition to racial integration. But the mistakes of the war and the ideological attacks from a conservative movement reinvigorated by the Southern white backlash against integration put the Democrats on the defensive, eroding their ability to innovate and to maintain their role as the party of the future.

Gardner Ackley was right. Unlike World War II, which began in a depression, the Vietnam War came in the midst of an economy that was reaching the full capacity of its industry and the full employment of its workforce. Suddenly adding another hundred billion dollars in demand, without offsetting it with higher taxes or a drastic cutback in domestic spending, was a recipe for inflation.

Prices began to rise in 1965, accelerating as military spending soared past the original lowball estimates. Two years later, responding to public anxiety over inflation, Johnson finally acted, and the Congress passed a 6 percent income tax surcharge. In exchange for their votes, Southern Democrats and Republicans demanded cutbacks in the War on Poverty. Reluctantly, Johnson agreed, further angering the Democratic Party's liberal base, which was already angered by the war. His would-be successor, Vice President Hubert Humphrey, entered the election of 1968 with a severely divided party.

The domino of war inflation then fell against the U.S. dollar. As Europe and Japan had recovered in the 1950s and the early 1960s, they began to sell more goods to the United States and thus earn more dollars. The quantity of dollars, representing claims on U.S. production and wealth, grew faster than the capacity of the U.S. economy to produce. More dollars, increasing demand, and pursuit of the same supply of goods and services typically leads to inflation and a reduction in the value of a nation's currency.

Foreign investors had had faith that the purchasing power of the dollars they held would remain stable because of the U.S. government's Bretton Woods's commitment to buy back dollars for gold at a fixed price. So at first they were content to hold on to the dollars, generally in the form of U.S. Treasury bonds, which would pay interest. There was, of course, never enough gold at Fort Knox to redeem all of the dollars. This was not a problem as long as the world had confidence in the U.S. pledge.

But as the Vietnam War's escalation began to erode the dollar's purchasing power at home, foreigners became nervous. By 1968, a substantial number of foreign central banks were cashing in their treasury bonds for gold. The price of gold rose. Among other things, this meant that someone holding dollars could buy gold at thirty-five dollars an ounce from the U.S. government and sell it on the open market at a profit. Clearly this was an unsustainable situation.

Adding to the pressures on the dollar was the rather dramatic deterioration in the U.S. trade balance. The prominent economic historian Charles Kindleberger noted that the U.S. economy in 1970 was at the end of its golden age:

> The Golden Age from 1945 or 1950 for a quarter of a century was one of unchallenged American preeminence in economic questions, but with indications of catching up abroad and slippage on the part of the United States. In new industries—aircraft, computers, electronics, pharmaceuticals, inertial guidance that allowed humans to set foot on the moon, medical equipment like the cat scan—the wide gap of the 1950s was beginning to be narrowed in the following decade, especially by Germany, Japan, Sweden, and Switzerland, but also by France and Italy.[8]

In 1969, the trade surplus that the United States had enjoyed continuously for seventy-five years disappeared. Two years later there was a deficit, adding even more to the world's supply of dollars. Foreigners, sensing that the dollar would have to be devalued, rushed to redeem their dollars for gold. Finally, in August 1971, Richard Nixon unilaterally ended the U.S. commitment to buy gold and imposed a 10 percent across-the-board charge on imports. In December, he forced a 10 percent devaluation of the dollar. Devaluation raised the prices of imports, adding to inflation. To stop prices from rising, Nixon slapped wage-price controls on the economy.

Nixon was not blinded by conservative ideology. In *Nixon Agonistes: The Crisis of the Self-Made Man*, probably the most perceptive book on Nixon that has been written, author Garry Wills called him the "last liberal."[9] Nixon came to power as a virulent anticommunist but made a historic pact with communist China. And although he was willing to attack liberals mercilessly, he was in fact a supporter of using the federal government to guide and manage the economy.

The problem, as with so many of Nixon's policies, was that he abused the opportunity. While suppressing prices with controls, on the one hand, he and his federal reserve chairman Arthur Burns pumped up the money supply with the other hand, overstimulating the economy. Still, the controls had a net positive effect. When they were finally lifted, prices jumped, though not nearly as high as they would have without controls.[10] In any event, the move was popular, and it helped him win reelection in 1972.

The dollar devaluation then knocked over another domino: America's assured supply of cheap oil from the Middle East. The devaluation was a shock to many around the world who had been piling up dollars earned by exporting to the United States. But the kings and emirs who ran the Gulf Arab oil states were the most upset. The devaluation lowered the value of their dollars, and the import surcharge cut their revenues from sales to the United States, which was one-third of the world market.

In 1948, the United States became a net importer of oil. To secure future supplies, the United States took over the British role of protector of the political status quo in the Middle East. The goal was to keep the Russians out, the kingdoms and the emirates divided, and the oil fields in friendly hands.

When in 1953, the democratically elected Iranian leader Mohammad Mossadegh nationalized British oil interests, he was promptly ousted by a CIA-engineered coup and replaced by the shah. The coup created an anti-American sentiment throughout the Muslim world. But the coup's installation of a dictator in Iran also demonstrated the U.S. commitment to its alliance with the other autocratic leaders of the region, the theocratic Arab monarchs.

In exchange for protection and a modest slice of the oil profits, the kings and emirs provided access to their fields, suppressed their secular and religious nationalists, and kept their anti-Israel militants at bay. Most important, they could argue to their militants that the deal with the United States was generating the revenue they needed to modernize their countries.

But Nixon's dollar devaluation and import tax cut into those revenues. The Arab rulers suddenly felt that the United States was reneging on its deal. "What is the point of producing more oil and selling it for an unguaranteed paper currency?" asked the Kuwaiti oil minister, urging his Middle Eastern counterparts to cut back production in order to raise prices.[11]

After the United States sold weapons to Israel during the October 1973 Yom Kippur War between Israel and the Arab states, the Arabs placed an oil embargo on the United States. The U.S. government brokered a cease-fire in the same month, but the embargo continued for six months. When it finally ended, the oil producers had demonstrated their ability to control the flow of the essential ingredient of modern commerce and military might, and they would not go back to the old subservient relationship. The Organization of Petroleum Exporting Countries (OPEC)—a cartel of thirteen oil-producing countries founded in 1960 and dominated by Arab countries—would now set the world price of oil. The Western oil companies still controlled the technology, and their markets remained OPEC's biggest customers, but slowly, by fits and starts, the power over the flow of oil and the flow of money that it generated shifted from consumers to producers.

This arrangement became, in effect, the core of a new patchwork global financial system that replaced Bretton Woods once the dollar ceased to be quite as good as gold. The Arab states of OPEC, despite building their entire modern national infrastructures from oil revenues, still had more money than they could possibly invest at home—or even spend on lavish vacations abroad. So they deposited much of their earnings in New York and London banks, which then recycled the money in the form of loans to the rest of the world. This kept the world's nonoil states supplied with the dollars they needed for growth.

It was a complicated, informal arrangement that depended on, among other things, a responsible well-regulated banking system at its core. At the same time, however, the political seeds were being sown for the deregulation of money markets and their transformation into a destabilizing speculative casino.

The U.S. corporate class had had to accept the New Deal, but most had never liked it. The more enlightened capitalists understood that during the Depression, Roosevelt had saved them from something much more radical. And after the war, the menace of communism pushed them into a reluctant recognition of the need for some sharing of the wealth to keep the U.S. working class content. But it rankled them that the prosperity and political power had to be shared; in their own workplaces, there were now federal laws and labor unions that constrained what had been the absolute power of the boss.

By the end of the 1960s, the Western elites' fear of communism began to shrink. The suppression of dissidents in Hungary and Czechoslovakia and Nikita Khrushchev's revelations of Joseph Stalin's crimes alienated much of the Left in the West. After Khrushchev was removed from power in a bloodless coup, the Soviet Union was taken over by a sluggish conservative leadership, China left the Soviet orbit, and the gap between living standards in Western and Eastern Europe widened, reducing whatever appeal communism may have had to workers in the capitalist West.

In the United States, this gave new life to the embryonic political counterrevolution against the Roosevelt era that had begun in the late 1950s when William Buckley Jr. began the *National Review*. Urbane and aristocratic with a biting wit, Buckley and his magazine became the center of a network of conservative activists recruited on university campuses and at business conventions and country clubs. Compared with the old stodgy Republican conservatism with its isolationist bent, Buckley's crowd was aggressively internationalist, religiously broader (Catholics and Jews were welcome), and more intellectual.

Their inspiration on economic matters came from a small international movement led by an Austrian economist named Friedrich von Hayek, a critic of John Maynard Keynes. Von Hayek was the classic free-market fundamentalist; he believed not just in the efficiency of markets but also that supply and demand was the basic organizing principle of society. Among von Hayek's acolytes was a British conservative politician named Margaret Thatcher.

Milton Friedman, a brilliant economist and organizer of intellectuals from the University of Chicago, brought von Hayek's ideas to the United States and spread them. Rich conservatives put up the money for conferences and books and the promotion of the academic careers of the next generation of conservative economists and journalists. Eventually, Friedman's vision dominated the arriving cohort of conservatives who came to dominate the Republican Party.

In 1971, Lewis Powell, who a year later was appointed to the U.S. Supreme Court by Richard Nixon, wrote a widely influential memorandum for the U.S. Chamber of Commerce in which he outlined a long-term program of subsidizing academics and journalists, organizing legal challenges, and financing politicians in order to change the way Americans thought about economics.

The conservative intellectual renaissance would have remained largely an elitist rearguard action against the historical social democratic trend in U.S. politics had Republican Party politicians not linked it to the angry white reaction, especially but not exclusively in the South, to the civil rights movement. The Buckley-Friedman attack on the federal government provided the moral cover for Nixon's Southern strategy, in which "state's rights" became the code word for the resistance to the political emancipation of African Americans. Suddenly, what had seemed a hopeless romantic stand against progress by a beaten aristocracy gained a mass constituency.

Moreover, the Vietnam War, the civil rights movement, the rise of the counterculture, and the attacks of the rejuvenated right wing had unnerved the Democrats. Trust in government, critical to a democracy's capacity to shape the future, had substantially declined. The new generation of Democrats was of a different stripe from their New Deal predecessors. Passion, political imagination, and big ideas were out. The party had a more suburban base and a suburban style. It supported modest progress in racial integration, sexual equality, and environmental regulation. It was colder toward big government and warmer toward big business. In effect, while the Republicans were consolidating the alliance between big business and right-wing populism, the Democrats were breaking up their old alliance between Southern politicians (social conservatives and economic populists) and Northern liberals.

Increasingly sophisticated attacks from the Republican Right and the growing indifference from within the Democratic Party itself put the New Deal on the defensive. Its intellectual energy sputtered just as the country needed to address the market signals of the erosion of U.S. economic power.

Jimmy Carter was the transitional figure. He prepared the ideological ground for Ronald Reagan just as Herbert Hoover had prepared it for Franklin Roosevelt. Contrary to popular impression, Hoover was not a laissez-faire conservative. As secretary of commerce in the 1920s, he increased the regulation of business, advocated more progressive taxation of the rich, and supported a pension for every American. Faced with the Great Depression in his first year in office, he increased public works and initiated a number of programs that Roosevelt would later build on.

In a similar way, Carter began the process of deregulating the airline, banking, trucking, and telecommunications industries that Reagan later built on as he unraveled the economic base of the Roosevelt social contract. Carter provided a bridge from the age of Roosevelt to the age of Reagan.

At the same time, Carter, more than any president since, seemed to understand the geopolitical lesson of the 1970s oil shocks: that the United States had become dangerously dependent on foreign supplies of oil. A year after he became president, Carter proposed a comprehensive multiyear plan for conservation and the development of new energy technologies. He spent most of his political capital trying to convince Congress and the people that (aside from the prevention of nuclear war) energy dependence was "the greatest challenge our country will face during our lifetimes," as he told the nation in a televised speech on April 18, 1977. It was "the moral equivalent" of war.

Two years later—frustrated with the lack of a national response— Carter was scolding Americans for their self-indulgence, worship of consumption, and setting a higher value on what one owns than what one does. "This is not," he said from the White House in a speech to the nation on July 15, 1979, that reflected his Christian convictions, "a message of happiness or reassurance, but it is the truth." His earnest talk to the nation was mislabeled the "malaise" speech (although he never used that word) by the media. It was denounced for blaming the people for the president's own failures by both Senator Ted Kennedy, who challenged Carter in the 1980 primary, and by Reagan, who ran against him in the 1980 election.

One may quarrel with the details of Carter's programs, but there is little doubt that had the nation begun and continued down the road that Carter laid out, we would now not only have a more efficient and competitive economy, we would also be much more in charge of our political destiny.

But Carter was also the first of the Democratic neoliberals, social liberals who were fiscal conservatives. Like many in the military—the most socialized enterprise in the United States—and despite his liberal stance on many social issues, he embraced a laissez-faire view of the world that endeared him to his big-business backers. The result was that Carter, who was no fool, made two disastrously foolish decisions.

In December 1976, a month after he was elected president, he held a press conference in Washington, D.C., at which he announced, among the other things, that he was rejecting the Democratic congressional leadership's routine offer to renew presidential authority to impose wage-price controls during an economic emergency.

Carter had promised in the campaign that he would keep the authority to control prices and wages that Nixon had used. But at the press conference, he asserted his faith that the free market would prevent inflation from getting out of hand. Scarcely noticed at the time, this assertion was the first of a series of episodes in the next several decades in which Democratic presidents moved further to the right of Eisenhower and, on economic issues, Nixon as well.

"Government cannot solve our problems," Carter lectured the country in his 1978 State of the Union address. "It cannot set our goals. It cannot define our vision. Government cannot eliminate poverty or provide a bountiful economy or save our cities." He continued, "I do not believe in wage and price controls. A sincere commitment to voluntary constraint provides a way, perhaps the only way, to fight inflation without Government interference."

Thus, on the one hand, Carter was attempting to mobilize the nation under government leadership to deal with energy dependence, but on the other hand, he was lecturing them on the ineffectiveness of government leadership. The message was, to say the least, confusing.

Carter's rejection of wage-price controls guaranteed that he would be a one-term president. When oil prices skyrocketed again in the late 1970s, he was helpless, having given away the one instrument he needed to both contain inflation and show the country that he cared. He then desperately tried to convince business and labor to pledge to keep their wages and profits below the rate of inflation. It was a nonstarter.

The inflation of the 1970s was not driven by the classic case of excess demand described in the economic textbooks. Its source was three separate jumps in the price of oil and, at the end of the decade, the failure of the Russian wheat crop, which raised global food prices. These outside shocks set off a spiral of inflationary expectations that drove businesses and labor unions to demand higher prices and wages in anticipation of further inflation. As the Nixon experience had demonstrated, temporary controls could alter those expectations and break the wage-price spiral.

But having denied himself the power to impose controls, Carter's only weapon against a new round of inflation was to squeeze demand out of the economy by slowing down economic growth. He hired Paul Volcker to be the chairman of the Federal Reserve, who immediately raised interest rates and plunged the economy into stagflation: a politically deadly combination of rising unemployment and rising prices. Carter cut domestic spending. But to impress conservatives, he also cut taxes for business and increased military spending.

On election day of 1980, despite the daily headlines about the crisis of the Americans being held hostage in Iran (including Carter's botched rescue attempt), the voter exit polls showed that the economic woes were the chief reasons voters gave for voting for Ronald Reagan. Two months before the election, 62 percent of voters had cited the "high cost of living" as the most important problem facing the nation. Fully 52 percent of American voters supported the imposition of wage-price controls.

In his history of Carter's economic policies, Georgia Institute of Technology economist W. Carl Biven concluded, "The Iranian crisis and the split in the Democratic Party were contributing factors in the electoral outcome, but the inflation that dogged the Administration from its first days in office, and which crested in 1980, was probably the decisive reason for his defeat."[12]

In January 1981, Stuart Eizenstat, Carter's chief domestic policy adviser, was asked by a historian from the National Archives what he thought the administration should have done differently. Eizenstat answered: "First, we should have sought wage and price control stand-by authority in 1977 as the President had suggested he would do in the [19]76 campaign."[13]

After his inauguration, Ronald Reagan ripped out the solar panels that Carter had had installed on the White House roof. The market would decide the future.

Not all Democrats were willing to give up on government. The energy crisis and the appearance of the first trade deficits in the twentieth century were early warnings that the country's post–World War II hegemony was eroding. It set off the last serious debate within the governing class on how the nation should respond. The debate centered on the question of whether the country needed a specific industrial policy to save its manufacturing base. If the argument that it did had prevailed, the country might have entered the third stage of the Roosevelt era. The New Deal had been about building a vibrant middle class from the ashes of the Great Depression. The Great Society had been about bringing in the people left behind. An innovative industrial policy would have reorganized the economy to deal with the growing competition as the world recovered from World War II.

For its advocates, industrial policy seemed a no-brainer. The manufacturing sector was the generator of productivity and innovation. It had been the engine of the nation's rising prosperity and the bedrock of its political as well as economic power. Without the U.S. capacity to become the arsenal of democracy—churning out the tanks, ships, planes, and ordnance that overwhelmed its enemies across two oceans—World War II might very well have ended differently.

If our government could help to rebuild the manufacturing capacity of Germany and Japan through the Marshall Plan, why shouldn't it help U.S. manufacturing stay competitive? Moreover, aid to those economic sectors deemed critical for our future was an American tradition. In the nineteenth and twentieth centuries, tariffs, taxes, procurement, and even public ownership had been employed to pick such industrial winners as clipper ships, railroads, airplanes, telephones, long-distance radio, and television.

In fact, went the argument, government policies were constantly affecting the allocation of investment to private enterprise, but with little regard for the long-term development needs of the country. Conscious, direct aid—such as the 1970s bailouts of the Penn Central Railroad, Lockheed, the Franklin National Bank, and the Chrysler Corporation—was ad hoc, panic driven, and crudely political. This might not have mattered when the United States was the industrial king of the global mountain, but it was now time to get our act together.

Incredible as it might seem today, the point was endorsed by a wide range of corporate leaders, who still saw their future as tied to the U.S. economy. "The time has come in my view," said prominent

Wall Street financier Robert Roosa, "to develop a truly homegrown American form of national economic planning." According to J. Irwin Miller, president of Cummins Engine: "Government must now become systems manager of the total potential of society." Thorton Bradshaw, CEO of Atlantic Richfield, observed, "Since so many government regulations are nothing more than stopgap efforts to compensate for failure to plan, it follows that government planning of a high order—including especially the setting of specific goals and plans for achieving them—would reduce the amount of government regulation with which we have to contend."[14]

Other business supporters of government planning included Henry Ford II of Ford Motor; William May, chairman of American Can; and Michael Blumenthal, chairman of the Bendix Corporation. In 1975 Democratic senator Hubert Humphrey and Republican Jacob Javits introduced the Balanced Growth and Planning Act to require the president and Congress to debate and establish national economic goals. Specific proposals included a national development bank, tax-code revisions, the end of a bias toward foreign investment, the use of procurement contracts to spur technological innovation, and generous government financing of technical education and training.

Opposition from conservative Republicans was to be expected, especially given the Reaganite takeover of the GOP after the party's defeat in the 1976 election. But with Jimmy Carter in the White House and his party in control of Congress, the critical debate was among Democrats. Its outcome had a profound impact on the course of the U.S. economy in the next three decades.

Interest in planning ahead was not limited to the Washington elite. Organized around the celebration of the nation's bicentennial in 1976, citizen forums were sponsored by hundreds of state and local governments around the country to develop plans for what their communities might look like by the year 2000. We had Atlanta 2000, Iowa 2000, California 2000, and so on.

The results varied. In some areas, the effort shifted people's focus from the issue of cheap gas to how they could create sustainable communities. In others, it led to innovative ideas for land-use planning. In others, focus was on schools. And in still others, citizens tackled difficult underlying problems of race, poverty, and the mutual responsibilities of citizens, business, and local government. But the important point is that these plans could have been the beginning of the process of developing a "homegrown American form of national economic planning." In this context, citizenship was being defined as more than simply going to the polls every several years. People were coming together collectively, as neighbors, as citizens, to ponder and discuss what future they wanted for their community.

Within the administration, opposition to national planning was led by the chairman of the Council of Economic Advisers: Charles Schultze from the Brookings Institution. His argument was basically ideological. Government could not make better decisions than the market, he said, and even if it could, what the private economy produced—or whether it should have a manufacturing sector at all—was none of the public's business.

Schultze's view reflected the postwar neoclassical synthesis of two strains of capitalist economic thought. One was the post-Depression *macroeconomic* focus on economywide aggregate numbers, symbolized by the Gross Domestic Product, or GDP: the dollar value of everything the economy produces. The other strain came from nineteenth-century *microeconomics*: the model of how perfectly informed autonomous individuals who maximize short-term profits respond to price changes. The political implication of merging the two strains of thought into one economic theory was to concede to the liberals that government has a responsibility for fiscal and monetary policies to stabilize the overall economy and concede to the conservatives that all other decisions should be made by the unfettered market.

About the vast, messy *metaeconomy* in between, where most corporate managers, workers, investors, speculators, inventors, schemers, and rent seekers actually lived and worked, synthesis economists had nothing to say. This world could not easily be fit into the mathematical model that they thought was necessary to claim their discipline as a science. Moreover, understanding it required tools beyond the economists' training: engineering, psychology, politics, management, marketing, labor relations, law, and, most of all, the study of how complex institutions behave and change over time.

This broader, more eclectic "institutionalist" approach to economics has a distinguished U.S. intellectual tradition reaching back to figures such as Thorstein Veblen, John R. Commons, and Adolph Berle. But by the late 1970s, their work was largely swept outside the economic policy mainstream—as were prominent contemporary economists who pushed at the narrow boundaries of the profession.

These included John Kenneth Galbraith, whose widely read books dissecting the behavior of the modern corporation were deemed by the synthesis majority as insufficiently mathematical; Nobel Prize winner Wassily Leontief, whose very mathematical "input output" methodology analyzing the flow of resources to and from economic sectors made him seem too friendly toward planning; and the younger Lester Thurow of the Massachusetts Institute of Technology, who seemed too interested in studying the way businesspeople actually behaved and the effect of their behavior on the distribution of income and wealth.

Underlying this debate were two different implicit assumptions about the United States and the world. For the neoclassical economists, the rest of the world was not important. The United States was so powerful and self-sufficient that its policy makers simply did not have to worry about the competitiveness of its goods and services or the incomes of the workers who produced them. Americans were therefore defined as consumers, and maximizing their welfare meant making sure they had as many choices as possible at the cheapest prices. This could best be accomplished by maximizing free competition. The more competition, the cheaper the goods to the consumer, and it did not matter much where they were produced.

For the institutionalists, the U.S. dominant position among global producers was not carved in stone. History moves on, and it was already signaling that the post–World War II legacy of economic dominance was beginning to fade. Therefore, government policies had to define the well-being of Americans as workers and not just as consumers. Living standard depended on more than cheap prices. After all, goods had been cheap in the Depression. One's standard of living depended on having a decent job.

The debate among economists was also a proxy for the conflicts of interest among those with power and money at stake. For example, the State Department represented the foreign policy establishment and favored helping foreign industries to capture U.S. markets as a way to gain Cold War allies, so it was opposed to policies that might restrict the off-shoring of U.S. jobs. So too was the Treasury Department, which represented the interests of financiers who were against giving the government power to guide private investment in ways that would serve the interests of U.S. producers rather than U.S. global investors. The financial elite was also aware that if manufacturing industries shrank, so would the political power of its strongest class adversaries, the unions.

Opposition to industrial policy consummated the marriage of Wall Street financiers and mainstream professional economists that continues today. Believers in the neoclassical synthesis tend to idealize, if not idolize, financial markets; buyers and sellers react almost instantaneously to minute price changes that are supposed to reflect all of the available information on businesses, about which neither buyer nor seller has to know anything at all. This idealized market lent itself to the mathematical models required to gain tenure and win Nobel Prizes in economics. To global investors, the economists were useful allies who rationalized government policies that were indifferent to where in the world, exactly, investment goes, as long as it maximizes what economists call *efficiency* and financiers call *profit*.

A dowry helped. Wall Street firms contributed funding to friendly economics departments and think tanks and gave consultant contracts to economists to build models that would prove the social value of unregulated business.

On the other side of the debate, the institutionalists' support for industrial policy within the Carter administration came from the Departments of Commerce, Transportation, and Labor, where economist Ray Marshall, an institutionalist from the University of Texas, was secretary. Although most of the business press was skeptical, the editors of *Businessweek* were friendly. Even a few Wall Street mavericks joined up. Felix Rohatyn, of the investment bank Lazard Freres, commented that "the thought that this nation can function while writing off its basic industries . . . is nonsense."[15]

Carter himself seemed conflicted. On the one hand, he was ideologically a free-market advocate, as his fatal rejection of wage-price controls demonstrated. On the other hand, he knew the value of long-term planning from his work in the U.S. Navy's nuclear submarine program. And he certainly understood the role of government in maintaining his family's peanut business. But Carter never quite grasped that the energy crisis signaled a general weakening of U.S. global economic power that would require government intervention to remedy.

Had Carter won a second term, industrial policy, manufacturing, and energy policy might have been integrated, which could have significantly changed the direction of the U.S. economy for the next thirty-five years. At the very least, our country would have become much less dependent on Middle Eastern oil, removing the motivation for both the Persian Gulf War and the Iraq War. We would certainly be way ahead of where we are now in the development of green industries, energy-efficient transportation, and a twenty-first-century workforce. We would most likely have a much smaller trade deficit and foreign-debt burden.

Furthermore, having a Democratic Party conscious of the importance of a healthy domestic industrial base could have prevented the Clinton administration from making two decisions that undermined the long-term health of the U.S. economy: the deregulation of finance, which shifted the engine of growth away from production toward overleveraged consumer debt, and the abandonment of U.S. industry to unwinnable competition with countries where wages are suppressed (Mexico), where government runs effective industrial policies (Germany), or both (China).

The discussions and debates about industrial policy continued in Congress during the first Reagan term. Carter's vice-president, Walter Mondale, was for a while a champion. But when he began to raise money from Wall Street, he lost interest. The financiers' advice was to make Reagan's deficits the focus of Mondale's 1984 campaign. He did, and he was clobbered. With Reagan's landslide election, the federal government was out of the business of thinking about the future.

4

The Age of Reagan: Americans Abandoned

Americans in 1980, like Americans in 1932, went to the polls more to vote out the old president than to vote in the new candidate. But once elected, Ronald Reagan, like Franklin Roosevelt, seized the opportunity to make a historic shift in the way the country thought about the future.

Just as the Republicans Dwight Eisenhower and Richard Nixon ruled within Roosevelt's political framework, so have the Democrats Bill Clinton and Barack Obama ruled within Reagan's. When Clinton left office, he said that his greatest accomplishments were balancing the budget, expanding free trade, and reforming welfare. His budget policy was hostage to Reaganomics, his trade and welfare reform were Reagan designs, and he extended Reagan's deregulation and privatization agendas. "The era of big government," he famously said in his 1996 State of the Union Address, "is over."

The impact of Reagan on the Democratic Party was, arguably, even greater than his impact on the GOP. As he moved the country to the right, the Democrats convinced themselves that they could capture a big-business constituency without undercutting their working-class and middle-class base, or at least not so much that they would lose its votes. Instead, they became hostage to Wall Street money. Economic class questions got in the way of business support, so the liberal energy and passion of the Democrats turned to social issues. They became embroiled in identity politics, representing the separate claims of the various subgroups of American society. By definition, this is a politics of division, not unity; it encouraged the Democrats to emphasize how different they were from one another, not their common interests.

Reagan did not plan all this, of course. Neither did Roosevelt plan the far-reaching effects of his own presidency. And it is impossible to draw a clear line of distinction between Reagan the man and Reagan the movement. Certainly his accomplishments were the product of believers in and out of the government who translated his few ideas into tens of thousands of decisions and actions. But although liberals then and now think of Reagan as a charming boob at best, manipulated by his conservative handlers, the major ideas that drove the era were his. In the most important accomplishment of his term—accommodating the dramatic transformation of the Soviet Union—he overruled his hard-line followers and legitimately earned his place in history.

Yet Reagan the actor also understood the uses of illusion. He picked his military entertainments carefully. The invasion of Grenada gave him the mantle of a hero with all the risk associated with attacking (as one sailor put it at the time) a golf course. When a bomb killed 241 U.S. marines and sailors in Lebanon in 1983, Reagan beat a hasty retreat. Whatever he might have had in his heart, Reagan's public image as a superpatriot was largely fake—arguably to his credit, however. It was based on the same illusions that made actor John Wayne an icon of military heroism, even though he had maneuvered his way out of serving in World War II.

Similarly, Reagan brought Christian fundamentalists into his political coalition with his speeches echoing early American evangelists' dream of a theocratic city on a hill. But he ended up giving the religious Right very little. There was no abortion ban, no nationwide prayer in public schools, and no censorship of the media; in fact, in the 1980s the use of sex in advertising accelerated. Reagan was a creature of Hollywood and big business: General Electric, which used him as a television spokesman in the 1950s, had transformed him from a fading midrank movie star to a popular politician. His covenant was not with God, it was with corporate America.

Economics was always the main game, and Reagan won it. He not only reversed the momentum of Roosevelt's social democracy, he altered the very way we treat economic time and space. After Reagan, the nation's investment horizons—both private and public—shrunk dramatically. At the same time, the definition of U.S. economic interests became imprecise, confused, and indeterminate.

In the past, despite great conflicts among various classes and groups over the benefits of economic growth, the fact that all Americans relied on the same national economy forced compromise and eventually forged the social contract. Capitalists and workers, farmers and city dwellers, blacks and whites, immigrants and the native-born, and men and women were mutually dependent on a prosperous United States. After Reagan, the people who manage large U.S. corporations—by far the most powerful influence on public policy—increasingly saw their future in a global economy disconnected from the future of their country.

Helped by Jimmy Carter's antigovernment rhetoric, Reagan the illusionist rode to victory on the myth that the government had caused inflation through excessive and wasteful social spending. The charge was dramatized by his inflammatory fable of the "welfare queen" riding around in a Cadillac. Cutting welfare for the "undeserving" poor was popular, but the real money—other than in the military—had been spent on the protective cushion surrounding the middle class, such as housing, transportation, unemployment compensation, Social Security, and national parks.

So instead of a direct assault on the spending programs that benefited the middle class, Reagan countered with another popular program: tax cuts, which had the strategic advantage of choking off the government revenues that fed domestic spending. He forced the Democratic-controlled House of Representatives to cut tax rates, and in a strategic masterstroke, he cajoled them into agreeing to eliminate the way the progressive income tax automatically accelerated federal government revenues as the economy grew. Because the tax rate was progressive (the higher the income, the higher the tax rate), a rise in incomes that was caused by inflation would produce a more than proportional rise in income tax revenues. By linking the income tax rates to the change in consumer prices, Reagan effectively shut off the revenue stream that had funded Lyndon Johnson's Great Society programs.

Reagan was no fiscal conservative. Contrary to popular perception, Reagan was indifferent to balancing the federal budget. "On the question of fiscal deficits," his chief economist Murray Weidenbaum later said, "I recall [Reagan's] views going through three stages: one, they won't occur; two, they'll be temporary; three, when they stick, they serve a good purpose—they keep the liberals from new spending programs."[1]

Reagan was just as strategic in his attack on the Social Security system, by far the most popular government program in U.S. history.

Social Security was a pay-as-you go system; each generation of workers paid the taxes that financed the payments to the retiring generation. Whereas the payments are progressive—low-income people get more money relative to their incomes—the tax, a simple percentage of wages, is not. Sounding an alarm that the government would have to raise taxes or cut spending in the future to pay for the bulge in retirements represented by the baby boomers beginning in 2011, Republicans demanded that the system be "reformed" to be put on an actuarially sound basis.

The problem was vastly overstated and could have been resolved with modest changes. Instead, a bipartisan commission headed by Reagan's Federal Reserve chairman, Alan Greenspan, persuaded Congress to raise the full retirement age and to increase the payroll tax. Democrats on the commission went along. The public was told that the money would be "saved" for future retirees. But there was no safe-deposit box in which the new revenue was stored away for the future. Instead, the new revenue was used to pay for the deficits resulting from Reagan's tax cuts and military spending spree.

Reagan's fiscal recklessness laid an elegant trap for the Democrats. It completely ensnared Clinton, ironically one of the smartest, most policy-wise presidents we've ever had. Believing that Reagan's deficits were a political opportunity for the Democrats to ingratiate themselves with Wall Street, Clinton made "fiscal responsibility" (balancing the budget) his political mantra.

Clinton had come to the White House having promised his constituency that he would expand government spending on the social safety net, particularly health care. But his chief adviser on economic questions was Robert Rubin, a cochairman of Goldman Sachs who had been a major fundraiser for the Democrats in the 1980s and was appointed secretary of the treasury in Clinton's second term. And Rubin's chief adviser was Alan Greenspan.

Together they convinced Clinton that the financial markets would cause a flight from the dollar unless Clinton cut the fiscal deficit left to him by Reagan and George H. W. Bush. Clinton, whose success taught him the value of close Wall Street connections, agreed. He spent much of his presidency shortchanging the Democratic Party's constituency so he could pay off the debts run up by his two Republican predecessors' spending on their constituency. In his last two years in office, the federal budget moved into a surplus.

A few days after the inauguration of George W. Bush in January 2001, the trap was sprung. Greenspan announced his support for Bush's proposed $1.6 trillion tax cut over the next ten years. The media reported that the Democrats were "shocked" and "stunned." How could Greenspan, the symbol of financial probity, support a tax-cut proposal that would spend the surplus and have the government borrow money to pay for it? How could Greenspan, who had lectured the Democrats for eight years that deficits were the root cause of runaway inflation and would destroy the Social Security system, so cavalierly dismiss his own doomsday scenario?

The only answer that fits the facts is that for Greenspan, as for Reagan, balancing the budget was not his true priority. Nor, despite his constant lecturing, was he convinced that budget deficits were the cause of inflation. His real interest can only have been to keep the Democrats from expanding domestic government services after Clinton won the election.

Having balanced the federal government's books, Clinton and the Democrats set the stage for George W. Bush's tax-cut frenzy.

In 1981, reacting to a dispute over wages and working conditions between the air traffic controllers and the Federal Aviation

Administration, Reagan broke the air traffic controllers' union by firing and replacing the striking workers. Since the consolidation of the New Deal social contract at the end of World War II, employers had generally not attempted to permanently replace striking workers. In effect, if workers can be fired for striking, then they do not have the right to strike; they simply have the right to quit.

Reagan's act signaled that the government would sanction a return to the pre–New Deal hard-line war against organized labor. Employers responded eagerly by stiffening resistance across the collective bargaining table, daring unions to strike, and creating sophisticated defenses against attempts to unionize. A new industry of consultants arose to run antiunion campaigns, teaching management how to threaten, bribe, and harass workers when union organizers showed up. Many of these tactics were illegal, but Reagan appointed antiunion hard-liners to the National Labor Relations Board, where they blocked, delayed, and denied complaints. Newspaper corporations—including the "liberal" *New York Times* and *Washington Post*—broke their printing unions and joined the chorus of business pundits who were assuring the public that unions were both an obstacle to progress and no longer necessary in an era of enlightened and compassionate management.

Without the mobilization of trade unions on election day and their financial contributions throughout the election cycle, the Democratic Party would simply not be competitive. Despite that, Clinton was largely indifferent to their fate. When asked to help pass a bill that would have once more restored the right to strike by making the permanent replacement of striking workers illegal, Clinton told the unions that he couldn't deliver the votes of the two senators from his home state of Arkansas. Yet one of them, Dale Bumpers, was close enough to Clinton that he acted as his defense attorney in the impeachment trial.

The leaders of the trade union movement certainly bore some responsibility for their own decline. They were often unimaginative in organizing and slow to accept the economic changes in their industries and the racial and sexual changes in the composition of the work force. And they allowed the Democratic Party to feed on their dwindling resources while getting very little in return.

When Reagan became president, 26 percent of American workers were unionized. Twenty years later, union membership had been cut by more than half. Throughout these years the legal balance shifted to employers. By 2009, the penalties and risks to bosses were so small that eight thousand workers were illegally fired for union activities. The response of the mainstream media has been that this simply represents the lack of appeal of unions to workers. Yet polls show that if given an opportunity, many more workers would join a union.[2] What has kept them from doing so is fear. Gordon Lafer of the University of Oregon found that 41 percent of nonunion workers believe that "it is likely that I will lose my job if I tried to join a union."[3]

However you want to allocate the causes of labor's decline, the net result is that it represents a major shrinkage of the protections surrounding *all* working Americans.

The post–World War II global boom widened the geographic horizons of American chief executive officers and investors. The world, it turned out, was filled with cheap workers and weak governments where, with a little bit of training and bribery, the costs of production could be substantially lowered. U.S. laws protecting workers and the environment stopped at the border, but production for the U.S. market did not.

To make it easier, American businesses pressured the U.S. government to sign a series of radical "free-trade" agreements that put high-wage American workers and businesses that produced in the United States under even greater pressure from foreign competition. The ideological framework was Reagan's, but the heavy political lifting was done by Clinton, who allied with Congressional Republicans to pass the three most important treaties: the North American Free Trade Agreement (NAFTA, 1994), the World Trade Organization treaty (1995), and the Permanent Normal Trade Relations agreement (2000), which opened up U.S. markets to China.

In return for giving foreign governments unprecedented access to U.S. markets for their goods, the American financial elites got the right to invest in low-cost overseas production, sell the products back in the U.S. market, and invest in other nations' banking, insurance, and financial institutions.

Selling these deals to the American public involved a relentless propaganda campaign masquerading as economic science. Free trade is close to a religious principle for American neo-liberal economists, and with some exceptions, they were constantly available to insist on its magical powers to bring prosperity in the form of cheap prices and high wages. The dissenters were attacked as ignorant about economics and prejudiced against foreigners.

But *free trade* was a misnomer. The argument for free trade is that it can allow nations to exchange the goods that each produces most efficiently. Thus, in the classic model, it would allow Portugal to concentrate on making wine and England to concentrate on making cloth. Intrinsic to such models is the assumption that investment stays at home. But the Reagan-Clinton deals were as much or more about freeing capital as expanding trade. Their purpose was to give U.S. corporations the right to produce offshore and sell to the U.S. market. As the president of Peru, Alan Garcia, told the U.S. Chamber of Commerce after the 2007 U.S.-Peru free-trade agreement in December of that year, "Come and open your factories in my country so we can sell your own products back to the U.S."

This is not what Adam Smith, David Ricardo, and the classical advocates of free trade had in mind. But the actual content of these agreements was unimportant to economists defending intellectual dogma. Indeed, a survey of the economists who supported the first of these deals, NAFTA, showed that only one in nine had actually read the treaty itself.[4]

Not even the venerable Nobel Prize winner Paul Samuelson, a founder of the neoliberal economics that dominated postwar economic policy and a staunch supporter of free trade, was exempt from the contempt of the academic inquisition that tolerates no heresy. When Samuelson suggested in a 2004 article that the United States might not, after all, benefit from free trade, he was dismissed as an old man who had lost his marbles.[5] His point was simply that the dogma that free trade was a win-win for everyone had become dubious as (1) highly skilled workers overseas became increasingly cheaper to hire, (2) the gains from producing goods more cheaply elsewhere went to capital rather than labor, and (3) the United States lost a comparative advantage in expanding industries.

Eventually, defenders of the free-trade deals admitted that they were not quite win-win for everyone. The very unskilled and uneducated, of course, might lose their jobs. But American workers were assured that their better education and access to superior U.S. technology would allow them to produce more high-value products. They would move up the global wage ladder, while the workers in other countries would get the vacated lower-wage jobs at the bottom.

Yet Americans kept slipping down the job ladder. At first it was jobs in the lower-paid sectors of manufacturing that went overseas. Then it was skilled work in automobiles, steel, machinery, and electronics. By 2008, 48 percent of all sales by Standard & Poor's top five hundred U.S. corporations were of items produced outside the United States. Not to worry, the laid-off workers and their children were told: they would be retrained and educated for high-paying service-sector jobs in the new world of computerized technology. Such jobs would always be generated in the United States because of our advanced technology, prestigious universities, and Nobel Prize–winning scientists.

The share of the workforce with college degrees doubled, and millions of students took out loans to learn computer science. But the rest of the world, now having access to American consumers, also went to school. India and China turned out scientists and engineers at a phenomenal rate, and the outsourcing of high-tech jobs spread throughout the economy. Projections by the Bureau of Labor Statistics in 2006 concluded that by 2014 the number of occupations filled by people with college degrees will rise by merely 1 percent, from 28 to 29 percent. The share of jobs for which a college education will actually be *required* is projected to be just 21 percent.[6]

It turned out that much of the job and wealth creation associated with the information economy was tied to the making of goods; success results from setting trained people to work on problems in the context of day-to-day production, whether of sneakers, automobiles, pharmaceuticals, or Hollywood films. The more we offshored production jobs, the more we offshored research and development as well. What had been touted as a natural comparative advantage for the United States in skills, technology, and organization was in reality duplicated or even surpassed by other nations. "American" transnational corporations were locating their research and development departments in India, Taiwan, and China, where the skills were high and came cheap. Soon IBM had more employees in China than in the United States. Apple had 25,000 workers in the United States and about 250,000 on contract in China.

An analysis of fifty-seven major research initiatives of the U.S. telecommunications industry showed that all but five were located outside the United States. According to one estimate, 80 percent of engineering tasks in product development can be "easily outsourced."[7] Jack Welsh, the celebrated CEO of General Electric, proclaimed a "70–70–70" rule: At least 70 percent of research and development would be outsourced. At least 70 percent of that would be offshored. At least 70 percent of that would be offshored to India. By the middle of the first decade of the twenty-first century, the majority of GE's employees were overseas.

During that decade, U.S. high-tech employment remained at 3.8 million jobs, and wages and salaries were stagnant. Meanwhile, multinational companies pressured the U.S. government to allow them to bring in foreign workers to be trained by Americans whose jobs they would take back home.[8] One result is to further obscure the effect of offshoring on high-wage jobs in the public debate. For example, Professor Ron Hira of the Rochester Institute of Technology points to the example of Cognizant Technology Solutions Corporation, a Fortune 500 company that has been on *Fortune* magazine's list of the 100 fastest growing U.S. firms for the last nine years. Between 2009 and 2010 Cognizant's sales to the financial and health care sector in the United States grew by about a billion dollars. Of the new jobs created 15,450 went to India. The company reported that the rest were hired in the United States, but as Hira points out, almost all of the U.S. hires went to foreigners on temporary work visas. So the net contribution to opportunites for U.S. workers was just about zero.[9] Hira estimates that some 1.3 million high-tech jobs were created in India for servicing the U.S. market.[10]

The economists who fervently supported the trade agreements they hadn't read are not stupid, but they are intellectually blinded by the free-market ideology that dominates their profession. The economic models they use to "prove" the benefits of globalization focus almost exclusively on consumer prices. The models conclude what is obvious to virtually anyone over the age of twelve: consumers will benefit from cheaper goods made by cheaper labor. What the typical American trying to understand the debate is not told is that these models invariably assume full employment. So it's no surprise that they do not find that trade deficits cost jobs.

Obviously, in the real world, economies are not constantly, or even typically, at full employment. So, unless compensated by an increase in consumer, business, or government spending, a trade deficit always means a slowdown in the growth of the GDP, which means a slowdown in job growth. Here the U.S. economics profession has disgraced itself over the trade issue. It has allowed the governing class to argue that these trade agreements increased exports. And so they do. But imports increased faster than exports. The net result was a reduction in jobs. As economist Thea Lee once quipped, the way the business media reported on trade is like the sports media reporting on a baseball game by giving the score of just one team.

Taking its cue from the authoritative economics profession, the media blamed the nation's crumbling competitiveness on American workers not being productive enough, on American students not taking enough math, on American schools for not making kids smarter and more motivated, on American consumers for not saving enough to pay for imports, and on other countries for not playing by the trading rules we had agreed on. All of these arguably contributed to the country's trade dilemma, but they begged the central policy question: Why is it in the U.S. interest to open up the country to more and more brutal global competition if doing so keeps driving up the trade deficit, our foreign debt, and domestic unemployment?

The question was rarely posed in the public debate. But when it was, the governing class's indifference to the fate of American workers was exposed. At a conference at the Brookings Institution in 2006, prominent Wall Street Democrats Robert Rubin and Larry Summers (who succeeded Rubin as Clinton's treasury secretary) assured the audience that they were in favor of more education, training, and other measures to alleviate the economic pain of trade-induced unemployment. All of this would, they agreed, make the United States more competitive in the global marketplace. That being the case, asked Larry Mishel of the Economic Policy Institute, why not do those things first so that American workers would be better prepared to compete? They dodged his question. Steven Pearlstein of the *Washington Post* asked it again. Rubin and Summers shook their heads. No, they were not in favor of putting anything ahead of the further opening up of the economy.[11]

Why weren't they? Rubin and Summers certainly knew enough about economics to realize that American workers could not maintain their wages in competition with China and India—or, indeed, with Germany and Finland—with the meager protections, support, and safety net available to them. Both men also certainly knew enough about politics to understand that the only way to get the business establishment and conservative Republicans to substantially expand the protections, support, and safety net was to withhold support for globalization until they agreed.

But there was never any such effort. The spending required to make Americans more competitive was merely a promise, broken with the next budget, in which the Democratic leaders collaborated with the Republicans to give priority to tax cuts and military spending.

Even dedicated free-trade advocates could see that Americans had become extremely vulnerable. A study by a Princeton economist and a former vice chairman of the Federal Reserve Board, Alan Blinder, stunned the economics profession by concluding that approximately forty-two million U.S. jobs were potentially offshorable. His focus was not on manufacturing jobs but on the high-tech service occupations that were supposed to compensate Americans for the loss of manufacturing jobs. Blinder pointed out the obvious: any task that could be done with a computer could be done anywhere.[12]

The implications of Blinder's analysis were enormous. It cut the heart out of the claim that free trade was increasing jobs opportunities for Americans, and it called into serious question the glib notion that workers would be protected by becoming computer proficient. Indeed, the evidence was that the only services that could not be offshored were those that involved personal, live, face-to-face contact.

The reaction to Blinder's study was, and continues to be, denial. His estimate of the number of jobs that are potentially offshorable was dismissed as too large, although a similar study by students at the Harvard Business School later concluded that if anything, his numbers were on the low side.[13] Most of the negative response consisted of a reiteration of the assertion that free trade always makes people better off because it lowers prices.

Blinder himself, embarrassed by the negative reaction of his colleagues, hastened to prove his free-trade credentials by insisting that cheaper goods were the ultimate criterion for prosperity. About the disappearance of the television-manufacturing industry, he later wrote, "The TV manufacturing industry really started here, and at one point employed many workers. But as TV sets became 'just a commodity,' their production moved offshore to locations with much lower wages. And nowadays the number of television sets manufactured in the U.S. is zero. A failure? No, a success."[14] Why? Because it led to cheaper TVs.

When he was asked by Diane Rehm of National Public Radio if his report meant that we had to become a nation of masseuses, waiters, and cab drivers, Blinder said no, there were other opportunities in higher-paying professions. "Like what?" asked Rehm. "Like brain surgeons," he replied.[15]

Americans who manage and own global enterprises might have as much personal concern about their nation's future as other citizens do, but they are paid to worry about their corporations, not their country. For decades, they had been making the point themselves, quite openly. As early as 1974, the CEO of Dow Chemical said he yearned to place his headquarters on an island "beholden to no nation or society and prevent the U.S. Government from attempting to force its subsidiaries to conform to American interests."[16] In 1995, the CEO of the Ford Motor Company said, "Ford isn't even an American company, strictly speaking. We're global. We're investing all over the world. . . . Our managers are multinational. We teach them to think and act globally."[17] In 2006, the CEO of Cisco Systems—poster company for the information economy—went a step further: "What we are trying to do is outline an entire strategy of becoming a Chinese company."[18] And the CEO of Intel—a company like Cisco, whose growth was built on technology paid for by the American taxpayer—stated, "Intel can thrive today and never hire another American. It is not our desire [to never hire another one]. It is not our intention, but we can do that."[19]

Ralph Gomory, a former IBM executive and later the president of the Alfred P. Sloan Foundation, noted, "There is and can be fundamental conflict between the goals of the company and the goals of the country."[20] Jeffrey Garten, a major architect of U.S. globalization policies and dean of Yale Business School at the time, observed that the United States "must adapt to the reality that U.S. multinationalists' goals may no longer dovetail with the national interest."[21]

As the globalizing economy relentlessly disconnected "U.S." corporations from U.S. interests, their influence on the U.S. government grew stronger. When lobbyists from Dow Chemical, Ford, and Cisco walked into the office of a member of Congress or into the Oval Office, it was assumed that they still represented the interests of something called the United States of America and the people in it.

But as David Rothkopf, a former partner of Henry Kissinger and a Treasury Department official under Clinton, noted, "In a global economy in which multinational corporations are no longer bound to any single country, they have gained a new kind of power over national governments that, by their nature, are confined by borders. Companies have created a new kind of marketplace in which governments compete with one another for investment, essentially undercutting in a fundamental way some of the most familiar, potent, and until recently enduring foundations of sovereignty."[22]

Between 1980 and 2006, finance replaced manufacturing as the driving force of the American economy. The banking and investment business expanded from 12 to 20 percent of the country's GDP, and its share of total corporate profits rose from 20 to 45 percent. Meanwhile, the manufacturing sector shrunk from 21 to 12 percent, and its share of profits dropped from 45 to 5 percent.

Some modest rise in the importance of finance was to be expected. As the United States prospered, it would naturally devote more of its resources and attention to the management of its citizens' accumulated wealth. But in the age of Reagan, the financial sector was dramatically transformed from mainly providing investment to enterprises that produced goods and services to diverting credit to unproductive short-term speculation on the prices of assets. As this transformation occurred, the U.S. business culture's concept of economic time dramatically shrunk, and in many places the future just disappeared.

Investment shapes the future. Credit creates investment. The primary function of banks, brokerage firms, and other financial institutions is to transfer capital from those who save from today's income to those who invest to produce tomorrow's income. Since in a growing economy the amount of credit that is necessary to support tomorrow's investment is greater than today's savings, banks are given license by the government to issue more credit than they can back up with deposits—that is, they have been given the power to create money.

Economic development requires patient capital. It takes years to go from a marketable idea to building production capacity, hiring and training people, creating distribution systems, developing marketing campaigns, and doing all the other activities required to make a start-up a successful business. Banks borrow money from savers on a short-term basis and lend it out on a long-term basis, making their own profit on the normal spread between lower short-term and higher long-term interest rates.

When capitalism is working as it should, finance is a rather conservative, if not dull, business. On Wall Street, it was traditionally a world of "white shoe" Ivy League culture run by the sons of the moneyed class, whose main task was to preserve capital with cautious investments. When they wanted excitement, they went sailing or took a few years off to work for the CIA. On Main Street, finance was a job with "bankers' hours," with plenty of afternoon time for the golf course and the Rotary Club luncheon.

But finance has a split personality. Lurking in the soul of the cautious, conventional Dr. Jekyll is an economically murderous Mr. Hyde who breaks out from time to time in a destructive speculative rampage. Virtually from the beginning of capitalism, money markets have shown a tendency to become casinos. In his classic study, *Manias, Panics and Crashes: A History of Financial Crises*, economic historian Charles Kindleberger observed that financial booms had led to busts in virtually every part of the capitalist world since the seventeenth century.

The objects of financial desire differ—coins, tulips, real estate, commodities, mines, oil wells, housing, canals, roadways, government bonds—but the manias and panics follow a similar pattern. Normal business expectations are suddenly displaced by the prospect of quick profits by trading in the next new thing. The sober world of the banker is suddenly filled with intoxicating visions of fabulous wealth. Credit loosens and time horizons shrink. Investors and lenders no longer need to judge whether the business can last or the managers have integrity and staying power, because they now expect to get their money back in months—if not weeks or days.

As asset prices escalate, the fever spreads. Ordinarily cautious souls see others making huge gains, and the pressure to join the frenzy becomes irresistible. Easy credit in turn attracts—and often turns—formerly honest players into swindlers and crooks. The financial speculators are typically aware that they are in a bubble, but no one knows when it will burst, and meanwhile there is still money to be made. At some point, an event—often what would ordinarily be inconsequential, such as a minor business defaulting on its loan—triggers a panic, and the house of cards tumbles down.

In modern economies, the products that the finance industry knows best are its own: bonds, stocks, credit instruments, and other paper assets, the value of which are abstracted, or "derived," from real-world investments. As the boom develops, these abstract investments offer quicker returns than the real-world investments. A trader from Citigroup or Goldman Sachs can make a sizable gain buying a security at 10 a.m. and selling it at 10:30 a.m. Such profits come not from any change in the inherent value of the company but from price changes based on what buyers and sellers are guessing— that is, speculating—that other buyers and sellers will buy or sell at any given moment.

In the wake of the crash of 1929, the New Deal created a grand bargain between the government and the financial sector. The banks, the principal institutions of finance, were given a government safety net in the form of deposit insurance, which guaranteed bank customers that they would not lose the money they had deposited if their bank failed. In return, the banks were prohibited from making risky investments, and it was assumed that this prohibition would block the reappearance of the speculative Mr. Hyde. The Glass-Steagall Act of 1933 separated banking from the stock market, a Securities and Exchange Commission was set up to regulate security fraud and abuse, and a network of state and federal regulation was placed over insurance, savings institutions, and pension funds.

The new system worked. The financial markets grew with the economy, but not much faster, and often slower. The 1929 average of stock market prices was not recovered until 1954, despite an almost 360 percent rise in GDP.

But Mr. Hyde kept gnawing away at the grand bargain that had kept him caged up. Gradually, government protections for U.S. capital expanded while the restrictions fell away.

In the winter of 1979–1980, "Bucky" and Herbert Hunt, sons of the right-wing oil billionaire H. L. Hunt, cornered three-quarters of the world's silver market. In a little more than six months they drove the price of silver from five dollars to more than fifty dollars an ounce. But they overreached and were caught in a cash-flow bind. In March 1980, they could not meet their obligation to take delivery on nineteen million ounces. The Hunts appealed to Federal Reserve chairman Paul Volcker, who, in a late-night deal (Volcker was said to have been in his pajamas), injected more than a billion dollars into the Hunt operation—this at a time when the Carter-Volcker high-interest austerity program was, in effect, denying credit to tens of millions of homeowners and small-business owners in order to fight inflation.

Reagan extended the Carter-Volker plan to fight inflation with high interest rates. One result was to squeeze the savings and loan banks, which had to pay more for savings deposits than they were receiving in mortgage revenue. The savings and loans successfully lobbied Washington to demand that their clients be freed from restrictions on making more profitable, and therefore riskier, consumer and commercial real estate loans. At the same time, the Reagan government loosened accounting rules and effectively abolished the regulations against self-dealing that prevented managers from using their banks to finance their personal business.

The result was predictable. Overnight, the savings and loans went from being benign local institutions serving their communities to being sources of guaranteed money for financial adventure. They were quickly bought up by high rollers who paid themselves sumptuous salaries and borrowed money from the banks they now owned to finance vacation homes, lavish parties, expensive cars, and private jets. Loans were made to cronies and family members, who used the money to invest in high-risk ventures that it was hoped would pay high enough returns to cover everyone's rear end.

During the boom stage there were more than enough respectable Wall Street lawyers and accountants to assure the government and the public that these were sound business practices. Indeed, just before the scandal broke, Alan Greenspan was hired by the notorious savings and loan manipulator, Charles Keating, to testify that Keating's Lincoln Savings and Loan bank was "a strong institution that poses no risk, with a management that was extremely seasoned and expert." Keating was later convicted of using the bank for fraud, and he spent four and a half years in prison. Sixteen of the seventeen savings and loan banks that Greenspan had certified as sound went out of business within four years.[23]

When the savings and loans finally crashed in a pile-up of rascality and incompetence, the Reagan administration bailed out the depositors and closed down approximately a thousand institutions at a cost to the taxpayers of about two hundred billion dollars. According to one estimate, the share of savings and loan deposits that were paid off by the U.S. government exceeded the share of bank deposits lost in the 1929 crash.

In a related debacle, the Reagan regulators looked on benignly while reputable firms like Salomon Brothers created the junk bond securities that were hyped by slick salesmen as safe and high yielding. High yielding they were, but hardly safe. The junk bonds were the fuel that fired the merger and leverage buyout bubbles in the 1980s.

In a leveraged buyout, investors and specialized private equity investment firms buy controlling interests in a well-run company with little debt and a healthy cash flow. They pay for the company not with their own money but with loans, such as junk bonds, that put up the company's assets as collateral, burdening the firm with debt. They then typically make the firm more "efficient" in the short run by selling off assets, laying off workers, and lowering wages. In the long run, this often makes the firm less able to compete, but before that happens, the private equity fund has sold out at a profit, blessed further with a special tax break.

Bankers and investment brokers are supposed to be experts at their trade. And the first thing that one learns in business school is that risk and yield go together. The greater the return on an investment, the higher the risk. That is what has traditionally given bankers their dour and stodgy reputations. But throughout the buildup of the great leveraged buyout bubble of the 1980s, such as in the dot-com bubble of the 1990s and the subprime mortgage bubble of 2000–2008, Wall Street assured itself and its customers that the rewards of these exotic schemes were coming at little or no risk. Moreover, their customers were often not just the average small investor but people in charge of large institutions, including pension funds, responsible for huge pools of money.

When the junk bond–propelled market inevitably crashed in 1987, the Federal Reserve promptly flooded the market with cheap loans, keeping companies that should have been bankrupt afloat. Junk bond king Michael Milken was eventually indicted on ninety-six counts, including insider trading, illegal profiteering, and tax evasion. But the actual lesson was that crime pays. It cost Milken about six hundred million dollars in penalties, but he got to keep about a billion dollars for himself after spending less than two years in a minimum-security prison. That's a deal that a lot of Americans would be quite willing to make.

Each cycle of boom, bust, and bailout was accompanied by the media chorus of cheerleaders for the Wall Street wizards during the boom stage, horror and surprise during the bust, and a brief period, during the bailout, of moralizing on the spectacle of people who were making exorbitant incomes being coddled by administrations that could not bring themselves to provide health insurance for working people. Then, inevitably, came a shrug of the shoulders, a sigh, and a moving on to the next cycle.

Future cycles included Reagan's bailout of the Continental-Illinois Bank, Citibank, and the Bank of New England as well as Clinton's rescue of the Wall Street holders of Mexican bonds in 1994–1995, Asian securities in 1997, and the 1998 intervention to prevent the collapse of the Long-Term Capital Management hedge fund.

It is no surprise that the expanding finance sector has drawn in bright, ambitious, and creative people who a few decades earlier might have gone into other businesses. Their talents were well utilized by the nature of financial speculation. Financial markets became a frenzied search for arbitrage: buying an item in a market where the price was low and selling it in a market where the price was higher. Each time this was done, a broker took a fee. Aided by computers shifting through millions of data bits, the time frame for profiting from any transaction shrunk from days to hours. With the introduction of high-speed computers, this went from hours to minutes to seconds.

As the money poured into the financial sector, credit was cheap and easily available, offering investors the magic of leverage: the ability to buy assets with little money down so that a small rise in the asset price would bring a large return on one's equity. The grumpy caution of the old banker was replaced by the reckless flamboyance of a new generation of players, confident of their own brilliance, their technology, and their macho instincts. A fawning media indulged them with the title "masters of the universe."

"In effect," wrote the *New Yorker* economics correspondent John Cassidy, "many of the big banks had turned themselves from businesses whose profits rose and fell with the capital-raising needs of their clients into immense trading houses whose fortunes depended on their ability to exploit day-to-day movements in the markets."[24]

With the exception of the 1920s' credit bubble, American corporations had largely financed their growth internally, out of the corporations' own cash flow. As such, the company managers, who understood their own businesses, were both the source of the funds and the destination of the investment. But as financing increasingly came from banks and securities markets, corporate expansion was financed by investors who knew less and less about the actual business.

So the measure for judging the performance of managers and boards became the number that shareholders could easily grasp: the price of the stock. Wall Street justified its increasingly reckless behavior with extremely abstract academic theories of "rational expectations," a notion that at any given moment the stock price embodied the best possible judgment on the future worth of the business whose shares it represented. Thus, you didn't need to know anything about the business, the market, technology, or anything else to judge a company's performance. Managers of steel companies, supermarkets, restaurant chains, and other businesses were increasingly paid with relatively short-term stock options as an incentive to keep the daily price of the company's shares high.

Finance soon broke out of its traditional Wall Street confines. It absorbed more and more of the time and energy of those who managed firms in the real-world economy that produced goods and services. As foreign competition got tougher, business owners found it easier to make money in finance than in manufacturing. Companies like General Motors and General Electric were soon generating more profits from their consumer credit and banking operations than from making cars and washing machines. More important, they were making it faster.

In the 1990s, bank lobbyists descended on Washington, complaining that all of this was creating unfair competition. Unregulated investment banks were now taking deposits in the form of money-market accounts and investing them in higher paying, riskier securities that were off-limits to regulated banks because of the Glass-Steagall Act. The reasonable response would have been to extend federal regulation to these new banklike arrangements. But the bankers demanded that they be deregulated. Rubin, Summers, and Greenspan were in their corner, and so was Republican senator Phil Gramm, who chaired the Senate Finance Committee. The Glass-Steagall Act was repealed.

Perhaps even more important, the bipartisan globalization of finance had created a massively complex set of cross-border credit relationships that by itself put the large U.S. banks, investment houses, hedge funds, and leveraged buyout firms beyond the reach of U.S. regulators. With money free to cross borders at will and within the wink of an electronic eye, the capacity of the government to manage the country's money supply—and therefore economic growth—was seriously compromised.

By the end of the "liberal" Clinton years, financial regulation had been gutted and the regulatory agencies demoralized, a process that was then accelerated by his successor, George W. Bush. In 1979, the debt of the finance industry—the banks, the stockbrokers, the investment firms—was roughly one-third of the debt of nonfinancial businesses and 12 percent of all corporate debt. In the next three decades, the debt the financial sector owed to itself grew by 3,200 percent, compared with a rise of 800 percent in the debt of the producing sector. By 2007, the debt of banks and investment firms was more than 150 percent greater than the debt of the rest of U.S. business.

The stage was set for the mother of all financial bubbles: the boom in subprime mortgages.

Part II

What the Crash Revealed

The future, what's that?

—Belisario, after his tribe, the Nukak,
emerged from the Columbia jungle in 2006
to join the civilized world

5

Who Knew?
They Knew

Testifying before a congressional committee in October 2008, Alan Greenspan was asked why he didn't see trouble coming. He replied, "We are not smart enough as people. We just cannot see events that far in advance."[1]

"Nobody was prepared for this," Robert Rubin told the *Wall Street Journal*. We were faced, he said, with a "perfect storm": the extraordinary convergence of uncontrollable and unpredictable forces of nature. "What came together was not only a cyclical undervaluing of risk [but also] a housing bubble, and triple-A ratings were misguided. There was virtually nobody who saw that low-probability event as a possibility."[2]

The Greenspan-Rubin defense echoed throughout the Wall Street–Washington corridor in the winter of 2008–2009. Richard S. Fuld Jr., the last CEO of the destroyed Lehman Brothers, assured a congressional committee that no one "was prepared for this one."[3] Daniel Mudd, the disgraced former CEO of the giant mortgage financier Fannie Mae, insisted, "Almost no one expected what was coming. It's not fair to blame us for not predicting the unthinkable."[4] The CEO of J.P. Morgan explained away the loss of billions from betting in the subprime mortgage market with the observation that the housing market's direction is notoriously unpredictable.[5] "I wasn't good enough to tell you what was going to happen," said Jimmy Cayne, the ex-CEO of Bear Stearns who had driven his company into oblivion.[6]

Unpredictable, incredible, and *unbelievable* were the words used in the fall of 2008 to describe the economic crisis by newspaper columnists, TV talking heads, and caption writers for newspaper photos of slumping floor traders with their heads in their hands. A once-in-a-lifetime catastrophe that no one could have foreseen, wrote thousands of financial advisers to their clients, desperately explaining away the massive meltdown of the customers' 401(k) portfolios.

For years the influential *New York Times* columnist Thomas Friedman had been a breathless promoter of global financial deregulation. Through his columns, books, speeches, and TV appearances, Friedman had long rationalized the values of the get-rich-quick buccaneer economy. "International finance," he proclaimed from the vortex of the boom, "has turned the world into a parliamentary system" that permitted newly enfranchised global citizens "to vote every hour, every day, through their mutual funds, their pension funds, their brokers."[7]

As this glorious system unraveled, Friedman grasped Rubin's reputation-saving metaphor:

> We are in the middle of an economic perfect storm, and we don't know how much worse it's going to get. People all over the world are hoarding cash, and no bank feels that it can fully trust anyone it is doing business with anywhere in the world. Did you notice that the government of Iceland just seized the country's second-largest bank and today is begging Russia for a $5 billion loan to stave off "national bankruptcy"? What does that say? It tells you that financial globalization has gone so much farther and faster than regulatory institutions could govern it. Our crisis could bankrupt Iceland! Who knew?[8]

The question was rhetorical, designed to answer itself and thus put the issue to rest. If no one could have known, then everyone was off the hook.

But too much damage had been done. The economy had tanked, trillions in savings had been flushed away, and great financial houses had suddenly crashed. Reagan-style capitalism was in disgrace. In the 2008 presidential campaign, not just Barack Obama and Joe Biden but also John McCain and Sarah Palin raged against the "greed and irresponsibility" of Wall Street. "Who knew?" was not good enough.

In an early 2009 column, conservative columnist David Brooks of the *New York Times* addressed the question of whether the root cause of our financial calamity was greed, stupidity, or both. Worried that the greed story might end with calls to "smash the oligarchy" or at least "restructure the financial sector," Brooks opted for stupidity. Bankers were simply in over their heads, he wrote. They "got too big to manage. Instruments got too complex to understand. Too many people were good at math but ignorant of history."[9]

Since then, we have been flooded with books, news media features, congressional testimony, talk shows, and millions of blogs telling and retelling the tale from every conceivable angle. Economists and historians will forever argue over the weight to assign to the various causes, and new details will be revealed as the lawsuits and the government investigations drag on. But we *know* what happened.

First, the underlying economic condition was the thirty-year flattening of incomes, which drove consumers to take on more debt in order to keep up with the expanding American dream. In 1980, debt was about 70 percent of their disposable income. By 2007, it was almost 140 percent. Because of lower interest rates and stretched-out payments, the share of monthly income that people had to devote to servicing debt rose 23 percent—less than the increase in their total debt, which made it easier to pile up long-term liabilities.

The lower interest rates were made possible because foreigners were willing to lend back the dollars they earned by running trade surpluses with us. As wages flattened and consumers took on more debt, the personal U.S. savings rate dropped from 10 percent of income in 1980 to 2 percent in 2007. Although it wasn't clear how this would end, it was obvious that it couldn't last.

Second, since the collapse of the savings and loans in the 1980s, more mortgages were made by specialized mortgage brokers. Local banks were bypassed as mortgages were placed with the expanding national megabanks and other large investors. Since the brokers did not themselves lend the money, they had less incentive to make sure that the borrower was good for it in the long run.

In the mid-1990s, housing prices, recovering from a cyclical downturn, began to rise. Aggressive brokers encouraged consumers to refinance their homes in order to get more spending money, arguing that as the value of the houses rose, the homeowners could continue to refinance their mortgages even if their incomes did not rise. People who could not afford the monthly payments unless they refinanced their mortgages every few years were given mortgage loans. Each refinancing of these subprime mortgages, as they were called, came loaded with fees and balloon payments that made them more profitable for the brokers and investors.

Subprime mortgages were not limited to low-income families. They were also available to middle-class professionals upgrading into McMansions. This new flow of money pushed housing prices up almost everywhere and, in the faster-growing parts of the country, into the stratosphere. In real terms, average home prices in the United States almost doubled in a decade.[10]

Third, pressured by Wall Street and real estate lobbyists to continue the housing boom, the Clinton and George W. Bush administrations leaned on "Fannie Mae" and "Freddie Mac," the independent quasi-governmental agencies that bought mortgages from banks in order to free up capital for housing, to expand their operations ostensibly in the name of widening opportunities for homeownership. But we were now in the Reagan era of deregulation and privatization. So instead of keeping the expanding effort under the control of the agencies' cautious and reasonably competent bureaucracy, the Clinton and George W. Bush administrations encouraged the creation of an ad hoc web of banks, investment firms, congressional committees, real estate brokers, homebuilders, and political fixers eager to cash in on the housing boom.

In the process, standards for mortgage eligibility, down payments, and basic honesty in filling out loan applications were thrown out the window. Government inspectors, auditors, and regulators were pushed aside as banks and mortgage makers flooded Fannie Mae and Freddie Mac with a tsunami of new subprime mortgage paper. The story was not, as many conservatives have tried to tell it, the result of government mandates to help the poor own homes they couldn't afford. This, as *New York Times* business columnist Joe Nocera bluntly put it, is a lie: "Fannie and Freddie, rather than leading the housing industry astray, got into riskier mortgages only after the horse was out of the barn. They were becoming irrelevant in the most profitable segment of the market. And that *they* couldn't abide."[11]

"They" were the high-rolling, highly paid Wall Street–connected executives the Clinton and Bush administrations brought in to turn Fannie and Freddie from instruments of conventional housing finance to gushers of profit for financial speculators. Early on *Times* reporter Charles Duhigg captured the essence of what was going on when he wrote about a hedge fund manager who called a senior Fannie Mae executive to complain that the latter was not buying enough risky mortgages. "Are you stupid or blind?" the investor roared. "Your job is to make me money!"[12]

The reckless expansion of Fannie Mae was originally engineered by prominent Democrats, James Johnson and Franklin Raines, who were Fannie Mae's board chair and CEO, respectively. Johnson was a skilled political operator with close ties to Wall Street. Raines had been Clinton's budget director. But it was a bipartisan effort. Republican Robert Zoellick, whom Bush made his trade representative and later appointed as president of the World Bank, was Fannie Mae's general counsel, and, among others, Newt Gingrich was a highly paid consultant and prominent booster. When George W. Bush took office, he filled the government housing programs with more real estate and Wall Street people who pumped up the out-of-control federal subsidies even further. "They loved us," Democrat Raines later said of the Bush White House, recounting how he flew with Bush on Air Force One to a housing event.[13]

In early 2003, Armando Falcon, the head of the U.S. government office charged with overseeing Fannie Mae and Freddie Mac, issued a report warning that the two government-sponsored entities (GSEs) were overloading themselves with risky mortgages and complex derivatives. Raines complained to the Bush White House, and Falcon was fired.

When in 2005 concerned congressional Democrats proposed to put Fannie and Freddie under stricter supervision, Bush refused to do so. As the *New York Times* later editorialized, "President Bush wanted to fully privatize them and feared that if they were adequately reformed, privatization would lose steam."[14]

Even with corrupt or negligent managers at the top, the government agencies performed better than the private industry. The Financial Crisis Inquiry Commission, set up to investigate the causes of the financial crash, reported that for loans to people of similar credit scores and down payments, the rate of serious delinquency on loans guaranteed by Freddie and Fannie was 6.2 percent, compared with the private financial sector's rate of 28.3 percent.[15]

The fourth, and by far the most important, cause of the economic crisis was the behavior of the deregulated private banks and financial firms that turned a large but not extraordinary credit bubble in the housing market into a general economic collapse. The creation of this massive pool of IOUs, presumably backed by tangible collateral—American houses and real estate—was just what a Wall Street reeling from the collapse of the high-tech bubble at the beginning of the twenty-first century was looking for.

Investment firms bought mortgages, commingled the subprimes with the primes, and marketed the new securities as safe and high yielding. This new debt paper was then peddled to investors, who used it as collateral for margin loans to buy yet more stocks and bonds. At each change of hands, fees and underwriting charges added to the total claims on the monthly mortgage payments of questionable credit risk at the bottom of this upside-down credit pyramid.

The expanded use of options provided investors with the leverage that was key to getting rich in a rising market. Options are bets on the future price movements of a security. Because the price of an option is a small fraction of the price of the security itself, it offers the opportunity to profit on the rise in value of an asset without having to pay its full price. Thus, if it costs 5 cents per share for the right to buy a stock that is priced at $1.00 per share, and the stock price rises 10 percent to $1.10 per share, your option allows you to buy a share at $1.00 and sell it at $1.10, a 10-cent profit. Inasmuch as you only risked a nickel, this translates into a 100 percent profit. If you had originally bought the share at, and therefore risked, $1.00, you would have made only a 10 percent profit. The risk with options is that they have a time limit. If the stock moves in the opposite direction by the time the option expires, you lose your nickel. If you had put all your capital—say, $100—into buying such options, when the market dropped only 5 percent, you would be wiped out.

In the 1970s, a variety of university economists developed theories of how to judge the value of options.[16] Wall Street firms then started using these formulas to convince their customers that their highly leveraged investments were guided by computer programs developed by Nobel Prize winners. In fact, many of these models were run by midlevel salespeople who had learned that if they made small changes in the model's assumptions of such things as future interest rates, repayments, and defaults, the computer would substantially reduce its estimate of the investment's risk.

The result was a frenzied bidding up of prices for a bewildering maze of arcane securities that neither the buyers nor the sellers could accurately value. Hedge funds—highly speculative and highly leveraged concentrations of short-term investment capital—brought what seemed to be an inexhaustible supply of fresh money into the mix. Through the extreme borrowing leverage provided by options, the investors were able to accumulate portfolios in which the ratio of the actual investment to the underlying asset was a staggering one hundred to one.

Business TV talking heads and financial columnists applauded the financial "innovations." This was American ingenuity at its best for all the world to see and admire. The commentators assured their audiences that by spreading risks among more people, the miracle of "diversity" was actually turning bad loans into good ones. And there was nothing to worry about, they said, for the banks were buying insurance policies against default.

In fact, these policies were quickly transformed into a set of even murkier derivatives called *credit default swaps*, which are bets on price movements of securities that in turn are bets on the default rate of loans held by other people. These swaps were marketed to hedge funds, pension managers, and, in some cases, back to the banks that were being insured in the first place. With money on all sides of every trade, it was hard for many players to tell at the end of the day whether they'd lost or won. At the end of 2007, the market for these swaps was estimated at $45.5 trillion—roughly twice as large as all U.S. stock markets combined.

The country's financial markets had gone from being decontrolled to being uncontrollable. But as long as the market expanded, the profits seemed enormous and apparently insured against loss. The operating margins at the giant insurer AIG on collateralized debt obligation (CDO) insurance rose steadily; by 2002 the margin was 44 percent of revenue, and by 2005, 83 percent. The profits of the unit that sold CDOs rose from $737 million in 1999 to $3.26 billion in 2005. Fat bonuses, lavish parties, and padded expense accounts for exotic travel followed.

The credit boom built on subprime mortgages also provided real, if temporary, benefits to a large number of Americans who never bought a derivative. The Wall Street booms trickled down to construction workers, real estate agents, and the workforces of the communities they lived in. Families were better housed, at least temporarily, and some permanently. College educations, vacations, and hobbies were paid for. Seniors sold their homes and lived their twilight years in comfort. Love was supported, marriage enabled, and divorce financed. Of course, the wealth created from installing new granite countertops and "flipping" two-hundred-thousand-dollar suburban homes for two hundred fifty thousand dollars never approached anything like the profits involved in trading the complex instruments that allowed for them.

In 2008, *New York Times* business columnist Gretchen Morgenson interviewed Keysha Cooper, a senior mortgage underwriter for Washington Mutual who was eventually fired for not approving blatantly fraudulent loans. Brokers, who easily made twenty to forty thousand dollars on a five-hundred-thousand-dollar loan, tried to bribe her to approve subprime deals. One offered nine hundred dollars to send Cooper's son to football boot camp. She refused to approve a loan for eight hundred thousand dollars that was obviously fraudulent. Six months later it defaulted, and when the bank went to foreclose, the address was found to be an empty lot.[17]

The fifth step down the lane to financial meltdown was the willingness of rating agencies and accounting firms to act as shills for the Wall Street sellers of the massively leveraged derivatives. Rating agencies (such as Moody's, Standard & Poor's, and Fitch) were assumed to be independent watchdogs that provided the investing public with objective evaluations of risk. The investor, not the company, issuing the security was assumed to be the customer.

But in the 1970s, deciding that they were not making enough money selling their services to investors, the rating agencies began charging the firms that were underwriting the securities. The customer was now the seller, not the buyer. Since every underwriter is looking for a favorable rating, competition among the rating agencies created a bias toward giving a rating with an eye to the next contract. In the late 1990s, every Moody analyst was expected to bring in at least a million dollars in new revenue. At the beginning of the twenty-first century, the rating agencies turned themselves into public corporations. Managers' pay was tied to the short-term price of the stock, creating even more pressure to raise sales and eroding the rating agencies' standards even further.

Similarly as demonstrated in the Enron, Global Crossing, and other scandals that erupted in the first few years of the new millennium, the accounting profession had been seriously compromised. The proliferation of complex securities and intricate financial deals made the selection of a friendly auditing firm much more important. Many had become public firms and were driven by the same need as the corporations they were auditing: to keep their stock prices up. To make more money, they began selling management services to the same companies that hired them to audit their books. So to some extent they were evaluating not only the people who were paying them but also their own performance.

Rules were stretched, and the concept of value changed. For example, assets were increasingly "marked to market," which means that the present value of future projected earnings could be claimed as income. And accountants regularly approved corporate shells that were set up to hide high-risk operations.

Investment banker Steve Eisman, who made a fortune betting on the collapse, told writer Michael Lewis that at first he didn't understand how securities backed by subprime mortgages were getting triple-A ratings. "I didn't understand how they were turning all this garbage into gold," Eisman admitted.

He would ask his colleagues, "Where are the rating agencies in all of this? And I'd always get the same reaction. It was a smirk." So

finally he called Standard & Poor's and asked what its rating formulas were assuming about how much the default rates on the bonds
would rise if housing prices fell. "The man at S&P couldn't say; its
model for home prices had no ability to accept a negative number.
They were just assuming home prices would keep going up." At that
moment Eisman understood "the total unabashed complicity of the
upper class of American capitalism."[18]

Finally, the sixth step in the economic crisis was that the boom
was internationalized. Given the U.S. trade deficit and low savings rate, much of the run-up in subprime-infected securities was
financed with foreign money. Since capital was now free to roam
the globe, it was impossible to identify the limits of the U.S.
financial system. The large American banks—like the largest banks
in Europe, Japan, China, and the rest of the world—had branches
and subsidiaries everywhere. Accountants juggled financial state-
ments among these entities to minimize the tax liabilities, but
even so, the connections had become so complicated that when
the crisis finally hit and the responsibilities had to be unraveled,
the corporate managers themselves could not sort out who owed
what to whom.

Real estate remained a local phenomenon, and each nation had
its own laws and its own capacity to enforce them. Nevertheless, the
techniques of leveraging mortgage credit spread throughout the
global financial web. Housing booms in Britain, Iceland, Ireland,
and Spain soon produced similar upside-down pyramids of massive
complex credit and abstract speculative paper resting on the shoulders of home buyers whose ability to repay their mortgages depended
on the ever rising prices of their homes.

The Bank of International Settlements—the clearinghouse for
the world's central banks—estimated that by the end of 2007 the
global market for derivatives was $516 trillion. At the time, the U.S.
GDP was $15 billion, the entire global GDP was about $50 billion,
and the total actual value of the world's real estate was about
$75 billion.

In the end, someone had to run out of money, and it was homeowners. When housing prices eventually flattened out, refinancing
stalled. Subprime-mortgage homebuyers had to rely on their inadequate incomes to make their rising mortgage payments. They fell

behind. The revenues to the mortgage holders declined, and their payments to the banks became delinquent. The value of the securities based on the mortgage payments fell. The banks demanded that their loans be repaid or that more collateral be put up.

But the assets of the people who had borrowed were tied up in the securities whose values were plummeting. They couldn't pay. When the day of reckoning arrived, like water cascading through widening cracks in a dam, the money gushed out faster than it had come in, draining the financial lake behind and exposing the dried-up wreckage of the fraudulent loans and worthless collateral that lay at the bottom.

The rest is history: the crash of Bear Stearns, the bankruptcy of Lehman Brothers, and the panicked response of the Republican White House and a Democratic Congress to pour massive amounts of money into the banks, investment companies, and insurance firms that were deemed "too big to fail."

Although there undoubtedly were challenged intellects among the public and business leaders who were most responsible for the economic crisis, David Brooks's stupidity explanation does not fit.

As John Maynard Keynes, Charles Kindleberger, and many, many other economists, such as Hyman Minsky, had shown, financial excesses were built into the modern economy. Economists might have different ways of explaining the boom-and-bust cycle, but it is inevitable: what goes up must come down. This was no secret on Wall Street. The term *Minsky moment* was coined by an investment banker for the turning point that kicks off a panic in which investors begin dumping even high-quality assets in order to cover their debts.

In September 2007, as the mortgage market was cracking, the Brookings Institution brought together Robert Rubin, Larry Summers, Ronald Steel (George W. Bush's treasury undersecretary), and other Republican and Democratic policy makers. There was not much difference in the views of the Clinton and Bush people. Roger Altman, who was a deputy treasury secretary in the Clinton administration, commented, "How did we get here? We got here because this is how markets typically operate."[19]

Except for Bush's first two treasury secretaries—Paul O'Neill and John Snow—who both came from industry, all of the major figures in the financial tragedy were smart and capable individuals with extensive knowledge of and experience in the way financial markets work. They were on every influential person's short list for the jobs that they held, and they were widely applauded by the established media.

Alan Greenspan and his successor as chairman of the Federal Reserve, Ben Bernanke (also a Republican), were both reappointed by Democratic presidents. There may have been other people as qualified and as acceptable to the financiers of the governing class, but there were none who were more so.

These men had at their command thousands of economists, statisticians, and market observers as well as easy access to the best and brightest analysts of capitalism in the world. When Greenspan, Rubin, and Summers got together—whether at formal meetings, for lunch, or on the tennis court—their aides describe their conversations as a movable seminar in economic statistics.

All of these people were well aware of the great flattening in American incomes. Rubin and Summers spent large amounts of time lecturing anxious liberal Democrats that the problem was not off-shoring or corporate power but a lack of education on the part of American workers.

Greenspan, the conservative Republican, had no such constituency conflict. Wage stagnation and the growing insecurity of workers, he repeatedly argued, were actually good for the economy. The growing gap between wages and productivity meant lower labor costs and therefore higher profits and a rising stock market.

On the question of how an economy in which more than two-thirds of its income was generated by consumer spending could continue to grow if consumer incomes were not rising, Greenspan answered that what consumers were missing in their paychecks was made up by the rising value of their homes, their stock portfolios, and their pensions.

Greenspan's formula had a double benefit for Wall Street. First, it pulled the rug out from under the demands that Washington do something about the increasingly skewed distribution of income and wealth that was now affecting the middle class. The days of any serious concern for the plight of the poor were long gone, of course, but as the wages-and-salary gap between the rich and the middle class grew, it represented a more serious political threat.

Secondly, Greenspan's formula rationalized the diversion of investment into financial markets, whose importance was now supposedly critical to the well-being of the middle class. In the new economy, workers would get ahead not by joining a union but by investing in companies that successfully kept out unions.

However, the overwhelming majority of Americans still depended on their paychecks, not their dividend checks, to put bread on the table and a roof over their heads. Even at the height of the late 1990s dot-com boom, only 22 percent of households directly owned shares in a company. Including the ownership of shares in mutual funds, 401(k) plans, and other savings programs brought the total to 52 percent. The richest 10 percent of Americans owned more than 80 percent of corporate stock directly or indirectly, with the richest 1 percent owning more than 60 percent. In 1968 the richest 1 percent of Americans were 168 times wealthier than the average American. In 2001, they were 173 times richer, and by 2004, 190 times richer.

Greenspan later said that he was not aware of the speculative housing boom until late 2005, shortly before he retired from the Federal Reserve. In 2002, he had told Congress not to worry. Rising prices were not being driven by speculation, he said, but by the following sustainable economic fundamentals:

- Population growth resulting from the baby boomers becoming adults
- An increase in incomes in the late 1990s
- A short supply of land suitable for housing development around urban areas
- Zoning laws and environmental regulations that impeded housing development[20]

Economist Dean Baker, who not only predicted the housing bust but also sold his home and moved into a rented house before it occurred, examined Greenspan's claims in that speech. None of them made sense.[21]

First, Baker noted, the baby boomers had entered the age of household formation many years earlier, and the percentage of the population that was buying homes was actually decreasing. Second, the rise in consumer incomes in the late 1990s was historically weak, and even in times of more robust income growth, housing prices had not boomed. Third, the supply of land had not suddenly shrunk relative to demand. If anything, the Internet was making telecommuting easier and allowing people to make a living farther away from their offices. Fourth, there was no evidence of an accelerated tightening of environmental restrictions since they had become common in the 1960s.

Finally, noted Baker, as the prices of owner-occupied housing accelerated, rents had actually declined, suggesting that the housing-price boom was being driven not by a supply shortage but by a speculative boom.

Other prominent analysts agreed. Robert Shiller, a codeveloper of the most widely used housing price index and the foremost U.S. housing economist, had been predicting a collapse of housing and stock market prices for several years. In a book called *Irrational Exuberance*, he wrote that "significant further rises in these markets could lead, eventually, to even more significant declines."[22]

The late economist Edward Gramlich, then a member of the Federal Reserve Board of Governors, raised concerns about subprime lending practices and an overheated housing market as early as 2000. Sheila Bair, a treasury official in 2001 who later became head of the Federal Deposit Insurance Corporation, called attention to the shady practices that were becoming standard in the mortgage business. Even after she watered down her proposals to a voluntary code of conduct, industry lobbyists beat her back.

Moreover, those who lived in the metropolitan United States and in the fast-growing coastal areas—particularly in the South and Southwest—could see with their own eyes and hear with their own ears that the sale prices of the houses down the street were extraordinary. In Boston and New York, Las Vegas and San Francisco, and Denver and Phoenix, sales were regularly concluded at prices above what the sellers had been asking.

Testifying before the House Committee on Oversight and Government Reform in October 2008, Greenspan famously confessed to naiveté: "Those of us who have looked to the self-interest of lending institutions to protect shareholder's equity, myself included, are in a state of shocked disbelief."[23]

Greenspan can reasonably claim that he miscalculated, overlooked something, and did not give enough weight to this or that warning signal. But telling us that he was naive about the unwillingness of traders, brokers, and financiers to discipline themselves to forgo opportunities to become superrich is simply not credible.

According to his own memoirs, published in 2002, while he was telling Congress not to worry, he was also telling his own Federal Reserve Open Market Committee that there was "eye-catching" evidence of an uncommon inflation in housing prices: "It's hard to escape the conclusion that . . . our extraordinary housing boom and the carryover into very large extractions of equity, financed by very large increases in mortgage debt, cannot continue indefinitely into the future."[24]

Still, his public denial of a real estate boom that would inevitably lead to a bust continued. In a February 2004 speech to the Credit Union National Association, he actually chided American families for "losing tens of thousands of dollars" by not taking advantage of variable rate mortgages.

As early as 1996, when the Dow industrial index had jumped to almost sixty-five hundred, he uttered his famous comment about the dangers to the economy when "irrational exhuberance"—speculation—rules. But then he backed away from taking any responsibility for interfering with the market on the grounds of ignorance: "But how do we know when irrational exuberance has unduly escalated asset values, which then become subject to unexpected and prolonged contractions as they have in Japan over the past decade?"[25]

In his 2003 memoirs of his tenure as treasury secretary, Rubin repeatedly warned against the tendency of investors to "reach for yield"—that is, to buy securities without regard to risk. "I remember at the time of the South Korean crisis," he wrote, "being struck in a discussion with a prominent New York banker by how little he and his company knew about a country to which they had extended a considerable amount of credit. Though the basic hazard of investing in countries with major economic and political problems should have been obvious, the prevailing mentality was to downplay or ignore those risks in the 'reach for yield.'"[26]

It is simply not possible that throughout the 1990s Rubin and Greenspan were unaware of the carnival of delusion and incompetence that characterized American finance. If they needed to be reminded, hundreds of books were being written to expose the reckless and childish world that it was. One of the most widely read was Michael Lewis's best-selling *Liar's Poker*, which was published in the wake of the junk bond bubble in 1989. It's the saga of an art history major just out of college who became a twenty-four-year-old mortgage bond trader with Salomon Brothers. Later he wrote, "I'd never taken an accounting course, never run a business, never even had savings of my own to manage. I stumbled into a job at Salomon Brothers in 1985 and stumbled out much richer three years later, and even though I wrote a book about the experience, the whole thing still strikes me as preposterous."[27]

Yet throughout the 1990s, Rubin and Greenspan not only looked the other way, they also shot at any attempt to deal with the growing evidence of a bubble. In the spring and summer of 1998, Brooksley Born, who headed the Commodities Futures Trading Commission (CFTC), warned of the dangers of the ballooning derivatives market. She proposed a set of rules requiring transparency, limits on leveraging, and prudent accounting—including reserves against losses.

Greenspan, Rubin, and Summers, working with Phil Gramm, the head of the Senate Banking Committee who also had a doctorate in economics, came down on Born like a ton of brinks. They told her that she didn't know what she was talking about, and they engineered an extraordinary congressional resolution forbidding either the CFTC or the Securities and Exchange Commission to even propose rules to regulate derivatives, swaps, and other exotic securities.

The treatment of Born by Rubin, Greenspan, and Gramm was a warning to everyone throughout the government that dissent from the new economic orthodoxy would not be tolerated. There would be no questioning of the system that was feeding the global expansion of the U.S. finance industry.

Self-censorship followed. Robert Shiller, who was a member of the economic advisory panel to the Federal Reserve Board, observed that in professional circles, "people compete for stature, and the ideas just lag behind. The economists who advise the policymakers are no different. We all want to associate ourselves with dignified people and dignified ideas. Speculative bubbles, and those who study them, have been deemed undignified."[28]

Clayton Holdings is a firm that analyzed mortgage pools for Citigroup, Goldman-Sachs, and other prominent Wall Street firms. It reviewed more than nine hundred thousand of these packages from the beginning of 2006 through June 2007 and found that only 46 percent of the underlying loans met the underwriters' own professed standards. Gretchen Morgenson reported that "instead of requiring lenders to replace these funky mortgages with proper loans, Wall Street firms kept funneling the junk into securities and selling them to investors."[29] While Goldman-Sachs, for instance, was selling these mortgage pools to investors, it was betting against them with its own company portfolio.[30]

The minutes of the Federal Reserve Board meetings of 2006 (Fed minutes are released after five years) record officials laughing at the efforts of desperate homebuilders to attract buyers as their unsold inventories built up—giving away cars and dressing up homes in empty developments with curtains to make them appear to be occupied.[31]

In the face of the evidence that they were aware of the housing bubble, the "who knew?" apologists for the Federal Reserve now say they could not have known that an eventually bursting housing bubble could take down the entire financial system. Yet they were also aware of the massively leveraged securities market that had been built on top of the weakening housing market.

By 2005, the staff analysts at the New York Federal Reserve reported to Timothy Geithner that the market for derivatives was out of control—that is, the banks and investment firms could not track, evaluate, or rationally price them. Geithner's response was to urge Wall Street to update its computer systems so they could more efficiently process buy-and-sell orders.

The same year, foreign—not American—investigators turned up evidence that Citigroup was engaging in imprudent trading practices. The New York Federal Reserve suspended the Citigroup merger program but shortly rescinded the ban. As late as May 2007, when the evidence of a massive bubble was piling up, Geithner was proposing that banks be allowed to *lower* the amount of capital required against losses.

As part of the disclosures in response to Obama's nomination of Geithner as treasury secretary, Geithner's appointment books for 2007 and 2008 were made public, and the *New York Times* reported, "No institution shows up as frequently as Citigroup, the biggest bank company under the New York Fed's supervision. Among the numerous senior Citigroup officials recorded were Geithner's mentor Rubin, chief executive Charles Prince, and his successor, Vikram Pandit."[32]

Of course, these contacts are in the nature of the job. Bernanke told the *Times* that Geithner's Wall Street relationships had made him "invaluable" as they worked together to steer the country through crisis. "He spoke frequently to many, many different players and kept his finger on the pulse of the situation."[33]

The job of chairing the Federal Reserve of New York would hardly go to someone who was not close to the financial sector. Geithner's two predecessors left to work for investment banking firms, and his successor came from Goldman-Sachs.

Some of the actors in this tragic story could reasonably claim stupidity and/or ignorance. The working poor were assured that they could afford a home of their own by the real estate agent and the mortgage broker, and if they had any lingering doubts, they would be assured by the confidence of two presidents of the United States and the chairmen of the Federal Reserve Bank.

But as one moves up the ladder of responsibility, the stupidity defense fades quickly. As Barbara Tuchman noted, folly among the elite is rarely ignorance or stupidity. The country's economic managers knew that they were presiding over a giant unsustainable bubble. They did not know exactly how big and complicated it was. But they knew they didn't know, and they knew that the rating agencies and the accountants didn't know. That alone should have been a signal to responsible people that something had to be done.

Doing something about it would have required heroics, however, and you don't become a member of the governing class by challenging the status quo.

When asked about the Born episode after the crash, Rubin claimed that he had actually favored imposing margin requirements on derivatives. But, he added, Born had a "counterproductive" style.

"If you want to move forward you engage with parties in a constructive way," he stated.[34]

Yet if the problem was simply Born's style, why didn't the smooth and politically adept Rubin push for reform in his own less strident way? Alas, he sighed, "All of the forces in the system were arrayed against it. The industry certainly didn't want any increase in these requirements. There was no potential for mobilizing public opinion."[35]

Rubin also claimed that as secretary of the treasury, he had had little real power: "Even if I'd taken a placard and walked up and down Pennsylvania Avenue saying the financial system would come to an end without strict regulation of derivatives, I would have had no traction."[36]

But in a host of other issues, the lack of public support had not seemed to deter him. He led the fight for the unpopular NAFTA, the even more unpopular 1995 Mexican peso bailout, the unpopular opening up of the U.S. market to China, and the repeal of the Glass-Steagall Act.

"As long as the music is playing, you've got to get up and dance," said Citigroup CEO Charles Prince in 2007, suggesting that he knew the music would stop.[37] Yet Prince was, in fact, just doing his job. He was being evaluated by his board on the performance of his stock, which in turn rested on his ability to turn short-term profits as least as much as his competitors were doing—which in turn depended on him trading in riskier and riskier markets.

The problem was, of course, greed. The once-in-a-lifetime chance to get rich fast overwhelmed everything. But it's hard to believe that U.S. bankers and brokers had suddenly become intrinsically greedier after the election of Ronald Reagan than they had been before.

Moreover, crude personal greed did not completely explain the behavior of Greenspan, Rubin, and the other government officials. All of them earned much less working for the government than they would have earned in the private sector. What Joe Stiglitz said of Geithner is probably mostly true for all of them: "I don't think that Tim Geithner was motivated by anything other than concern to get the financial system working again. But I think that mindsets can be shaped by people you associate with, and you come to think that what's good for Wall Street is good for America."[38]

Still, one could have said that about every chairman of the Federal Reserve Board, every president of the New York Federal Reserve, and every treasury secretary in the modern era. What changed after the election of Reagan was that gradually most of the *political* system had also begun to think that what was good for Wall Street was good for the country. It had almost always been true of the Republican Party, but in the Roosevelt era, the Democrats had been a countervailing weight against the influence of big finance.

What changed for the Democrats was certainly the money. In the wake of Reagan's 1980 victory, Congressman Tony Coehlo of California became the chairman of the Democratic Congressional Campaign Committee. Coehlo dramatically expanded the party's fundraising from the finance industry in return for giving Wall Street more access to the House committees in which tax, spending, and regulation bills originated. At the time it was conventional wisdom that the Democrats had a permanent lock on the House of Representatives, where they had been in the majority for all but four of the past fifty years. Therefore, Coehlo assured the party's liberals that they did not have to worry about undue influence from big money. "Business has to deal with us whether they like it or not," Coehlo boasted.[39]

After Coehlo was forced to resign over an alleged sweetheart junk bond deal, he went to Wall Street, where he made millions. But he had permanently changed the way the Democrats raised money and from whom they raised it. After the Democrats lost the House in 1994, their bargaining position with Wall Street weakened. But they were hooked. Clinton, already a Wall Street favorite, took the corporate fundraising to another level. He got the corporate lobbyists to contribute not because *they* needed the Democrats but because they knew the Democrats needed *them*. In the 2000 presidential campaign, corporations gave the Democrats $340 million, dwarfing labor's $52 million. The Democrats' chief Wall Street fundraiser was Robert Rubin of Goldman-Sachs.

Gradually, the Wall Street connection became important for Democrats who were running not just for president but also for governor, for Congress, and even for state legislatures. Nor was the issue just campaign financing. It was not lost on the ambitious young Democrats that, as with Coehlo, an association with bankers and brokers could offer opportunities in business as well as in politics.

Wall Street's takeover of the commanding heights of the Democratic Party was critical to the transformation of the U.S. governing class's idea of the role of government in financial markets. No longer was that role to control the tendency of the markets toward speculative asset bubbles, nor was it to diffuse the bubbles before they popped. *It was to intervene only after the damage had been done.*

Before and after the crash, Greenspan maintained that the federal government was incapable of knowing when a market was over-priced. Therefore the only thing that it could do was to intervene after the bubble burst in order to pump it up again.

The rationale was also laid out by Bernanke in a scholarly paper he presented at the National Bureau of Economic Research conference in August 1999. The paper concluded, "Trying to stabilize asset prices *per se* is problematic for a variety of reasons, not the least of which is that it is nearly impossible to know for sure whether a given change in asset values results from fundamental factors, non-fundamental factors, or both."[40]

This was not just a technical point about monetary policy. It was a reflection of the Reaganite philosophy of government, which was now shared by the leadership of both parties. Despite the rhetoric of laissez-faire, the government's role in the economy remained critical. But that role had changed. Its purpose now was not to intervene in order to prevent large-scale damage. Rather it was to intervene after the damage had occurred to pick up the pieces, put them back together, and have the rest of the country pay for the damage.

6

Obama: Stuck in the Sandpile

In September 2008, Barack Obama was neck and neck in the polls with John McCain in their race for the presidency. When the stock market crashed, McCain and his running mate, Sarah Palin, looked erratic and shallow compared with the calm, cool Obama and Joe Biden, the experienced senator with a hint of the working class in his style. By election day, the crash had jolted enough white Americans to overcome their reservations and vote a black man with a Muslim-sounding middle name (Hussein) into the White House.

His election was, in itself, a historic event. Few adults had thought they'd live to see an African American president. His inauguration brought tears of joy to millions of eyes and lumps to millions of throats. Even many conservatives could not help feeling pride in our democracy. Foreigners expressed wonder at the capacity of the United States to surprise.

Obama's sober manner on the cold January day on which he was inaugurated reflected the enormity of the task ahead. He made a dramatic contrast with the swaggering adolescent style of his predecessor. The intended message was that an adult was now in charge.

His speech was largely standard inaugural fare: appeals to national unity, reverence for the past, and optimism for the future. He promised a fist for those who would be our enemies and an open hand for those who would be our friends. There were no truly memorable lines except for one dramatic sentence. "In the words of Scripture," he told his fellow Americans, "the time has come to set aside childish things."[1]

Childish was an inspired stroke. Rising out of Obama's unique mixture of the dry law professor and the pulsating preacher, it momentarily cut through the misty sentiments of national ritual to state why he had been elected; the country could not go on like this.

Most listeners surely understood what he meant. The class of culprits responsible for the financial calamity had been identified: greedy Wall Street bankers and brokers and corrupted Washington regulators. Obama would reap the whirlwind, but the seeds had been sown by previous administrations: Reagan, Bush the father, Clinton, and Bush the son. Anger with the Wall Street–Washington axis was widespread and hot.

The members of his audience also seemed aware of their own responsibility. A surprising number of Americans acknowledged through polls, talk shows, and blogs that they had been enablers, if not accessories, to the crime. No one, after all, had been forced to take out mortgages that they couldn't afford, overcharge their credit cards, or gamble in the stock market casino.

One Democratic pollster who conducted focus groups just before Obama's inauguration was shocked at the extent to which ordinary citizens recognized their complicity. "Their intellectual criticism was directed at the financial world," said John Martilla, "but their emotional criticism was directed at themselves."[2]

We had indulged in an orgy of consumerism, gorging on the sweet illusions of tax cuts, easy credit, and cheap imports. *We* had been swept away by the fairy tale that Wall Street would make us privately rich while the country's commons—health care, education, and transportation—were increasingly impoverished. *We* had responded to the erosion of the standard of living with tantrums against immigrants and dumb acceptance of tax cuts for the rich. Many people did not even seem to mind that our government had financed two wars with a credit card. *We* had reelected George Bush, who had lied to take us to war and like a spoiled teenager financed it with a credit card that someone else would pay for—or whatever.

The new president, whose campaign had championed "the people" against the Washington elites, built on this sense of wider culpability to make a tentative suggestion for shared sacrifice. Our condition, he said, was "a consequence of greed and irresponsibility on the part of some, but also our collective failure to make hard choices and prepare the nation for a new age."[3]

Unlike George W. Bush, Obama seemed to understand the basic economic imperative. In March 2008, as Wall Street was beginning to feel the tremors of the coming financial earthquake, his speech to the Economic Club of New York competently analyzed the flaws in the free-market fundamentalism of the past decades. He reminded his audience that at the beginning of the republic, the Founding Fathers had recognized the need for government to set the rules of the marketplace.

He was specific; he condemned the repeal of the Glass-Steagall Act and said it was aimed more at "facilitating mergers than creating an efficient regulatory framework." It was not simply some policy mistake, he noted. It was the work of a three-hundred-million-dollar lobbying campaign financed by many of the people in his audience. "This was not the invisible hand at work," he noted. "Instead it was the hand of industry lobbyists tilting the playing field in Washington."[4]

Throughout the campaign he eloquently indicted Wall Street and the compromised regulators in Washington. When the bottom finally fell out in September 2008, Obama had been right on the money.

Moreover, Obama's words demonstrated that he understood that the country's economic problems could not be solved by just patching up the holes in Wall Street regulation. The relentless trade deficit, the addiction to foreign oil, the offshoring of jobs, the increasing reliance on foreigners for high-technology products, and the growing gap between the incomes and wealth of the rich and that of everyone else were signs of widespread rot at the core of the economy.

Invoking a metaphor (building a house on a firm foundation of rock) from Jesus's Sermon on the Mount, Obama declared, "We cannot rebuild this economy on the same pile of sand. We must build our house upon a rock. We must lay a new foundation for growth and prosperity, a foundation that will move us from an era of borrow and spend to one where we save and invest, where we consume less at home and send more exports abroad."[5]

If by rebuilding the country's economic foundations, Obama meant what most people understood him to mean—doing what was necessary for the revival of rising prosperity for the majority of working Americans—it was obviously a huge task. It meant immediately reversing the cascading loss of jobs in the wake of the financial crisis. It meant shifting investment from financial speculation to the production of competitive goods and services. It meant squeezing the waste out of the bloated health-care system. It meant stopping the ever worsening lopsided distribution of income, wealth, and opportunity.

It was a program to begin a new era, not a fiscal year. Given the resistance to such change among the U.S. elite, it could not have been completed in Obama's first or even second term. Therefore, success required that Obama exploit the educable moment to establish a wide durable political base that could support these goals even after he left office.

It was not unprecedented. Both Franklin Roosevelt and Ronald Reagan had demonstrated the political leverage available to a determined leader who comes to power because of an economic crisis that can be blamed on his predecessor and his predecessor's party. The crash had discredited George W. Bush and the Reagan-inspired cowboy capitalism he represented. It gave Obama the greatest opportunity for serious change that any Democrat had had since Lyndon Johnson's ascension to the presidency in the wake of John Kennedy's assassination.

Like Johnson, Obama had absolute Democratic majorities in both houses, though short of enough votes in the Senate to override a filibuster. And even though the country was divided in 2008, there was nothing like the bitter racial conflict that Johnson faced when he became president in 1963. Certainly, the conservative opposition within Johnson's party at the time was at least as hostile to his Great Society agenda as the Blue Dogs, the conservative wing of the Democratic Party today, were to Obama's.

Nor did Obama have to face a powerful unfriendly faction within his own party as Johnson had faced in those around Kennedy.

Obama's clever selection of Hillary Clinton as secretary of state eliminated his only serious Democratic rival of national stature. And in
the space of a little more than a year, his campaign had created a formidable national grassroots political machine of its own, capable of
raising money, generating volunteers, and challenging Obama's
opponents in state and local politics.

Certainly, Obama had the intellectual equipment. He had a crisp
intelligence, an open mind, and a talent for strategy. He chose his
words carefully. As a professor of constitutional law, he had been
steeped in the logic and history of American democracy more than
any president since Woodrow Wilson. He was charming to insiders
and appealing to the public, with a demeanor as modest as a successful politician's can be. As a black man who had risen to the top of a
white-majority nation, he clearly understood how American society
worked.

Thus, it was hard to imagine anyone else who could have been
elected in 2008 who had as great a personal capacity and as much of
an opportunity to lead the nation through the hard choices that it
faced. Obama arguably represented the country's last best hope, the
most inspiring leader that the two-party system could have produced
at this moment of crisis, and the most equipped to persuade Americans to put away the most "childish' of things: the notion that the
future will take care of itself.

The leader and the historic moment seemed to be in sync. The
United States would once more demonstrate its exceptional capacity
for self-renewal. "You never want a serious crisis to go to waste,"
quipped Obama's chief of staff, Rahm Emanuel, after the election.[6]
The crisis was serious. But it was wasted. The American people continued to sink into the same pile of economic sand from which
Obama had so eloquently promised to save them.

In late August 2011, the Congressional Budget Office (CBO), the
country's most authoritative statistical forecaster, projected that at the
time of the November 2012 election the unemployment rate would
be 9 percent and that it would remain at at least 8 percent through
2014. Built into the CBO forecasts were large decreases in government civilian spending that President Obama and the Republicans in

Congress had already agreed to. These included sharp cuts in Medicare and further large cuts over the next ten years in discretionary domestic federal spending, the category that includes the investments in education and training, infrastructure, and research and development that virtually every politician and pundit in the country acknowledged were essential for rebuilding the economy.

The financial markets were left in the hands of the speculators who had just run it over the cliff. Millions of homeowners were trapped in debt and threatened with foreclosure. The bloated inefficient health-care system remained a drag on the economy. The offshoring of jobs and the piling up of trade deficits continued. And the educable moment was surrendered to a reckless, reactionary movement to the right of Ronald Reagan.

The president's supporters maintained that he had done the best he could. Given the huge forces lined up against him, they said— from business to the growing right-wing populism of the Tea Party— he did as well or better than one could have expected. He produced a health-care law, which Bill Clinton had been unable to do. He persuaded Congress to approve some new financial-market regulation. And he produced an economic stimulus that stopped the free fall of the economy into a possible depression.

They are probably right; he did do the best he could. Furthermore, he was probably the best that we had of the group of presidential candidates who were electable. But the best we had of those who were electable was not good enough.

Even before Barack Obama was inaugurated, he and his advisers were making decisions that would put the president on the wrong side of the question that Ronald Reagan had famously asked the American people during his debate with Jimmy Carter in 1980: "Are you better off now than you were four years ago?" While Democrats basked in their postelection triumph and the political punditry filled the media with the notion that the Republican Party may have now become a permanent minority, the Obama team, with eyes wide open, was setting the stage for the electoral disaster two years later.

With the banking system paralyzed and interest rates already as low as possible, there was never any question that the shrinking economy needed a stimulus. The Great Depression had taught us that in a capitalist economy, if no one spends, no one works. Every U.S. president since World War II had allowed the federal deficit to rise during a recession. Reagan's recovery of the mid-1980s was driven by an expanded federal deficit, and so was George W. Bush's in his first term. When Bush urged people to "go shopping" in response to the shock of 9/11, he was widely mocked. At the moment of national tragedy, it was certainly in bad taste to remind Americans of the crass commercialism that underlay their society. But on the economics, Bush was right.

President Obama's economic team gathered in Chicago in December 2008 to recommend a plan that he could implement right after the inauguration. The team was talented and experienced. Larry Summers was in charge. Other veterans of the Clinton years were economic advisers Peter Orszag and Jason Furman. Highly respected Christina Romer from the University of California was in charge of the basic analysis, assisted by Jared Bernstein, one of the country's leading labor market economists. Timothy Geithner, the new treasury secretary, was there to advise them, along with Ben Bernanke at the Federal Reserve. It was a topnotch team of the country's political establishment.

Romer and Bernstein estimated that the shrinking economy had left a spending hole of about $2 trillion. The entire spending gap did not have to be matched directly by government deficits because an injection of federal money would generate further spending as it rippled throughout the economy. Romer, who was to become the chairwoman of Obama's Council of Economic Advisers, urged a stimulus of $1.2 trillion over two years.

It turned out that she and the other Obama advisers underestimated the hole. In fairness, so did most of the prominent private-sector economic forecasters at the time. It actually was $2.8 trillion. But no one questioned that it was *at least* $2 trillion. So Romer's proposal—a $600-billion-a-year plug in a $2 trillion hole—was at the low end of a low estimate of the necessary stimulus.

Even so, at a December 2008 decision-making meeting in Chicago, Summers and Emanuel overrode it on the grounds that the new Congress—which would be controlled by the Democrats and was not yet even sworn in—would not go along. Emanuel also believed that the public would not accept a higher federal deficit. So they presented Obama with a choice between $550 and $890 billion over two years.

The bill that finally passed the Congress settled on $780 billion over two years. To try to appease the Republicans and the Blue Dog Democrats, about 40 percent was in the form of tax cuts, which are about one-third less stimulative than direct government spending. Despite this concession, no House Republicans voted for the bill, anyway. Senate Republicans also mostly voted against it, thirty-seven to three.

Prominent economists, including Nobel Prize winners Paul Krugman and Joseph Stiglitz, said that the stimulus was too small. Krugman later noted that it was a matter of historical record that countries hit by a severe financial crisis normally experience long periods of economic pain, so "the inadequacy of the stimulus was obvious from the beginning."[7] When the plan was made public in January 2009, columnist Martin Wolf of the *Financial Times* complained that the deficit should be allowed to become larger—and continue for a long time. "The US," he wrote, "must run big fiscal deficits if it is to sustain full employment."[8] Summers himself told ABC News in February 2009 that the economic crisis was "worse than any time since the Second World War. It's worse than, I think, than most economists like me ever thought we would see."[9]

Some White House insiders later said that the stimulus had to be modest because it would have been hard to spend the money fast enough (and that it would take time for federal spending to work its way into the economy was an argument for moving fast). States and localities did not have enough "shovel-ready" projects, they claimed. Pushing the money out too fast would risk scandals that would undermine the administration's credibility. The next election was not for two years, which would certainly give enough time for the impact of the stimulus to be felt under any circumstances.

The stimulus spending, as far as it went, worked: it stopped the economy's free fall into a depression. In March 2009, as soon as the spending's impact began, the job losses that had been growing larger each month for a year began to decelerate, and by October the job rate had even turned slightly positive.

But it was not enough to bring back the jobs that had been lost. The official unemployment rate remained stuck at roughly 9.5 percent throughout 2010. Mortgage foreclosures and small-business bank-ruptcies continued. State and local governments, which, unlike the federal government, could not print money, were forced to lay off teachers, police, and firefighters; shut off essential services like street-lights and transit; and cut back on shelters, food banks, and other ser-vices needed by the rising population of the destitute.

When Americans went to the polls on November 2, 2010, there were three million more people out of work than when Obama had been inaugurated. Add in those who had stopped looking for work, whose hours and pay had been cut, whose homes or small businesses were gone and/or going, and whose education, careers, and pensions had been cut short, and you had the central cause of the Democratic loss in the midterm election. According to the CNN exit polls, 62 percent of those who voted said that the current state of jobs and the economy dictated their choice to vote against incumbents.[10]

The Democrats lost control of the House and hung on to the Sen-ate by just one vote. Moreover, the Republicans who took over were dominated by right-wing ideologues so extreme that they pushed the U.S. Treasury to the brink of default in the summer of 2011.

It is supposed to be an article of faith among Democrats that during unsettled economic times, elections are driven by—in the famous words of political consultant James Carville—"the economy, Stu-pid!" That is, voters tend to hold the incumbent responsible for whatever state the economy is in, regardless of how it got there and how long it might reasonably take to fix it. By that logic, it was a no-brainer that the American electorate would punish the Democrats for their failure to drive down unemployment in two years. In addition, there was widespread resentment that the bankers and the brokers who drove the country into the mess—having been bailed out by Bush and his treasury secretary, Henry Paulson, with a vote by Con-gress in early October 2008—were back again under Obama giving themselves record bonuses. The conservative media machine, led by Rupert Murdoch and Fox News, exploited this resentment (and the voters' short memories) by blaming Obama and the Democrats.

The assertion that a higher stimulus package had been politically unfeasible deserves more scrutiny. Clearly, in Congress the Republicans and some Democrats were more concerned with the deficit than with unemployment. But for the American people, just the opposite was true. A CBS poll in April 2010 reported that 27 percent considered jobs to be the most important issue, 27 percent said the overall economy was most important, and only 5 percent said the federal deficit was. In May, NBC and the *Wall Street Journal* polled 35 percent for jobs, 10 percent for the deficit. The same month, Fox News came in at 47 percent for jobs and 15 percent for the deficit. In June, the Pew Trust poll found 41 percent for jobs and 23 percent for the deficit, and Gallup reported 28 percent for the general economy, 21 percent for jobs, and 7 percent for the federal deficit.[11]

Moreover, voters who named the deficit as their first priority did not necessarily mean the difference between government spending and government revenues. Pollster Mark Mellman observed that the deficit had become a proxy for the real target of people's anger: who was getting the benefits. "They're particularly angry about those bailouts in the context where they see big corporations being saved and their own jobs being lost," Mellman told reporter Ryan Grim of the *Huffington Post*. "Something's being done for the big corporations but nothing's being done for them. It also is true that simply letting thousands of teachers and police and firefighters be fired in the name of deficit reduction is not going to earn kudos from anyone. That's not what they mean when they say they're concerned about the deficit."[12]

The pollsters and the political analysts in the White House surely understood this point. The obstacle, however, wasn't the politics of the country, it was the politics of the Congress. Emanuel told the Obama economics team that Congress would not pass a larger spending proposal. Maybe that was true, but why didn't they try? They had a newly elected, popular president with a large majority of Democrats in both houses.

The White House's excuse was that the Senate filibuster rule that requires a sixty-vote majority was too big a hurdle. But when George W. Bush was faced with the similar obstacle to passing his massive tax cut in his first year as president, he used a parliamentary device called "reconciliation" that permits a simple majority to pass budget issues. The same maneuver was available to Obama. Moreover, the filibuster is a Senate rule, not a constitutional mandate. Before a gentlemen's agreement in the 1990s that made life more convenient for Senators, a filibuster required members to actually talk continuously all day and all night to prevent a vote from taking place. So another option would have been for the Democratic majority to force Republicans to go through that ordeal, exposing their obstructionism in the face of a national job crisis. Meanwhile, with his still high political approval at the time, Obama could have barnstormed the country, educating Americans on the importance of an adequate stimulus.

Neither of these tactics would have been easy, and in the end may not have worked. But the stakes for Obama could not have been higher. Whether the new administration could deliver on jobs would determine the fate of Obama's presidency and his party. It is hard to believe that full-court political pressure by the White House for a stimulus that would solve the country's most pressing problem was not worth a fight.

When the proposal for a more adequate stimulus was blocked, Jared Bernstein remembers consoling himself with two thoughts. One was the hope that the administration would get lucky. "Maybe the economy was stronger than we thought," he told me. The other was an assumption that if the economy turned out to be weaker, the administration could always go back and increase the stimulus.

By the late summer of 2009, it was apparent that the stimulus would not be enough. At a private dinner meeting in August, Summers was asked what he thought the unemployment rate would be at the time of the November 2010 congressional elections. His answer was 9.3 percent, substantially higher than it was in George W. Bush's last year. Thus, more than a year before the election, the president's chief economic adviser knew that the economic conditions for the Democratic Party would be disastrous! And still there was no serious effort to change those conditions.

The explanation that best explains the administration's behavior in its first two years is not that Congress was too polarized with partisan bickering, but that Obama and his top advisors were more concerned with offending the financial markets than offending the electorate. *New Yorker* reporter Ryan Lizza, who obtained and read the fifty-seven-page decision memo Summers sent to Obama in

December 2008, reported that it "barely mentioned Congress." Instead, Summers warned that "an excessive recovery package could spook markets or the public and be counterproductive." Summers did not dispute the calculations that Romer and Bernstein had made and knew that his recommended stimulus would not bring unemployment back to where it was when Obama took office. But, he wrote: "To accomplish a more significant reduction in the output gap would require stimulus of well over $1 trillion based on purely mechanical assumptions—which would likely not accomplish the goal because of the impact it would have on markets."[13]

Paul Krugman told Lizza that concern that the financial markets would respond negatively (that is, raise interests rates) to more stimulative deficit spending was "a major economic misjudgment." And so it was. Three years later, the federal government had borrowed more than five trillion dollars from the financial markets and interest rates on U.S. Treasury bills remained at under two percent.

But Summers's—and ultimately Obama's—decision to low-ball the stimulus was not simply a technical misjudgment; it was a *values* judgment. Summers, a smart economist and a Democrat, was sensitive to the importance of using deficits to avoid a depression. But having been mentored by Bob Rubin and enriched by Wall Street, he was more sensitive to the anxieties of his friends in finance over the appearance of a threat of inflation. The compromise solution was enough stimuli to keep the jobless rate from rising further, but not enough to bring it down.

The tension between the goals of full employment and balancing the budget is an old debate in U.S. politics. The policy intellectuals who represent U.S. business have always resisted the idea that the government should promote a job for everyone who is willing and able to work. In that sense they illustrate Karl Marx's view that capitalists needed a permanent army of the unemployed in order to keep labor docile and wages as low as possible. But this also worked against their interest of having enough customers coming in the door with money in their pockets to buy their goods—or at least it did in the time before globalization. From a business point of view, the task of government policy was to maintain enough employment to keep the economy expanding but not enough to encourage workers to demand higher wages.

The financial industry is particularly hostile toward anything that might raise fears of inflation. Banks are creditors. They held promissory notes, mortgages, and corporate bonds that paid fixed interest rates. When prices rose, it reduced the real value of the earnings on the debt that they held. Moreover, rising prices meant rising interest rates, which reduced the value of the existing bonds (by paying lower rates) that investors held in their portfolio. As the finance sector grew in political importance, maintaining low interest rates to protect the bondholders grew in importance to the Washington politicians.

That high federal deficits always lead to inflation is an economic urban myth. In the modern American experience, there has been virtually no peacetime example of budget deficits triggering inflation and higher interest rates. The last serious bout of U.S. inflation had occurred in the 1970s, and it was driven not by federal deficits but by three separate oil shocks generated by the global oil cartel. The previous episode of inflation resulted from the cost of the Vietnam War added to an economy already at full employment. The episode of inflation before that was fueled by the Korean War, and the one before that was caused by the pent-up demand for consumer goods and the loosening of price controls after World War II. In the 2009–2010 recession in which the Obama administration found itself, the threat from inflation being generated by too much money in circulation was as close to zero as one could get.

Moreover, the economy arguably needed a little *more* inflation in order to revive the housing market and induce consumers and businesses to spend now in anticipation of higher prices later. It was a point that Bernanke himself had made in scolding the Japanese in 2000 for not doing enough to get their economy out from under the implosion of their real estate market a few years earlier.

Summers certainly understood that inflation was no threat. He was not arguing that a higher fiscal stimulus would lead to immediate inflationary pressures in the economy. Nor was he arguing that higher federal budget deficits would crowd out private borrowers from the credit market. Rather, he was arguing that the Wall Street people he knew were anxious that maybe inflation would happen sometime in the future—tomorrow, next month, next year? Who knew? What was important was that their anxiety had to be mollified. If it wasn't, the bond market, which had not lost faith in the U.S.

economy after the destruction of twelve trillion dollars of financial wealth, would somehow lose confidence in the United States if the government ran a large deficit to regenerate the economy.

It is a mistake to see Summers, Orszag, and the other economists who opposed an adequate stimulus as individual villains in this drama. In the end, they were agents representing what Stiglitz had called the Wall Street "mindset"—the inevitable result of the finance sector's influence over the policy soul of the "liberal" wing of the two-party system.

Summers, whose Wall Street connections have already been noted, was Obama's chief economic adviser. Geithner, his treasury secretary, had been a protégé of Henry Kissinger as well as of Rubin, had worked at Goldman Sachs, and had been hired as the president and CEO of the Federal Reserve Bank of New York by the bank's chairman, leverage fund buyout king Pete Peterson. Bernanke, besides being a protégé of Alan Greenspan, was the chairman of George W. Bush's Council of Economic Advisers as well as the Federal Reserve chairman.

At the Treasury Department, Geithner's three chief counselors were all Rubin protégés: Gene Sperling, who the year before had made $887,727 consulting for Goldman Sachs and $158,000 for speeches mostly to financial companies; Lee Sachs, formerly with Bear Stearns, who made more than three million dollars as a partner at Mariner Investment Group; and Lewis Alexander, who had been the chief economist at Citicorp.

Geithner's deputy was Neil Wolin, yet another Rubin acolyte, who had been CEO of Hartford Financial Services. Herb Allison, a former CEO of Merrill Lynch, was made head of TARP to replace the outgoing Neel Kashkari, who had been Paulson's protégé at Goldman Sachs. Geithner's chief of staff was Mark Patterson, a former lobbyist for Goldman Sachs—despite Obama's formal ban on hiring ex-lobbyists. For those without Wall Street connections, however, the ban was strictly enforced. For example, it prevented the appointment to a government job of human rights advocate Tom Malinowski on the grounds that he had been a lobbyist—for genocide victims in Darfur!

The list goes on. Chief of staff Rahm Emanuel had made more than eighteen million dollars in just two and a half years on Wall Street, and he was only next to Rubin in his ability to raise money for the Democrats in New York.[14] Peter Orszag, the budget director, was another protégé of Rubin's and two years later quit to become a vice-president at Citigroup Global. Michael Froman, a managing director at Citigroup, was given the job as deputy assistant to the president in charge of international economic affairs. Steven Rattner, the founder of the leveraged buyout firm, Quadrangle, was made auto czar, in charge of the bailout of General Motors and Chrysler.

By late 2008, one would have thought that the point of view represented by these people would no longer be taken seriously. Not so. A convenient belief in what Paul Krugman called the "confidence fairy"—that is, the importance of boosting morale on Wall Street— still set the limits on what this Democratic administration would do to bring the real economy of jobs and production back to health.

As the effect of the stimulus faded, the economy stumbled again. The numbers of those out of work for more than six months was at an all-time high. Foreclosures were mounting. The president fell steadily in the polls.

Congressional Democrats urged Obama to propose another stimulus. Summers said he agreed but did not press the case. Republicans, now the majority in the House and sensing political blood in the water, ridiculed the idea; if it didn't work once, they claimed, how absurd to argue for it again. That the economy would have been far worse without it was lost in the political static. Obama gave up control of the political debate and began to follow the GOP lead in making the deficit his priority. Several members of his staff told me that Obama several times referred, inside the White House, to his "inner Blue Dog."

With less than two months to go before the 2010 midterm election, Rahm Emanuel resigned as chief of staff and announced that he was running for mayor of Chicago. Obama replaced him with William Daley, the brother of Chicago's retiring mayor and an executive at Morgan Stanley, who weeks before had publicly diagnosed Obama's problems as having moved too far to the left. A little more than a year later, Obama replaced Daley with budget director Jack Lew, who among other credentials, had been CEO of Citi Global Wealth Management.

After the election, and the triumph of the Tea Party Republican faction, any hope for a renewed stimulus of any size was dead. Indeed, the president was now a budget hawk. He made deal after deal with the aggressive Republicans to cut domestic spending. Going into each negotiation, he asked that taxes also be raised on the rich in order to share the sacrifice. The Republicans refused, demanding instead that taxes be cut. Obama conceded, time after time. Every honest federal budget analyst in the country knew that the short-term budget deficit was being driven by the recession and spending on the Iraq and Afghanistan Wars and that the long-term "structural deficit," the deficit that would remain even after a recovery, was the result of George W. Bush's 2001 tax cuts and the escalating costs of health care. No matter—the Republicans blamed domestic federal spending.

Because there was little effective resistance from the president, the media bought into the argument. A *National Journal* survey of newspaper coverage in May 2011 reported that references to unemployment fell, despite its continuing importance to the public, while references to the deficit soared.[15] The ideological positions in Washington moved farther to the right. The conservative position was that the deficit problem should be solved with spending cuts. The liberal position was that there should be a balance between spending cuts and tax increases. But the idea that the deficit should be raised in order to create jobs was now beyond the pale. "It would be political folly to make the argument that government spending equals jobs," said Dan Pfeiffer, Obama's communications director.[16] But the argument was true, and since jobs were the most important issue in voters' minds, the real political folly was in not making it.

The president not only followed Republican policy, he publicly echoed the powerfully misleading analogy between the family budget and the federal budget that has sustained the Right for decades. "Families across this country understand what it takes to manage a budget," Obama declared in a radio broadcast on August 25, 2011. "Well, it's time Washington acted as responsibly as our families do." Week after week, he reiterated this simple-minded homily that reinforced the destructive notion that when hard times come, the government should cut back its spending. So much for the educable moment.

The President then appointed a commission to recommend ways to cut the budget deficit. Its cochairmen, former Republican senator Alan Simpson and Democrat Erskine Bowles, an investment banker (and member of the board of Morgan Stanley) who had been President Clinton's chief of staff, were outspoken advocates of cutting Social Security. In August, Simpson publicly compared Social Security to "a milk cow with 310 million tits [*sic*]."[17] Obama had no comment.

In November, Simpson and Bowles released their recommendations, the most prominent of which were cuts in Social Security benefits, a permanent cap on federal spending and revenue, and a series of tax reforms that eliminated middle-class benefits. They left the tax loopholes for Wall Street and Americans who invest overseas untouched while actually reducing revenue from the progressive income tax.[18] The plan received enormous media coverage and was hailed by the mainstream print and electronic media for its courage in recommending the "hard" decisions that faced the country.

A week before the November 2010 election, Obama defended his economic record on Jon Stewart's *Daily Show*. If he had been told two years earlier that he would be able to "stabilize the system" for less than 1 percent of GDP, "I'd say," Obama told Stewart, "we'll take that."

What about the fact that "unemployment will be near 10 percent?" asked Stewart.

The question hung in the air. Finally, the president replied that he had inherited the crisis in the job market.

Obama had inherited the crisis in the financial market as well. But his response to the bankers, brokers, and bondholders had been, like his predecessor's, swift and lavish.

When the markets crashed in the fall of 2008, George W. Bush's government—treasury secretary and former Goldman Sachs CEO Henry Paulson, Federal Reserve chairman Ben Bernanke, and New York Federal Reserve president Timothy Geithner—frantically huddled with the panicking heads of the largest financial firms.

Teams of lawyers and accountants from Washington and Wall Street quickly organized a rescue involving loans, loan guarantees, government purchases of preferred stock, mergers approved on the spot, and frantic efforts to assure other countries' central banks that Wall Street would be saved. In a three-page memo, Paulson sketched out the Troubled Asset Relief Program (TARP), the centerpiece of what eventually became an infusion of more than three trillion dollars in government cash and guarantees to the country's largest banks, including investment firms like Goldman Sachs, which quickly became banks in order to qualify.

After initial resistance from Congress, the plan was passed by both houses and signed by George W. Bush on October 3, 2008—a month before the election. Advised by Rubin and Summers, Obama publicly endorsed the program. Once Obama was elected, TARP became his to enforce, and he gave the job of managing it to Wall Street.

There does seem to be little doubt that in the fall and winter of 2008–2009, the financial markets had to be rescued quickly. Otherwise the credit system that supported the economy would surely have fallen apart. Given the urgency and fact that the system had become so complex that it was impossible to trace who owed what to whom, the only option was to keep the entire system afloat. Rescuing the system from insolvency, however, did not require putting a permanent government safety net under privately owned banks and brokerages houses such as Citigroup, Morgan Stanley, Merrill Lynch, Bank of America, and Goldman Sachs.

The crash and rescue provided Obama with the rare opportunity to rein in the bloated, out-of-control financial sector and shrink the speculative markets it fed on. But with Wall Street of Washington negotiating with Wall Street of New York, that opportunity was tragically lost. TARP was an early and dramatic signal that both the Bush and Obama administrations were not just rescuing the perpetrators of the crime but coddling them.

Even though the government was now a major shareholder—and in some cases the majority shareholder—Geithner, Summers, and the others rejected any suggestion that the government take over and reorganize the banking sector; or, if not, that it require an end to its speculative excesses; or, if not, that it at least demand that the financial executives who were receiving the government's welfare cut out the lavish lifestyles that they had all come to take for granted. Without any of these conditions, the bailout was seen by the public for what it was: corporate welfare.

When the stories leaked out that CEOs were continuing to pay themselves bonuses, fly in private jets, and sponsor lavish retreats at luxury resorts, the public was outraged, the pundits professed shock, and Congress held hasty hearings. Inside the administration, all of this was seen as an unfortunate media side show, driven by the emotions of an unsophisticated public.

In a speech at the National Press Club in February 2009, Bernanke acknowledged that citizens were "concerned" that the people who caused the problem were being rewarded. But, he admonished, "extraordinary times call for extraordinary measures."[19] His only real regret was that the government had let Lehman Brothers fail the previous September. The system, after all, had to be saved. The bonuses, the lifestyle, and the question of whether financial executives were getting paid more than they were worth was a matter for the other shareholders and unimportant to the government. So suck it up, he basically advised. "Our economic system is critically dependent on the free flow of credit."

And so it is. But on what, the concerned citizen might ask, does the flow of credit depend? In the fall of 2008, one could have reasonably argued that the lenders, because their capital had evaporated in the crash, had no money. The TED spread, which tracks the difference between Treasury Department and interbank interest rates and is the most closely watched measure of credit availability, was then at an all-time high (460 basis points), reflecting the heavy risk that premium banks were charging one another.

By January the spread was back to its precrisis level of less than 100 points, indicating that the banks were lending to one another again. Given the new government safety net, they now trusted that they would get their money back with interest. But they still weren't lending to the rest of the economy; because with rising unemployment and falling incomes, making loans to businesses was generally too risky.

The core problem of the recession was insufficient demand, which in turn was caused by rising joblessness and the huge excess of debt. Those who had jobs were paying off their credit cards rather than using them for new purchases. There was a depression in the housing market. With the prices of their homes now below what they owed on the mortgages, millions of Americans were struggling to make payments on an asset they could no longer afford to own, so they were falling behind on the payments and stumbling into foreclosure and bankruptcy.

Meanwhile, the lenders who held the mortgages still carried them on their books as though their value hadn't changed, even though they were not earning money on them. In other words, both the consumers and the banks were trapped by the fact that the financial system had not adjusted to the real condition of the housing market. Until those assets were written down for their real worth, it would take a very long time before the inevitable bankruptcies and foreclosures would clean up the nation's collective books so that confidence would return. The fact that the Japanese economy had still not rebounded from the implosion of its real estate market in the 1990s suggested that it could easily be a decade or more.

There was little mystery about how to clean up the housing credit mess. The answer was to force the banks to renegotiate the mortgages with the homeowners, reducing the principal according to the lower, real-world price. Obama provided several modest incentives for banks that voluntarily reduced the principal according to the lower, real-world price. But this would have meant that the banks absorb or at least share the losses from the drop in housing prices. Most refused.

Had Obama been willing and able to kick-start faster growth with spending, the economic knot might have been loosened. Consumers would have had more income, banks could have started making profitable business loans, and housing prices might have stabilized. But in the absence of growth, the Federal Reserve kept the leaking system afloat by pumping up the largest banks with cheap money.

In the fall of 2010, Obama and Geithner announced that several of the banks had paid off the initial loans and were buying back the government's preferred stock. What they failed to say was that the repayments were being subsidized. The banks were borrowing money at virtually 0 percent from the Federal Reserve and buying long-term, no-risk U.S. Treasury bonds for 3 or 4 percent. They were also lending at 5 percent to investors, who were buying high-yielding (and high-risk) Brazilian, Turkish, and other emerging countries' bonds at 10 to 12 percent. Very little of this money was finding its way to investment in the anemic U.S. economy.

Moreover, the policy of trying to reflate the economy primarily through providing low-interest rates to banks and investment houses, who could then use the funds to get higher yields around the world, squeezed the small U.S. savers and 401(k) contributors. Retiring workers who had carefully saved for years on the assumption that they could get a 5 percent annual return on their small nest egg found themselves getting less than 1 percent and trying to make up the difference with a part-time job at Burger King.

The combination of a Wall Street–owned Republican Party and a Wall Street–rented Democratic party ensured that the political system would not use the crisis to put in place safeguards against another crash or to curb the financial system's destructive diversion of the capital necessary for the long-term growth of the economy.

After a year of agonizing negotiations with an ungrateful Wall Street and obstructionist Republicans, the Democratic Congress and the administration finally produced the Wall Street Reform and Consumer Protection Act, sponsored by Congressmen Barney Frank of Massachusetts and Senator Christopher Dodd of Connecticut, in the summer of 2010. The legislation made some improvements. It extended the government's regulatory authority and required more transparency in the trading of exotic securities. It also created a government subagency within the Federal Reserve to protect consumers from abuses.

But Dodd-Frank, as the law is known, restored none of the Glass-Steagall Act's firewall between lenders and borrowers. It allowed trading in the most volatile and dangerous derivatives, credit default swaps, and other securities that represented exotic gambling with other people's money. It did not end the embedded conflict of interest among securities underwriters and rating agencies, accountants, and insurers. And it did little to curb the influence of the financial sector over its regulators through the corrupt revolving door between Washington and Wall Street.

There was some shifting of organizational charts, the result of which was to strengthen the authority of the Federal Reserve. So, for example, the new Consumer Financial Protection Agency was placed in the Federal Reserve, which sees its primary function as protecting the banks. This virtually guaranteed that consumer protection would be, at best, a secondary priority. Despite the 2,300 pages, Dodd-Frank's core premise was to give the same regulatory system that was in the pocket of Wall Street the authority to monitor, discipline, and reform Wall Street.

On issue after issue, the final bill failed to specify remedies, instead leaving them to the regulatory agencies. It also provided no incentive for talented dedicated people to devote their lives to policing the financial markets and to protect them from the political interference of the powerful special interests.

By omission, Dodd-Frank codified the de facto and bipartisan policy of "too big to fail." During the debate, Democratic senators Sherrod Brown of Ohio and Ted Kaufman of Delaware offered an amendment to put a cap on the size of banks. The administration was against it. According to Bloomberg News, Timothy Geithner told Kaufman that "the issue of limiting bank size was too complex for Congress and that people who know the markets should handle these decisions." What Geithner did not tell Kaufman or Congress or the public was that the total amount of the federal bailout of the banks had come to an astonishing $1.2 trillion in one day and that the financial sector had make an additional $13 billion in profits on the cheap money supplied by the Federal Reserve.[20] The Republicans in Congress killed the amendment.

Bank size had been the condition that forced the government to bail out the large banks. Because they were so big, their failure threatened to bring down the entire financial system. The top five banks and investment firms in 2006 had 25 percent of the sector's revenues; by 2009 they had 40 percent. Two years after the bailouts, they were 20 percent larger and controlled $8.6 trillion, about 60 percent of the country's GDP. Thomas Hoenig, the outspoken president of the Kansas City Federal Reserve, noted six months after the passage of Dodd-Frank, "The economic influence of the largest financial institutions is so great that their chief executives cannot manage them, nor can their regulators provide adequate oversight."[21]

The financial reform codified the Reaganite policy of corporate welfare that Greenspan, Rubin, Bernanke, and the governing class had been managing for the past thirty years. It could not do much to prevent another bubble, but it would be easier to pay for the damage once it occurred. The day the reform package was approved, bank stocks rose.

Obama, Frank, Dodd, and most Democrats undoubtedly would have preferred a better and stronger bill, just as Summers would have preferred a lower unemployment rate, but they did not want it enough to challenge the corporate lobbies and take the issue to the people. That would have been called "class warfare." As with Obama's fiscal policy, inside the Beltway this was the best they thought they could get. And it wasn't nearly enough.

The precrash Reagan-era corporate excesses soon returned. Golden parachutes once more cushioned CEOs as they jumped out of the companies they had damaged. Robert P. Kelly's severance pay after being fired from Bank of New York Mellon was $17.2 million. When the CEO of Yahoo, Carol A. Bartz, was let go, she took almost $10 million. After a disastrous eleven months as Hewlett-Packard's boss, Leo Apotheker was given a send-off worth $13.2 million.[22]

Within a few months, the media had begun producing feature stories on the rebound of extravagant spending by the rescued Wall Street masters of the universe. A Goldman Sachs analyst hosted a Halloween Party for a thousand people at a Manhattan nightclub. A Bank of America executive threw himself a birthday party in Hong Kong where "women [who were] dressed like Playmates, with feather boas and satin ears, danced behind a pink silk screen." The financial rich were again flocking to expensive restaurants. Summer rentals in the Hamptons were booming. Investors were pouring back into the auction market for art and antiques.[23]

Four years after the crash, Phil Agelides, the former California state treasurer who chaired the Financial Crisis Inquiry Commission, ruefully observed that charges of fraud against firms like Citigroup and Bank of America had been settled for pennies on the dollar and executives who bilked consumers and investors for trillions "remain largely unscathed."[24]

By January 2012 the Securities and Exchange Commission had penalized only twenty-five people, largely with a slap on the wrist. As Gretchen Morgenson reported, most of the fines were paid by the companies, not the individuals. The one exception involved a bankrupted West Coast mortgage company. The CEO agreed to give back $542,000 in illicit earnings. His incentive pay for the two years before the company crashed had been at least $2.9 million.[25]

This sorry record should be no surprise. The Obama SEC continued the bizarre Bush SEC practice of asking suspected financial firms themselves to hire lawyers to tell the government whether the firm has broken the law. And the result is predictable. As law professor and former assistant U.S. attorney Mary Ramirez commented, "If you do not punish crimes, there really is no reason they won't happen again."[26]

"If you thought the 'too big to fail' issues of 2008–9 were bad in the United States," commented former International Monetary Fund chief economist Simon Johnson in an article he co-wrote with investment banker Peter Boone, "wait until our biggest banks become even bigger."[27]

Just before the 2010 election, a *Wall Street Journal* poll reported that Americans thought that free trade had harmed rather than helped the country by 53 to 17 percent. Among Tea Party supporters, the negative view was shared by 61 percent.[28] A few months earlier, a Pew Research Center poll reported that 83 percent of the American public thought that protecting U.S. jobs should be a national priority.[29] But only 21 percent of the elite membership of the Council on Foreign Relations agreed.[30]

During the Democratic presidential primary campaigns of 2008, both Barack Obama and Hillary Clinton had promised to do something about the offshoring of jobs. Both pledged, for starters, to renegotiate NAFTA to give workers some of the protections that the treaty gave exclusively to corporate investors. Their comments were immediately denounced by the mainstream media as "protectionist," a word that in the columns of the *Wall Street Journal*, the *Washington Post*, and the *New York Times* had replaced "communist" as the epithet that stopped serious political conversation.

Within the Beltway, the lobbyists told their clients not to worry. Noting that both Obama and Clinton were surrounded by Wall Street advisers who were dedicated free-trade advocates, they dismissed the candidates' pledges as cynical pandering to win voters in the downsized industrial heartland. When it became public that Obama's economic adviser, Austin Goolsbee, had assured the Canadian Embassy that Obama had no intention of fulfilling his pledge, Obama vigorously denied it.

But the cynics were right. Shortly after election day, Obama unceremoniously reneged on his promise. There would be no renegotiation of NAFTA or any other free-trade agreement. For virtually every job in his administration that had anything to do with trade, he appointed people who were committed to the continuation of the policies of the last thirty years that had led to a relentless hemorrhaging of jobs, incomes, technology, and opportunities.

As Bill Clinton had done, Obama allied with the Republican-controlled House, the Business Roundtable, and the Chamber of Commerce to approve the trade deals that the preceding Republican president had negotiated—in this case, with South Korea, Colombia, and Panama. Like Clinton, he ignored the evidence showing that imports would rise faster than exports and that more jobs would be lost than created. To make matters worse, Obama agreed to a Republican demand to cut the already meager assistance to workers laid off because of increased imports. As had been the case with NAFTA, a majority of Democrats in the House voted no.

Obama and his trade negotiators claimed that the deal would allow more Americans to sell more cars in South Korea. At the time, the United States was selling six thousand automobiles a year in South Korea, and the South Koreans were selling five hundred thousand cars a year here. South Korean autoworkers made roughly one-third the wages of U.S. workers and were just as efficient. Moreover, the administration agreed to define a "Korean" auto as any car that was 35 percent or more made in South Korea, which meant that South Korean companies could import to the United States cars and parts that had been 65 percent produced in countries like China, North Korea, or Vietnam, where wages are one-tenth or less of those in the United States.

Even the government's own pro–free trade U.S. International Trade Commission had admitted that the Korea Free Trade Agreement would increase the U.S. deficit and reduce the number of high-wage jobs in automobiles and electronics while increasing the jobs in low-wage areas like meatpacking.[31] The Economic Policy Institute estimated a minimum net loss of approximately 160,000 additional jobs.[32]

This was a drop in the bucket of the U.S. labor force, scoffed the free-trade advocates, completely ignoring the question of why, at a time of stagnant wages and rising trade deficits, the U.S. government would pursue a policy that was certainly going to lose high-wage American jobs.

The AFL-CIO opposed the deal. But in an embarrassing and tragic display of how weak unions had become, the president of the United Auto Workers agreed not to oppose it in exchange for a delay of five years in the implementation of the automobile sections of the treaty.

Like the four presidents before him, Obama assured the nation that free trade would create good jobs and a balanced trading account with the rest of the world. There were the ritual visits to a U.S. factory that had succeeded in finding an export niche somewhere in the world. Obama—like Bush the son, Clinton, Bush the father, and Reagan—proclaimed it the wave of the future. Over the years, there were token rescues of one or another particular plant or industry from being swamped by foreign competition, but in general, the erosion of U.S. jobs and technology continued.

The treatment of economic globalization in Obama's annual *Economic Report of the President* echoed George W. Bush's and Clinton's. It was full of assertions of trade-driven prosperity based on hoary theoretical arguments for free trade that had long been out of touch with the reality of the modern global marketplace. The fact was ignored that hundreds of millions of new workers, hungry and willing to work for peanuts, were pouring into the world's labor markets; that other nations were also counting on growing by selling to foreigners; and that our nation's comparative advantages were rapidly disappearing. Also ignored was the major implication of the report's own logic: that Americans would have to compete by lowering their wages. Again, it was not that the economists who wrote these reports were ignorant of the world, it was just that they were working for interests for whom these facts were best Photoshopped out of the picture.

By the end of September 2010, the stimulus had added $551 billion to U.S. growth, but the trade deficit had subtracted $674 billion from that growth. This blunt reality remained beyond the range of the establishment's discussion of the country's economic plight.

The ideological constraints on industrial policy meant that Obama's modest efforts to support the country's position in the global race to market new energy technologies had to be made under the cover of the short-term stimulus to create jobs. To serve the immediate goal, the money had to be shoveled out quickly in loans to help already existing companies to expand. Thus, Obama's Energy Department made a large loan to the Solyndra Corporation, a solar panel manufacturer, despite warnings from the bureaucracy that the company was in trouble. Solyndra's presumed market advantage was that it could successfully compete because it used less high-priced silicon than its rivals. When the price of silicon fell—partly because of the global recession—the company went under.

Obama and his energy secretary, Steven Chu, defended the loan on the grounds that in order to spur technological growth, the government had to take risks that the private sector would not take. They were right. The problem was that the program was pinched and piecemeal. Successful government interventions like this require a long-term commitment to a strategic program, not a series of ad hoc projects.

Thus, for example, at the end of World War I, when the U.S. government determined to make the nation a leader in long-range radio transmission, Franklin Roosevelt, then secretary of the navy, organized American business to buy up patent rights and pool them into a new company called the Radio Corporation of America (RCA). Succeeding governments subsidized and nurtured RCA in a number of ways. One result was that superior U.S. long-range radio communication proved decisive in World War II against Japan.

Another example was John Kennedy's project to put a man on the moon. The government did not simply make loans to private business and hope for the best; it totally organized the new space industry, which required nearly ten years of trial and error before the goal was reached.

It would have taken an enormous public education effort by Obama to create the political consensus for a serious energy technology program. Because he was stuck in Reagan's sandpile of antigovernment ideology, he could not and would not do it.

By his second year, he had already committed himself to cutting the domestic discretionary part of the budget, which contains the spending for the human and physical investments he had argued were essential to restore American competitiveness. The president urged Congress to spend six billion dollars for high-speed rail, but the Republicans in the House would have none of it. Meanwhile, the Chinese government had already committed a hundred billion dollars to their high-speed rail system.

The stimulus had provided an initial billion dollars in energy grants to local communities. When it was revealed that 84 percent of the money was going to German and Chinese manufacturers of wind turbines, the administration placated the public outrage by getting agreements to do more of the work in the United States. Even so, in August 2011, the largest U.S. manufacturer of solar panels, Evergreen Industries, filed for bankruptcy and announced it was moving production to China.

Other U.S.-born solar companies have moved to the Philippines and Malaysia. "Quite frankly," commented a Wall Street stock analyst of the solar industry, "as a solar manufacturer it is a lot better to pay workers $1 an hour in China than $15 an hour in Massachusetts."[33]

Based on their experience building huge projects at home—such as the massive Three Gorges Dam, the Beijing airport, and the world's fastest high-speed trains—the Chinese were fast elbowing U.S. firms out of infrastructure and civil engineering projects in Africa, South America, the Middle East, and the United States itself. The $7.3 billion new bridge across the San Francisco Bay was engineered and manufactured in China. Said the project director for the U.S. general contractor, "I don't think the U.S. fabrication industry could put a project like this together. Most U.S. companies don't have these types of warehouses. equipment or the cash flow."[34]

In August 2011, a stone memorial to Martin Luther King Jr. was unveiled on the National Mall in Washington. The work was controversial; for many, the stern-looking figure of King with his arms folded across his chest misrepresented the man's spirit and life. But artistic merit aside, it was another symbol of the governing class's lack of interest in nurturing our country's ability to make things. The sculptor was a Chinese artist whose previous work included statues of Mao Tse-Tung. The granite was shipped from China, and the work was done largely by Chinese stonemasons.[35]

The project cost $120 million, most of it raised from private donations. The U.S. government contributed $10 million, and China gave $25 million. The bipartisan commission in charge of the memorial said that it saved $8 million by having it made in China.

7

The Shaky Case for Optimism

R emember," admonished President Obama in his 2011 State of the Union Address, "for all the hits we've taken these last few years, for all the naysayers predicting our decline, America still has the largest, most prosperous economy in the world. No workers—no workers are more productive than ours. No country has more successful companies or grants more patents to inventors and entrepreneurs. We're the home to the world's best colleges and universities, where more students come to study than any place on Earth."[1]

In his next State of the Union address he declared, to bipartisan applause, "Anyone who tells you that America is in decline or that our influence has waned doesn't know what they [sic] are talking about."[2]

The important thing was not to succumb to pessimism. Vice President Joe Biden lashed out against "those who suggest that—I don't mean foreigners, I mean domestic critics—that somehow, we are destined to fulfill [historian Paul] Kennedy's prophecy that we are going to be a great nation that has failed because we lost control of our economy and overextended, then we might as well throw it in now, for God's sake. I mean it's *ridiculous.*"[3]

But exactly why was it ridiculous? As the country's economy soured, a growing number of pundits took up the task of providing the upbeat answer. The United States would continue to be number one because of its can-do spirit and multicultural makeup. So, ultimately, it really didn't matter that much if the political system was dysfunctional or even corrupt. The market would determine the future, and the nation's assets—its people, their unique combination of morality and materialism, and their love of freedom—were sure to prevail in the global economic competition. The government should, of course, do whatever it needed to help. But this was still the age of Reagan; the government would follow, not lead.

At the end of a long book detailing the history of foreign policy tragedies because of the overconfidence of U.S. leaders, Peter Beinart, a former editor of the *New Republic*, tells us that "tempered by wisdom, American optimism is—and always will be—one of the great wonders of the world."[4]

Fareed Zakaria—once an editor and a columnist for *Newsweek*, *Time*, and the *Washington Post* and a commentator for CNN, denounced the "cottage industry of scaremongering."[5] His book, *The Post-American World*, published as the economy was crumbling in 2008, acknowledged that China and India might grow faster, but because of the United States's great lead in technology, they could not possibly catch up in the foreseeable future. Indeed, he dismissed Chinese engineers as largely "auto mechanics and industrial repairmen"—no match for the much more sophisticated Americans.[6]

"Relax, we'll be fine," wrote the establishment conservative David Brooks of the *New York Times* on April 2010, one in a series of columns he wrote over the next year about U.S. prospects. "The fact is, despite all the problems, America's future is exceedingly bright."[7] Leaving aside that there are no facts about the future, Brooks is an intelligent, widely read center-right pundit. We can trust him to give us the best available arguments for an optimistic tomorrow.

Two books impressed him: *Rebound: Why America Will Emerge Stronger from the Financial Crisis* by economist Stephen Rose and *The Next Hundred Million: America in 2050* by Joel Kotkin, whom Brooks calls an "über-geographer." Rose and Kotkin are smart analysts. They are both former left-leaning thinkers who have moved to the center-right in the last twenty years.

Rose begins his case in *Rebound* with a statistical argument about living standards in the recent past. Showering the reader with graphs and tables, he writes that the middle-class squeeze is a left-wing myth, perpetrated by people who don't understand the dynamism of American free enterprise.

Economist John Schmitt reviewed Rose's book and demonstrated that Rose spends most of his time knocking down straw men and ignoring the mass of evidence of an upward redistribution of wealth and opportunity *before* the crash of 2008. Thus, for example, Rose's own numbers show that the richest 10 percent took two-thirds of all of the income gains since 1979, whereas in the previous three decades they received one-third. Meanwhile, the rate of growth in overall income had fallen by half. Despite being more educated and more productive and having more capital equipment to work with, the majority of American workers for the roughly thirty years before the 2008 crash saw their wages remain stagnant.[8]

Sugarcoating yesterday allows Rose to sweeten tomorrow. He dismisses China and India by answering a question that no one asked: Are these countries so large that they can produce enough for the whole world? Of course his answer is no. And Rose is confident that our huge debt to China guarantees that the Chinese can continue to lend us the money to buy their goods. Besides, they can't start exporting cars to the United States until 2020!

Rose predicts that Americans will have better jobs because they will be better educated for what he calls the office economy. They will outdo the world based on their renowned technological superiority. Personal 401(k)s will bring more security in their old age than guaranteed pensions. This future seems embarrassingly dated, however; even before the crash, the correlation between education and income had deteriorated, the country was running a chronic deficit in high-tech trade, and business schools were teaching that virtually any office function could be offshored. As for the idea that the average working person can provide for his or her old age by outsmarting the fast-buck hucksters who dominate the stock market, that too does not pass the laugh test.

"The kind of society that will emerge after the crisis passes," Rose assures us, "will be very much like the one that existed before the crisis."[9] But, ironically, to provide this happy ending he has to turn back to the political agenda of the left-wing doom-and-gloomers he devotes his book to slamming. For example, he proposes a tough ten-point program for strict controls over Wall Street, which includes having the federal government choose the banks, accountants, bond rating agencies, and real estate appraisers. Good idea—and one that would have been laughed out of the editorial board of the *Wall Street Journal*, which happily publishes Rose's attacks on liberal pessimists. Echoing Robert Rubin, Rose dismisses the financial crash as a rare "perfect storm." Once the recession ends, Rose says, "economies throughout the world will rebound and first reach, and then surpass, their former output levels."[10]

In a bravura display of naiveté, Rose assures us that such reforms surely will be drawn up and that we will therefore have a smaller financial sector because "we" have undoubtedly learned our lesson. Likewise, Rose thought that soon we would have some form of socialized medicine to keep the costs down, as Britain does, and he blithely suggests that the government needs a more proactive "industrial policy" in order to develop technologically advanced products.

The second guide to Brooks's positive future, Kotkin's equally upbeat *The Next Hundred Million*, asserts that Americans will prosper because their mobility allows them to choose the most efficient and profitable places to live and work.

Like Rose, Kotkin envisions a United States in 2050 that will be much like the United States in 2010, only more so. He predicts prosperous suburbs, green industries, planned communities, extended families, wholesome religious activism, and farmers' markets linked by the Internet. The trend away from the cities will continue. He forecasts that the prairie heartland will be repopulated as advanced telecommunications allow families to live and work where land is cheap. But all of this, he cautions, can happen only if bottom-up local markets are left to flourish free of the heavy hand of centralizing government. Globalization, Kotkin glibly asserts, is decentralizing.

Kotkin's localism is more mainstream Chamber of Commerce than it is radical Tea Party or back-to-the-land communitarian. But like the Tea Party elderly man who demanded that the government keep its hands off his Medicare, Kotkin shares the contempt for big government while happily enjoying its benefits. Thus, for example, he writes that the suburbs and the rural United States spontaneously generate their own economic growth, with little reference to the massive government subsidies that support them.

Like Rose, Kotkin assumes that prosperity is America's natural condition and that the polity will make whatever decisions it must to keep the market healthy. His key argument is that our nation's greater openness to immigration will keep our labor force, and therefore the economy, growing faster than Europe's or Japan's. Thus, he envisions an American heartland that might compete with India for call centers—not what most U.S. workers would regard as a happy future.

As for China, he is not impressed: "The country's lack of democratic institutions, its cultural hegemony, its historic insularity, and the rapid aging that will start by the 2020s do not augur well for its global preeminence."[11]

Like Rose, Kotkin hedges his bets and so does not quite deliver the conclusion that Brooks has claimed for him. Kotkin admits that the United States faces class divisions, crumbling infrastructure, and energy dependency. Still, these are isolated problems that will surely be resolved, somehow and in some way, even as our federal governmental functions are being redistributed among 150,000-odd municipalities, school districts, and zoning boards.

A few months later, Brooks cited Anne-Marie Slaughter, a prominent governing-class intellectual, to support his "we'll be fine" thesis. Slaughter was dean of the Woodrow Wilson School of International Affairs at Princeton University. President Obama and Secretary of State Hillary Clinton appointed her as the director for policy planning at the State Department, where the future of U.S. foreign policy is defined.

Slaughter's optimism comes from her faith in cross-border "networking," which she and Brooks think is the way in which the post-recession new world order will be organized. "In this world," wrote Slaughter in a well-circulated 2009 article in *Foreign Affairs*, "the measure of power is connectedness."[12]

The idea that connections matter in the world is hardly new. The ability to climb the ladder of power and money in most of our society has always been understood to depend on the help of other people. "It's not what you know, it's who you know" is fundamental folk wisdom among all social classes. Indeed, your class can be defined by your network. In our iconic inspirational literature of upward mobility, from the works of Charles Dickens to those of Horatio Alger, the young hero almost always rises from rags to riches—not because he spent a lifetime working hard and saving his money, but because he is helped by a well-connected wealthy mentor, whom he usually meets by accident.

Reducing the serendipity involved in making the connections to help one up the career ladder has long been a middle-class preoccupation. Dale Carnegie's 1936 book, *How to Win Friends and Influence People*, the granddaddy of self-help books, was a milestone. It legitimized the manipulation of human relationships in the service of career and provided the psychological techniques for doing it. Selling themselves with these techniques, clever ambitious outsiders might bypass the "old boys'" network in their ascent up their career ladders.

The Internet has revolutionized networking—Rolodexes replaced by e-mail lists replaced by Facebook and Twitter—and according to Slaughter, therein lies America's great advantage. Slaughter notes, "Every CEO advice manual published in the past decade has focused on the shift from the vertical world of hierarchy to the horizontal world of networks. Media are networked: online blogs and other forms of participatory media depend on contributions from readers to create a vast, networked conversation. Society is networked: the world of MySpace is creating a global world of 'Our Space,' linking hundreds of millions of individuals across continents."[13]

Slaughter's vision of a networked global economy is a reasonable projection of current trends in technology and the internal transformation of institutions. But it is class bound. It ignores the fate of ordinary workers with ordinary goals of steady work, rising wages, and a family life centered on the place of residence. She presents us with an elite paradise. Even more than Rose and Kotkin, she does not distinguish what is good for her definition of "America" and what is good for the vast majority of people who live here. Slaughter gushes in wonder at the flexibility of the global corporations, like IBM and Boeing, morphing into "systems integrators" that funnel "tasks to wherever they will be done best," with no curiosity about the effect on the Americans whose lives depended on doing those tasks. What she calls business "networking" is also known as offshoring, which makes up most of the production of Boeing and IBM.

Like Rose and Kotkin, Slaughter has an optimistic vision of a bright future that requires her to dismiss China's potential. After visiting a supermodern industrial complex in Shanghai, she admits it is awe inspiring. "But," she writes, "the Chinese government is determined to develop innovation as if it were developing a fancy variety of soybeans."[14] Slaughter is unfortunate in her simile; soybeans loom larger in America's future than in China's. Government-supported agribusiness is responsible for our largest net export to the world— and soybeans are our largest export to China. In technology, we continue to run deficits.

Slaughter's snobbish dismissal of China's technology strategy blinds her in several ways. First, the purpose of these Talent Highlands, as the Chinese called their state-of-the-art industrial complexes, is to capture markets to put their people to work. And their politically rigid authoritarian system has produced a remarkably flexible and well-networked manufacturing machine to do it. Thus, for example, a few weeks before Apple was scheduled to begin selling the iPhone, Steve Jobs decided that he wanted the screen to be glass not plastic. Apple executives frantically called the Chinese contractor that assembles iPhones for Apple at the very facility Slaughter visited. As the *New York Times* reported: "A foreman immediately roused 8,000 workers inside the company's dormitories. . . . Each employee was given a biscuit and a cup of tea, guided to a workstation and within half an hour started a 12-hour shift fitting glass screens into beveled frames. Within 96 hours, the plant was producing over 10,000 iPhones a day."[15]

Over 90 percent of the iPhone is produced overseas, with the high-tech components coming from Japan, Germany, Korea, and Taiwan. But, it has little meaning for Slaughter, who is indifferent to where the jobs, wages, and community benefits are located, as long as it is in the most profitable location.

Second, Slaughter ignores the fact that technological progress requires a close connection to production. The steady movement of corporate research and development operations to China and India is a stark refutation of Slaughter's happy notion that Americans will prosper by designing and buying the products that the Chinese and Indians will make.

In this new networked world "that favors decentralization and positive conflict," writes Slaughter, "the United States has an edge."[16]

But who is this "United States" that has the edge? It is not the Americans who used to make things for Apple, Boeing, and IBM. Nor is it the vast majority of citizens of the United States whose future depends on having those companies' "tasks" performed in the United States for wages that can sustain a rising standard of living. It is a small subset of the professional elite in the service of their own individual futures who have decreasing links to the future of their country.

Slaughter echoes pollster John Zogby's name for the new generation of eighteen- to twenty-nine-year-old Americans: First Globals—"more networked and globally engaged than members of any similar age cohort in American history." According to Zogby, more than half of Americans in this age range say that they have friends or family living outside the United States—vastly more than any other U.S. age group. A quarter of this group, according to Zogby's data, believe that they will "end up living for some significant period in a country other than America."[17] Slaughter then leaps from the sunny prospects of 12.5 percent of young people to the conclusion that the future of the other 87.5 percent of America is bright.

Even so, what gives the United States an "edge" in networking? Slaughter says it's our creative culture, which rests on our diversity. "This diversity, and the creativity that it produces, is visible everywhere: in Hollywood movies, in American music, and at U.S. universities. At Princeton University this past fall, five of the six student award winners for the highest grade point averages had come from abroad: from China, Germany, Moldova, Slovenia, and Turkey."[18]

There is much reason for us to be proud of our multicultural society. But Slaughter is not echoing the Statue of Liberty's call to bring us the tired, the poor, and the wretched refuse from the world's teeming shore. Like Kotkin, she believes that America's future lies with the world's rich, educated, and restless, who will bring back to us the money they made on the back of our massive trade deficit.

But why would these mobile networking elites have any more loyalty to the United States than they have to China, Germany, Moldova, Slovenia, or Turkey? Why would they have more loyalty than the native-born Americans running offshore corporations, busily disconnecting themselves from the fate of their own nation? In the same way that Obama's description of global trade stops with exports and ignores imports, Slaughter's vision of the larger process of

globalization works only if the United States accrues all of the benefits of global mobility but none of the costs.

After telling us that the United States will triumph by selling citizenship to the well educated and well-off, she acknowledges that our
society could become "radically inegalitarian if only a relatively few
have the chance to prosper financially."[19] She casually disposes of the
problem of inequality by declaring it a political choice—that is, choos-
ing between Democrats, who care about decreasing inequality, and
Republicans, who don't. But the globalization that Slaughter promotes is an inequality machine, busily siphoning away the benefits
that once trickled down from the rich to the rest within the national
economy as a result of the tax structure. In the past thirty years, this
globalization has swamped the feeble attempts by liberals to restrain
the relentlessly growing imbalances in income, wealth, and power.

Slaughter is nevertheless relentless in her insistence on a happy
future through networking. She reports that the divisive and warlike
nation-state system is being undermined by the multiplication of
networks of individuals and small groups who bypass the traditional
vertical structures of business and government. The networkers are
evolving toward a "disaggregated state," which have the speed and
flexibility to "perform many of the functions of a world government—
legislation, administration, and adjudication—without the form."[20]

Her claim that global networking creates greater accountability
and democracy really makes no sense. By its very nature, global networking shifts individuals' allegiance from their institutions to their
peer groups of professionals in other institutions and countries who
are more reliable allies in the struggle to climb the global career ladder.

Professor Janine Wedel, author of *Shadow Elite*, notes that these
global networkers perforate the dividing boundaries of institutions,
sectors, and nations. They "snake through official and private organizations, creating a loop that is closed to democratic processes." She
concludes that terms like *conflict of interest* and *corruption* cannot
adequately describe "how agenda-wielding players actively structure,
indeed create, their roles and involvements to serve their own agendas—at the expense of the government agencies, shareholders, or
publics on behalf of whom they supposedly work. These players not
only flout authority, they institutionalize their subversion of it."[21]

● ● ●

Rose, Kotkin, and Slaughter are fuzzy on the difference between what might be good for the people who manage the United States and what might be good for the majority of U.S. citizens. They reflect the national political discussion that is routinely sprinkled with references to undefined "national interests." When examined, these usually turn out to be the interests of people nestled in the networks that surround Wall Street and the Pentagon.

The geopolitical forecaster George Friedman is clearer about what he means by "America." He is a geopolitical realist; his unit of analysis is the nation-state, which he sees as being in an eternal power struggle with other nation-states. Leaving aside tactical disputes over hard and soft power, Friedman reflects the perspective, though not necessarily the conclusions, of the bulk of the U.S. foreign policy and military establishment.

The American Empire, he tells us in *The Next Hundred Years*, is not only not declining, it is ascendant. There are two reasons for this. One is the nation's overwhelming advantage in military technology. For the next century, Friedman writes, we will dominate the seas with our high-tech navy, the land with robot soldiers, the sky with aircraft, and outer space with solar-powered attack satellites and telecommunications systems. What appears to many to have been a catastrophe in Iraq and Afghanistan is, to Friedman, a sideshow. He thinks that the current war against Islamist terrorism is already over. As an imperial power, the United States does not have to actually *win* conflicts against nuisances on its periphery; all it has to do is keep them off balance and divided. Al Qaeda's goal to unite Muslims in a jihad against the United States has failed. Islam will remain in chaos and rife with religious, ethnic, and political conflict for at least another century.

The second reason Friedman thinks that imperial America will prevail is demographic. As global birth rates decline, he predicts, there will be a worldwide labor shortage by midcentury. Like Kotkin and Slaughter, he believes that the U.S. tolerance for immigration will keep the country supplied with workers and low labor costs. For the nation-state, he says, per capita income is not what is important. He is indifferent to the fate of the U.S. standard of living. The key, he believes, is to keep total income high enough to support the military-industrial complex.

Friedman too is not worried about China. Like the other happy-face forecasters, he believes that China is permanently hooked on

U.S. markets and will always need us. For the next few decades, at least, China's navy is too weak and its military electronics too primitive to undercut our strategic position in the Pacific. After that, China will "implode" because of internal ethnic and regional tensions. "China," writes Friedman, "is held together by money, not ideology. When there is an economic downturn and the money stops rolling in, not only will the banking system spasm, but the entire fabric of Chinese society will shudder."[22]

Friedman's confidence in China's meltdown is shared by a significant portion of U.S. policy intellectuals. It rests on an assumption that China's ethnic conflicts make it an inherently unstable country, unnaturally held together by Mao's revolutionary dictatorship and then by the wealth generated by crony capitalism. But British journalist Martin Jacques has pointed out that the Han Chinese represent 92 percent of the population and consider themselves not only one people but one race. "The explanation for this," writes Jacques, "lies in the unique longevity of Chinese civilization, which has engendered a strong sense of unity and common identity while also, over a period of thousands of years, enabled a mixing and melding of a multitude of diverse races."[23]

Jacques reminds us that the overwhelming majority of Chinese have lived in the same regions for about two thousand years, "acquiring a unity which has, despite long periods of Balkanization, lasted until the present."[24] From the mid-nineteenth century until the 1949 revolution, the country was exploited by outsiders, and this created a profound sense of nationalism. After the Chinese government massacred demonstrators in Tiananmen Square in 1989, many in the West predicted that China would break up as the Soviet Union later did. That this did not happen deserves some serious pondering.

Instead of worrying about China, writes Friedman, we should keep our eyes on Japan. Japan's technological prowess makes it a challenger to U.S. preeminence, and its aging population will drive it to dominate neighboring countries that have large pools of cheap labor. Friedman projects a midcentury war, with the United States and a floundering China fighting a coalition led by Japan and Turkey, which by virtue of its own demographics and strategic position would dominate the Middle East. The United States will triumph, of course, and North America will remain the economic and political power center of the world. But because conflict among nation-states is a permanent condition, the century's end will see the United States menaced by a resurgent, nationalist Mexico.

Friedman does not expect that we will completely swallow his predicted scenarios. But he reminds us that the "black swan" thesis of financial contrarian Nassim Nicholas Taleb (see chapter 1 of this book) taught us to expect the improbable. And Friedman's improbable future is built on assumptions about military technology, demographics, and the maintenance of global hegemony that are widely accepted by the U.S. governing class and are generally compatible with the beliefs of Zakaria, Slaughter, Rose, and Kotkin.

As for the domestic political economy, Friedman seems less naive than the others. He thinks that the U.S. government will not, or cannot, regulate asset price speculation, and therefore we can expect more credit booms and busts. He also recognizes that open economic borders bring lower wages, inequality, and constant dislocation. But no matter—revolt from below is remote. The governing class will impose open immigration on the United States, and a docile population grateful for cheap imports will keep coughing up the revenue to finance our superior military power.

Perhaps the most comprehensive and balanced effort to support the optimistic case is journalist Paul Starobin's *After America*.[25] Starobin accepts that we are at the end of U.S. global hegemony. The United States has already lost its ability to organize and exploit the global political and economic system, and it cannot get it back. China, he thinks, is no paper tiger. Whereas Friedman sees China as hopelessly dependent on the U.S. market, Starobin argues that the creditor always has the upper hand over the borrower. China and India are using their surplus to build up their navies, which could gradually push the U.S. out of the trade routes in the Indian Ocean and the South Pacific.

Starobin lays out several possibilities for what might follow the decline of U.S. global power. The first is chaos. If U.S. imperialism has been the bulwark against a return to a geopolitics of savagery and war, then its shrinking authority will leave anarchy in its wake. Europe before 1945 might be the model for the world, or as former

Republican congressman and 2008 presidential primary contender Tom Tancredo put it, "We go under, Western civilization goes under."[26]

The second scenario Starobin lays out is a multipolar world, a favorite among the big thinkers of the foreign policy establishment. In this vision, the United States, China, the European Union, Russia, Brazil, and India carve up the world into spheres of influence and work out their frictions in more or less peaceful ways. For this to happen, Starobin rightly observes, nationalism would have to suddenly turn into a benign force.

The third scenario is that China takes the place of the United States as the world's solo power. Its huge financial reserves gradually make the yuan the world's go-to currency. China's investments and professed lack of imperialist agenda elbow aside U.S. influence in Latin America, Africa, and the Middle East.

Whichever declinist scenario plays out, writes Starobin, it might not be such a bad thing for the United States. Of course, the nation in decline could go down a bitter, jingoist "dark path." But he quickly moves on in search of hope, and he finds it in the kind of technology-driven social decentralization celebrated by Slaughter and Kotkin. So, like Slaughter, Starobin thinks we might have a "happy chaos" with thousands of points of light, in which the "distinguishing feature would be the ability of technologically equipped individuals to form their own connections, their own social patterns, absent controlling influences."[27]

Like Kotkin, Starobin imagines a future of decentralized governance. The United States might just be too big to manage, anyway, so he paints a picture of the power in Washington devolving to the states, whose urban areas become global cities much more connected to the rest of the world than to one another. California is the model: multicultural, technological, libertarian—"an experimental model of an anti–Big Brother, personal choice–oriented, Kantian-enlightenment society."[28] As Governor Arnold Schwarzenegger boasted, "We are a nation-state. . . .We're acting as a new country."[29]

If California could move away on its own and live on its own, without the United States, why couldn't other places do so, too? Sure enough, Starobin notes that more and more U.S. cities are globally connected. Happily enough for the multicultural Democratic Party, the biggest—New York, Chicago, Los Angeles, San Francisco, and Miami—tend to vote Democratic. Thus, the Democrats, whom Starobin thinks are the natural allies of the secular, internationally mobile, postindustrial voter, will be the great beneficiaries of the new global city future.

The first and most widely shared assumption of the optimists is that globalization and free trade will be America's salvation. Like all articles of faith, it needs no proof. The facts of history are ignored; U.S. development behind protected walls, the chronic trade deficit, and the relentless offshoring of technology and jobs do not fit with the happy-ending scenario and are therefore left out of the picture. A sentence or two about the threat of protectionism is deemed sufficient. Only Friedman, whose focus is exclusively geopolitical, acknowledged the consequences for ordinary Americans—and he couldn't care less.

The second shared assumption is that U.S. openness to immigration will give the economy a comparative advantage over its rivals. There is some logic to this, if one's definition of the economy does not include most of the country's workers. But it collides with other kinds of logic. One is the resistance to more immigration by Americans who are facing diminished job opportunities. Another is the assumption of great economic benefits. Studies of the economic impact of immigration over the past several decades are, at best, mixed. On the one hand, new immigrants have clearly been a net burden on state and local governments, raising the costs of education, health, and social services. On the other hand, illegal immigrants, who pay taxes but do not get benefits, have been a net gain to the Social Security system. The impact on wages in the short run is negative, which is the core argument for the economic benefit of immigration—that it lowers labor costs.

The third shared assumption is that government policy matters little. Rose assumes that the U.S. governing class simply will do the right thing. Friedman thinks that it will be driven by the ancient thirst for power built into human nature. Slaughter, Kotkin, and Starobin think that networking, decentralizing Americans will get along fine with a vastly diminished federal government. Starobin suggests that the city of Washington might survive merely as an attraction to foreign tourists to gaze on the colossal monuments of a bygone empire.

After raising the probability that English may no longer be the world's international language ("Not even in America can the dominance of English be assured"), Starobin writes, "The good news is that learning a second language is the sort of thing that Americans, the younger, the better, can do in their schools, even on their computers. Nobody has to wait for Washington." He then describes how an elite school in suburban Washington is teaching first graders the Chinese word for *rat*.[30]

The future of the United States, in the view of David Brooks, lies in allowing the private sector free reign to build a "crossroads nation" where global talent congregates and collaborates. "Parents in middle-class nations around the world should want to send their kids to American colleges. Young strivers should dream of working in Hollywood or Silicon Valley. Entrepreneurs from Israel to Indonesia should be visiting venture-capital firms in San Francisco or capital markets in New York. Global engineers should want to learn the plastics techniques in Akron, and retailers should learn branding and distribution in Bentonville and Park Slope."[31]

Many indeed may want to *come* here. But why, when Hollywood, Harvard, and Silicon Valley are abandoning the United States, should the world's middle class want to *stay*? If it makes sense for Dick Cheney's superpatriotic military contractor Halliburton to move its headquarters to Dubai, what will halt the outflow of talent and capital represented by global institutions even less connected to the federal government?

These optimists all turn up their noses at the notion of crude ethnocentric American exceptionalism. Starobin lauds Wall Street and the multinational corporation because they are "not held hostage to the mythology of American exceptionalism and the fate of the American Imperium."[32]

Nevertheless, exceptionalism is key to their optimism. That is, Americans will find their way back to prosperity because they are practical, innovative, and confidant, and more so than other people. At least some Americans will: the extraordinary and the privileged who learn Chinese in grade school, learn networking in the best schools, and are in demand by powerful rootless global institutions.

What will happen to the rest—the majority who, by definition, are ordinary? These are the people whose standard of living had been cushioned by their citizenship in the United States of America, enabling them, as less than 5 percent of the population, to use one-third of the world's resources.

In the past, a share of the wealth generated by talented and privileged elites did trickle down to those below. The wealth was largely reinvested and spent in the United States, and, after the New Deal, governments and unions enforced its wider distribution. But as more of the flow of investment, jobs, and opportunities is channeled into the global economy and as the social contract keeps shredding, the assumptions of the past that what is good for the Americans at the top is good for the rest of them—which is at the core of the case for optimism—no longer holds.

In the end, David Brooks seemed to understand that his "we'll be fine" narrative needs a better change agent than Slaughter's hyper-strivers zipping along the global network. And, like Rose, he seems to have discovered this change agent in, of all places, big government. After assuring us that the "entrepreneurs, corporate executives, line workers, and store managers handle the substance of the economy," Brooks outlines the requirement for a very active government to locate the United States at this global crossroads: "First, government establishes an overall climate, with competitive tax rates and predictable regulations and fiscal balance. . . . Then government actively concentrates talent. . . Finally, the government has to work aggressively to reduce the human capital inequalities that open up in an innovation economy. That means early and constant interventions so everybody has a chance to participate."[33]

So the narrative of an optimistic free-market future brings us back full circle to the need for a competent intervening government. And the effort to get around that problem by imagining a shift in responsibility to the states and the cities has run into the brick wall of fiscal reality.

When the national recession began, California—the poster child of the new, independent, decentralized global economy—imploded. Its prosperity turned out to have been based on the same credit bubble as that of the rest of the country. The state still had its global connections, of course. Silicon Valley was still selling technology to the world, and university professors were still flying around the globe to give lectures and lure students to their campuses. But it turned out that the major source of California's growth was firmly connected to Washington and Wall Street.

By the end of 2010, the state's official unemployment rate was 12.4 percent—the same as "old economy" Michigan. The state's budget deficit had soared, the pension system was sixteen billion dollars in the hole, twenty-two thousand teachers had been laid off, and hospital and other public facilities in the global cities of Los Angeles and San Francisco were being downsized or shut down altogether. The head of J.P. Morgan suggested that California was a bigger risk than Greece.[34]

This was surely an overstatement. Silicon Valley will produce more technological breakthroughs, some of which will produce the next big thing for the consumer market. But as we learned from the experience of computers, the Internet, solar power, and robot technology, the globalized business model of U.S. corporations now guarantees that the benefits of technological breakthroughs in American universities and research and development start-ups will be quickly dispersed throughout the world, in Anne-Marie Slaughter's words quoted earlier in this chapter, to "wherever they will be done best."

Thus, the evidence available at the end of the first decade of the twenty-first century provides little objective evidence for an eventual market-driven turnaround in the fortunes of the American middle class. One might imagine, of course, that the Chinese will keep buying the IOU's needed to support our civilian and military overconsumption for the next hundred years; that call centers in Nebraska can compete with India while paying higher wages; or that U.S. global banks and corporations might lengthen their time horizons and contract their global ambitions.

But that does not seem to be the wisest way to bet.

Part III

When What We See Coming Finally Comes

Not everything that is faced can be changed, but nothing can be changed until it is faced.

—James Baldwin

8

The Politics of Austerity

B anana republic, here we come," wrote Paul Krugman in December 2010 after Barack Obama and the Republicans agreed on a deficit-reduction plan that slashed social spending and continued George W. Bush's tax cuts for the wealthy.[1]

To be sure, Krugman's phrase—conjuring up the image of strutting generals, hacienda-owning oligarchs, and tin-shack poverty—was tongue-in-cheek. The United States is not a third-world country. Our generals tend not to strut, our oligarchs don't typically raise cattle, and our poor usually have indoor plumbing. But just as surely, a rough template of long-term austerity is slowly being fit onto American society.

Given the unequal distribution of income and wealth, widely shared prosperity wholly depends on rapid economic growth. The basic arithmetic is not controversial. The workforce is growing at roughly 1 percent per year. Worker productivity, which reduces the amount of labor required to maintain the same level of production, is on a long-term trend of 2.3 percent per year. Although productivity varies year to year, there is little reason to expect a substantial change in the next decade. Adding the annual growth in the number of workers and their productivity tells us that the economy has to grow faster than 3.3 percent per year in order to reduce unemployment.

Let's begin with the optimistic scenario. It is in any president's interest to look on the bright side. So we can be confident that the long-term economic forecast of the 2011 *Economic Report of the President*, produced by highly respected, competent economic analysts, represents as positive a case that the economic advisers to the governing class can make.[2]

The report forecasts that the economy will grow at 3.6 percent per year through 2017, when the unemployment rate will drop down to 5.3 percent and continue at that level for the foreseeable future. The significance of this number is that a Democratic president is admitting that after eight years of his administration, there will be at least 1.2 million more people out of work than in 2007 under George W. Bush, when the unemployment rate was 4.6 percent.

In addition, the report assumes that between now and 2017, fewer people who are of working age will want to work, and those who do will work fewer hours. Why this would happen is not clear. But the assumption is necessary, along with some other adjustments, to conclude that the economy needs to grow at only 2.5 percent per year to keep unemployment from rising. Since the report foresees a growth of 3.6 percent per year, unemployment will fall.

But how do we reach a 3.6 percent growth rate? According to the report, consumers will spend and borrow more. They will also increase their savings rate. With a higher supply of savings interest rates will remain low. But inasmuch as there is no projected acceleration of wages and no expectations that housing prices—and therefore refinancing—will rebound, both spending and savings cannot rise at the same time. So to achieve this kind of growth, consumers will have to take on even more debt, which can happen only if lenders become even more profligate than they were at the height of the credit boom. This is totally incompatible with Obama's pledge to dig the economy out of the sandpile of excessive consumer spending and debt.

The report also assumes a boom in exports that will accelerate job growth. But it admits, in an aside, that imports are likely to grow faster. Economics 101 tells us that the net effect of this growing trade deficit will be a further slowdown in job growth.

The report tells us that we can expect great, unspecified achievements in education, technological innovation, and the indomitable spirit of small business. All of this will supposedly happen while federal, state, and local governments are radically cutting their budgets, which will suck hundreds of billions of dollars out of an economy already suffering from insufficient demand.

This is truly an exercise in hope. The world implied by this economic report no longer exists, unless one believes that U.S. consumers can hop back on the credit boom that almost destroyed us. Even so, before they can do that, their debt burden would have to shrink back roughly to what it was when the boom started.

Financial analyst A. Gary Shilling—one of those who had predicted the 2008–2009 crash—points out that the ratio of consumer debt to after-tax income doubled during the boom years to about 130 percent. For consumers to adjust back to a more normal ratio of about 65 percent would take at least ten years of paying back loans and increasing savings, which can be done only if consumers spend less. Shilling estimates that spending less to pay off debt would drain the growth of the GDP by 1.5 percent per year, resulting in a 2017 unemployment rate of more than 23 percent![3]

Shilling does not actually expect the jobless rate to climb that high, because the government, under any administration, would not be able to withstand the pressure to create jobs. But an economy trending toward that level of unemployment would require a stimulus the size of World War II to compensate for the stagnation in consumer demand, and a shift from a trade deficit to a trade surplus of a size that is pure fantasy in a world of brutal competition made even more brutal by the spread of the financial crisis to Europe, South America, and even Asia (see chapter 10).

As the world around us has changed, so has the nation's central economic problem. With the shrinking of our historical legacy of competitive advantages, the problem is no longer simply stability, or the smoothing out of the business cycle. National adjustment to our new condition requires economic *redevelopment*: improving the basic capacity of the economy to compete in a way that generates rising living standards. Again, the United States is obviously not a third-world country. But its future, like that of a third-world country, depends on its ability to build infrastructure, to educate its people, and to set national priorities. Economics commentator Jeff Madrick has suggested, and even the hard-line economists at the World Bank and the International Monetary Fund have learned, that a country's economic development is a political process as much as an economic one.

Globalization accelerates the changes in the market and in technology. A nation's comparative advantages are constantly shifting. Governments therefore need to be able not just to invest in infrastructure, education, and research but also to continually monitor, evaluate, and reorder their public investment priorities. As we saw in chapter 7, even the free-market optimists eventually admitted that a successful future will require a competent, accountable, and interventionist government.

Thus, after having denounced as scaremongers those who worry about the future of the United States, Fareed Zakaria wrote a long essay for *Time* entitled "How to Restore the American Dream." It was the familiar list that corporate CEOs have been rattling off in after-dinner speeches for decades: lower business taxes, cuts in government pensions and health care, balanced budgets, and better education. But Zakaria sees that this will not be enough.

"The U.S.," he writes, "has to constantly ask itself what other countries are doing well and how it might adapt—looking, for example, at what other countries are doing with their corporate tax rates or their health care systems and asking why and where we fall short. Americans have long resisted such an approach, but if someone else is doing tax policy, tort litigation, health care or anything else better, we have to ask why."[4]

This kind of benchmarking has been going on for decades. Our national bookshelves are piled high with good ideas from abroad, and we know how these ideas are translated into policy. We know that the Germans and the Scandinavians maintain high wages and high productivity through a social contract that gives workers a stake in success. We know that they finance their public investments through higher taxes. We know that they produce better students by investing in high-quality teachers and schools. We know that they avoid the mountain of lawsuits and medical malpractice insurance with government-managed health care and social services that do not require you to hire a lawyer in order to pay your doctor bills and feed your family while you recover.

The problem is not that Americans "have resisted this approach" because we are too xenophobic to accept ideas from elsewhere. We happily accept others' electronics, skilled and wealthy immigrants, and cuisine. But Zakaria's admonition to the United States to "ask itself" has no meaning in the context of the structure of U.S. governance. There is no competent *we* anymore to think through the national interest. The more than 310 million Americans are not individually going to benchmark anything; this is the job of government. But after thirty years of a politics of tearing apart the capacity of the federal government to plan and act to shape the future, there is no *there* there.

Facing that reality would require Zakaria to make the case for a restoration of a strong social democratic government. So, as with many establishment pundits, his optimism dribbles away in vague references to what some unspecified "America" must somehow do.

Half of our two-party system is simply unable to grasp the country's dilemma. By the election of 2010, the Republican alliance between populist social conservatives and the business elite had taken another long plunge into know-nothingness and rampant corporate greed.

Today, the Republican side of the two-party system has virtually nothing serious to contribute to the discussion. Its economics are largely driven by faith, contradictory claims, and absurd policies that many of the Republicans themselves do not accept. The party's 2010 Pledge to America to extend the Bush tax cuts for the rich; maintain spending for seniors, veterans, and the military; and balance the budget by 2020 would require that the entire rest of the federal government—including Congress itself—be shut down.

It's not that the Republican Party lacks smart people among its leaders. But virtually all of them are imprisoned in a political iron cage bounded on one side by an irrational Tea Party political base and on the other by the more rational, but not necessarily less destructive and unyielding, corporate financiers.

House Majority Leader Eric Cantor of Virginia is not stupid. Nor is he an ideologically pure deficit hawk. Like most Republicans, when George W. Bush was in the White House, Cantor supported deficit-busting tax cuts and war spending. With Obama as president, however, Cantor insists that every new expenditure—even aid to victims of natural disasters—be matched with spending cuts elsewhere. Hypocrisy, of course, is not unknown among Democrats, either. But the Republican leadership's delight in taking the country to the brink of defaulting on its debts in the summer of 2011 in order to get more concessions on spending cuts was ample evidence of how deep their itch is for class warfare.

So within the confines of our two-party system, hope for the future lies with the ever hopeful Democrats. The good news is that compared with Republicans, Democratic leaders and the people they surround themselves with have a reasonably accurate understanding of the country's economic plight. The bad news is that they lack the will to lead the country out of it.

President Obama began his 2011 State of the Union Address with an eloquent call for the United States to invest in education, research, and public infrastructure in order to compete with the Chinese. Then, with the unemployment rate at 9.5 percent, he announced a five-year freeze on domestic spending and an intention to cut Medicare, Medicaid, and Social Security. At one dramatic moment, Obama said, "To every young person listening tonight who's contemplating their career choice: If you want to make a difference in the life of our nation, if you want to make a difference in the life of a child—become a teacher. Your country needs you."

Sustained applause followed. There was no mention that in that current school year, at least sixty thousand teachers had been laid off in 80 percent of the country's school districts. A month later, the president unveiled his new budget: increased military spending; a five-year freeze on domestic spending; and cuts in social services and education, including Pell grants for low-income students to go to college. By July, Nancy Pelosi, the highest ranking liberal Democrat, declared, "It is clear that we must enter an era of austerity."[5]

Liberal Democrats are heartsick that Obama seems to have thrown away the opportunity to impose the change he had promised.

In the pages of the the *Nation, Mother Jones*, and the *American Prospect*; among the liberal cable commentators like Ed Schultz, Rachel Maddow, and Keith Olbermann; and at virtually any gathering of the Democratic Left, Obama is considered a wimp who constantly caves in to the Republican bullies. Sharp-tongued Democratic consultant James Carville quipped that "If Hillary gave one of her balls to Obama, he'd have two."[6]

Many complained that he'd turned out to be a lousy political bargainer, violating common sense by prematurely making concessions even before the deal making had begun. Others complained that he was inept at public relations, not understanding the need for a clear "narrative" and the importance of "passion" in politics.[7]

To others, he was too smart. *Washington Post* political writer Dana Milbank noted that Obama was a puzzle to both sides of the political divide. So Milbank talked to three behavioral psychologists, and their diagnosis was that Obama was distant, intellectual, and too cerebral for rough and tumble politics. He has a high degree of "integrative complexity," they said; he's someone who sees all sides and is therefore always aware of "multiple variables and trade-offs." This was opposed to the more simpleminded George W. Bush, who looked at the world from one fixed and immutable idea.[8]

In conversations around the country, Democrats commonly shake their heads at Obama's naiveté. "He doesn't understand that you can't trust these Republicans," said a teacher from California. "Maybe it's that he doesn't know how these white conservatives think," a carpenter from Boston suggested.

Whatever Obama's inner psychological makeup, the notion that he is an over intellectualizing innocent in a world of political thugs doesn't quite fit. Obama is clearly a brilliant political strategist. Given the burden of his race and background, he engineered what was arguably the most successful long-shot victory in the history of U.S. politics. He had grown up in Indonesia being taunted for his African blackness, and in the Chicago streets playing basketball with people with sharp elbows. He'd spent a lifetime maneuvering through worlds dominated by powerful white people. That he suddenly froze up and lost his voice when confronted with the likes of Mitch McConnell or John Boehner, and that he could not see from the White House what others could see from their living room TVs, was not convincing.

Marshall Ganz, a legendary intellectual guru of community organizing in the United States who helped to design Obama's grassroots campaign for the presidency, wrote that Obama had shifted from being a *transformational* leader, whose purpose was to inspire the public to demand change, to a conventional *transactional* politician, whose purpose is to make insider deals, which disappointed the energetic young people who had created his political network. "He went," wrote Ganz, "from 'Yes, we can' to 'Yes, I can.'"

Ganz wrote that "Obama must reverse the leadership choices of the first half of his term. His No. 1 mission must be to speak for the anxious and the marginalized and to lead us in the task of putting Americans to work rebuilding our future. . . . And he must again rely on ordinary citizens to help us move forward."[9]

Ganz is a wise and seasoned political activist. Yet after accurately describing how the president had turned his back on the people who had elected him, Ganz, like virtually all of Obama's Democratic critics, assumed that Obama shared their politics but was not properly informed, was too naive, or was not politically astute enough to successfully pursue them.

Jewish villagers who suffered pogroms in nineteenth-century Russia consoled themselves with the phrase "If only the czar knew!" In fact, the czar *did* know. And so does the president.

Blaming Obama's political actions on his personal failings is comforting for Democrats. It offers hope that their agenda might still be fulfilled if they can get his ear and convince him of his errors. And it helps them to avoid succumbing to despair.

Eric Alterman, a columnist for the *Nation*, wrote one of the clearest-thinking analyses of the meaning of the Obama debacle in the summer of 2010, when the signs of a Democratic defeat in November were rapidly accumulating. Listing the variety of Obama's personal failings, he concluded:

> It does not much matter who is right about what Barack Obama dreams of in his political imagination. Nor is it all that important whether Obama's team either did or didn't make major strategic errors in its first year of governance. . . .
> Face it, the system is rigged, and it's rigged against us. Sure, presidents can pretty easily pass tax cuts for the wealthy and powerful corporations. They can start whatever wars they wish and wiretap whomever they want without warrants.

They can order the torture of terrorist suspects, lie about it, and see that their intelligence services destroy the evidence. But what they cannot do, even with supermajorities in both houses of Congress behind them, is pass the kind of transformative progressive legislation that Barack Obama promised in his 2008 presidential campaign.[10]

The system, of course, is "rigged" with money.

Money to finance the astronomically expensive election campaigns, which absorb the most important hours of the day—virtually every day—for all but the most enormously wealthy elected officials.

Money that the business-financed Right has invested in an electronic propaganda echo chamber, starting with Fox News, which has dominated the cable news ratings for more than eight years, and extending through a nationwide talk radio system whose audience is twice the size of the combined audience of the three TV network evening news shows, ten times the size of the audience for National Public Radio's most popular news show, and sixteen times the size of the audience for the liberal news comedians Jon Stewart and Stephen Colbert.

Money needed for the lobbyists who not only carry checks to their officials but who also carry with them the promise that the friendly member of Congress or head of a government agency might have a very lucrative business career after his or her "public service."

Money that generously supports the conservative think tanks, the academic chairs, and the careers of public intellectuals (of both parties) that provide the "expert" advice on how the public should think about policies.

Given the structure of U.S. politics, Wall Street has veto power over the fundamental economic policies on which virtually all other changes in the country's direction depend. Any potential Democratic candidate for the presidency, the Senate, and most House seats has to go with hat in hand to dinners in New York to gain acceptance with the seated Democratic contributors from Citigroup, Goldman-Sachs, Morgan Stanley, and the rest.

There they have an ostensibly relaxed, high-toned discussion about the country's economic problems, the proper role of government in the economy, and the importance of maintaining confidence among the world's major investors, but everyone understands the subtext: an examination of the candidate's understanding of the hosts' interests. There are no formal quid pro quos, but it is a deal nevertheless. The candidates signal their understanding of their hosts' needs and pledge to be accessible, always qualifying the pledge with the face-saving caveat that they may not see eye to eye every time. The hosts signal that they understand—within reason, of course—a candidate's need to play the populist on the campaign trail.

It is by far the most important constituency visit that a Democratic candidate makes. Walter Mondale, Michael Dukakis, Bill Clinton, Al Gore, John Kerry, and Barack Obama all made the trip and passed the test. Moreover, long before the meeting happens, any serious Democratic aspirant has to have developed relationships over the years with the people who are going to be at the table. They have to had already fit through the earlier holes in the vetting screen, already signaled that they would be sound on the money questions.

The influence of big business on the Democratic Party is hardly new or surprising, given that we live in a secular capitalist society. But by Obama's time, Wall Street had forced a model of thinking about the economy that set the standard for who is qualified for the jobs that manage economic policy. As long as the financial industry remains the driving force in the economy, is lightly regulated, and requires periodic government bailout, then only those with experience and expertise in financial markets and those who have the confidence of the bankers and brokers are considered to possess the credentials to manage the country's economic policy.

Obama's deference to Robert Rubin and his appointments of Larry Summers, Timothy Geithner, and all the others angered the party's left wing and exposed Obama—the candidate of change—to ridicule and the charge of political fraud. When Jon Stewart asked the president how he could square his campaign remark that "you can't expect different results from the same people" with hiring exactly the "same people" (such as Larry Summers), Obama replied that he needed experienced people with knowledge of Wall Street.

Certainly there were other people who understood Wall Street who were not in the pockets of the banks and investment firms. Nobel Prize–winning economists Joseph Stiglitz and Paul Krugman were two. But neither of them would have been acceptable to Wall Street and the economic policy establishment whose views the mainstream media—and thus the majority of the Congress—relied on to pass judgment on Obama's credibility.

Given that Obama's presidency has been transactional rather than transformational, the Wall Street people he brought in actually had the most appropriate set of skills to serve him. They are short-term deal makers, the talent most valued in a financial world in which the prize is won by those who are minutes, even seconds, ahead of the electronic herd when it turns around. These are the people you want to assure bankers and brokers that they will be okay. They have the skills to carry out the government's role as defined by Alan Greenspan and Ben Bernanke: to pick up the pieces after the financial train wreck.

But rebuilding an economy crumbling on a foundation of sand is quite a different economic problem. Ganz was correct; the task is transformational rather than transactional. For this you need people who can change the system's behavior, analysts who can think long-term and provide investors with the incentives to lengthen their horizons. You need leaders who can define the future and inspire citizens to work toward it. That task requires a different model of economic policy and therefore different people to run it.

In 1977, Thornton Bradshaw, the head of Atlantic-Richfield Oil and an advocate of national planning, pointed out that there were three ways to deal with energy prices: through the fee market, through OPEC, or through the federal government. The first was impossible, he said. The market was not reliable because there is always too much oil or too little, which provides exactly the wrong incentives to producers and consumers. The second, to let OPEC continue to decide, "is tantamount to handing over control of our national future to other nations."[11] Therefore, he concluded that there was no alternative to having the federal government set oil prices.

Ironically, raising taxes on gas to cut back consumption and force people to find alternatives is a popular proposal among many of the pundits and, in private, among many politicians as well. But it is politically toxic with opposition from both the Right and the Left.

The political antidote is for higher energy prices to be made part of an understandable long-term energy plan, with goals and strategies that lead to an attractive energy future: a national commitment to electric cars, mass transit, solar and wind power, and clean coal, with the jobs and economic benefits designed to stay in the United States. This in turn demands that the country's governing class abandon its discredited notion that the energy future can be left to the market.

Obama's bailout of General Motors is a vivid example of the way in which the transactional Wall Street mindset, with its obsession with the short-term bottom line, chokes off the possibilities for transformational politics. GM's bankruptcy would clearly have been a major blow to the economy, causing suppliers to go bankrupt, pensions to be forfeited, and massive unemployment to occur. Having rescued the Wall Street firms that caused the catastrophe, a Democratic administration could not have walked away from so prominent an industrial victim.

If Obama's plan for a new economic foundation was going to mean anything, U.S. manufacturing would have to be transformed and expanded. But instead of putting industrial people in charge—he had, after all, put Wall Street people in charge of rescuing Wall Street—Obama selected Steve Rattner, a Wall Street leveraged buyout artist, who had no background in manufacturing, much less automobiles. Rattner could define the task only in the short-term, deal-making transactional mode.

No one at the Treasury Department was worried that Rattner knew nothing about manufacturing, transportation, or cars. Nor was anyone worried that the attorney general of the state of New York had initiated an investigation into charges that Rattner had bribed state pension officials to give his firm billions of dollars of business, a matter suggesting that his success might not have been solely a result of his prowess with balance sheets.[12]

Summers, Geithner, and, by default, Obama defined the GM crisis not as an opportunity but in the most conventional, opportunistic way: as a way to save the company from bankruptcy at the lowest possible political cost to the president and financial cost to the treasury.

Rattner took the job in February 2009, invested eighty-two billion dollars of the government's money, and quit five months later.
Upon leaving, he declared himself a success—a judgment echoed by
the media and touted by the president. In terms of his job assign-
ment, to save the company from bankruptcy, it was indeed a success.
As with a leveraged buyout operation, Rattner took over the company, fired the CEO, and forced concessions from the union, the
suppliers, and the car dealers. Ed Whitacre, the new CEO, like
Rattner, knew nothing about the industry. Rattner hired him for his
"toughness" after reading how he killed rattlesnakes on his Texas
farm.[13]

Whitacre lasted nine months. He was then replaced by a managing director of another leveraged buyout firm, the Carlyle Group. In
his five months as auto czar, Rattner made only one trip to Detroit,
and it lasted just one day, on which he was briefed by officials at GM
and Chrysler, gawked at a modern assembly line, and flew back to
Washington.

At the end of 2010, GM initiated a new stock offering in which
the government sold about half of its shares. Assuming that it sells
the rest under more or less similar circumstances, the net loss to the
U.S. taxpayers will be about nine billion dollars, saving more than
twenty billion dollars in unemployment compensation and other
costs. It will be a successful transaction, but hardly transformational.

During that time, 21,000 more workers were laid off, at least
14 factories and 3 warehouses were closed, and 1,454 dealerships
were shut.[14] Rattner's long-term plan for GM shifted more production to China, South Korea, and Mexico.

Ironically, under the previous CEO, Rick Waggoner, the company—after having killed its electric car program several years ago—
had started down the road to building an all-electric car along with
its gas-electric hybrid, the Chevrolet Volt. But Rattner had little
interest in this. "The bottom line," he wrote in his memoir of his
five months in Washington, "was that there was no way for the Volt
or any other next-generation car to have a positive impact on GM's
finances any time soon. Certainly not within the five-year framework
that private equity firms typically use to evaluate investment opportunities."[15] Ironically, the day GM issued its new stock offering to

pay back part of the government loan, Nissan introduced its all-electric car for the U.S. market, priced at eight thousand dollars less than the GM hybrid.

The bailout of GM was just that and nothing more. It was unconnected to the long-term transportation and energy needs of the country, U.S. industrial redevelopment, or the kinds of autos that Americans should be producing and driving in the future. From Rattner's memoirs, we can assume that he never had a conversation with either the secretary of transportation or the secretary of energy.

In May 2009, Alan Reuther, the auto workers' chief lobbyist in Washington, wrote a letter to every member of Congress protesting the Rattner-GM plan to continue to import a large percentage of the cars sold in the United States. A few Democrats echoed his complaint, but it was shrugged off by the administration. The *New York Times* reported, "The Obama Administration apparently sees interference in such plans as crossing a line into industrial policy."[16]

Rattner also tells us in his memoir that Serjio Marchionne, the head of Fiat, which bought out Chrysler, told Ron Gettelfinger, the president of the United Auto Workers at the time, that Chrysler workers were going to have to substitute a "culture of poverty" for their "culture of entitlements."[17]

If neither the Democratic nor the Republican Party can or will address the fundamental questions of our economic future, why not start a third party?

It is not, of course, unprecedented. The Republican Party was born in the late 1850s in reaction to the inability of the existing parties to deal with the issues that led to the Civil War. But that was 150 years ago. Since then we have had dozens of attempts to breach the Democrat-Republican political duopoly. From time to time populist, socialist, and, more recently, the Green Party win local elections, and independents, such as Senator Bernie Sanders of Vermont, win election to Congress.

Nationwide, some third parties have made a difference in presidential elections. In 1912 Teddy Roosevelt's Bull Moose Party split the Republican vote and elected Woodrow Wilson. In 1992, Ross Perot drained votes from George H. W. Bush to give the election to Bill Clinton. And in 2000, Ralph Nader took enough votes away from Al Gore to trigger the events that led to the Supreme Court giving the election of George W. Bush. But each of these episodes was unique and built around a charismatic individual. And each soon faded.

The first reason for the failure of third parties is that in the states, where election rules are set, the major parties have collaborated in setting up substantial procedural roadblocks to third-party success. The second reason is the winner-take-all voting system for Congress, which does not allow small parties to accumulate legislative seats the way they can in most parliamentary systems. The third reason is that the media frames the way it presents politics in terms of two parties and instinctively marginalizes any efforts to widen it. As a result, establishing a serious third party whose agenda is outside the range of the Democratic-Republican debate requires an enormous and hugely expensive effort to get recognized even before an election campaign begins.

But the fourth and major problem for third parties is that there seems to be just enough difference between the two major parties to make most voters and political activists reluctant to risk splitting the vote on their side of the political divide. Democrats, in particular, are still haunted by the consequences of the Nader candidacy in the 2000 election.

If any third party should emerge, it will most likely come from the center—that is, the space between the two parties rather than from farther left or right. The notion that the central problem of U.S. politics is "partisanship" and a stubborn unwillingness to compromise pervades the mainstream media. So from time to time a call goes out from the punditry for a new politics of the "radical center" or a "third way," with centrist figures like New York mayor Michael Bloomberg offered as possible leaders. The hope is that the financing will come from the "centrist" rich: the hedge funders, the leverage buyout artists, and the financial fixers, who are more than happy to keep things roughly where they are.

Wall Street's stunning triumph during the initial Obama years is ample proof of the enfeeblement of the Democratic Party as a counterweight to corporate power. The signal is clear to the next generation of party leaders: to succeed they must plug themselves into the circuits that include members of Congress and their top aides, cabinet and subcabinet appointees, and K Street lobbyists for the great fountains of opportunity in the finance industry.

Democrats have adopted the established Republican career model. Young people who had been Treasury Department aides in the Clinton administration went to Wall Street and came back as crisis managers in the Obama administration. Once they finished the rescue of Wall Street, they began to move back to New York to resume their own moneymaking among grateful colleagues. In the next crisis and/or the next Democratic administration, they will return as seasoned, trusted, well-established people appointed to the critical cabinet jobs, and they will bring with them the aides who will be the next generation of the governing class.

At the base of this plutocratic political pyramid is the spiraling cost of electoral campaigns and the importance for politicians of both parties of raising the money from big business in general and Wall Street in particular.

In the past, direct corporate support for election campaigns was prohibited by law, and individual contributions to a candidate were capped at two thousand dollars. By having individual executives bundle their contributions with others in the same corporation or industry, the rules could be circumvented to some extent, but they remained important constraints on the development of a full-fledged plutocracy.

Those restrictions were removed on January 21, 2010, by the Supreme Court decision *Citizens United v. Federal Election Commission*, which declared unconstitutional any limits on what corporations could contribute to so-called independent campaign expenditures. The case had been brought by Citizens United, a corporate-funded group that had run TV ads attacking Hillary Clinton but was not formally connected to any other candidate's campaign organization. The court held that independent spending was a right of free speech, and it affirmed prior decisions that in other ways had defined corporations as citizens with constitutional rights. Therefore, corporations were said to have the right to spend unlimited amounts in an election, as long as they did not coordinate their activities with a specific candidate.[18]

The prohibition on coordination is a fig leaf. Since *Citizens United*, the creation of independent political action committees (super-PACs) is now a standard part of the strategy of virtually any candidate for major office. They are often run by people who come directly from a candidate's own fundraising staff. Thus, for example, the chairman of Mitt Romney's super-PAC resigned as the fundraising chairman of his campaign in order to start the "independent" super-PAC, Restore Our Future. On at least one occasion, Romney has spoken at a fundraising event for the group.[19] Barack Obama soon followed with his own super-PAC, set up by two of his former White House advisers as part of his plan to raise a billion dollars for the 2012 election. In the Republican primaries that spring, super-PACs were spending more than the candidates' own campaigns.

Even before the *Citizens United* decisions, the cost of campaigns was skyrocketing. In the 2010 election, the cost of winning a competitive race for Congress—one in which the victor won with less than 55 percent of the vote—was close to $2 million. In *supercompetitive* races, in which the incumbents lost, the cost averaged $3 million per candidate. All this for a job that pays $174,000 per year.

The U.S. Chamber of Commerce is already the largest campaign contributor in American elections. Among other activities, it secretly channels corporate funds to shift public opinion to the right. Although it claims to represent more than three million businesses, 96 percent of which are small, in 2010 the Chamber of Commerce received 55 percent of its operating revenue from sixteen firms that contributed more than one million dollars each.[20] In 2009, it took approximately eight-six million dollars from insurance companies for a campaign to defeat Obama's health care bill at the same time that the companies' lobbyists were negotiating with Democrats over the legislation.[21] In the 2010 election, the Chamber of Commerce spent thirty-two million dollars, "almost entirely in support of Republicans, FEC data show."[22]

In the 2010 election, which was too soon for business to take full advantage of the *Citizens United* ruling, conservatives outspent liberals two to one on independent campaign expenditures.[23] The top four business-backed candidates on the right alone spent twice as much as all labor unions. The labor union share of all "independent" spending dropped from 29 to 16 percent.

The story may not end there. The *Citizens United* decision held that U.S. corporations have all of the political rights of U.S. citizens. But it left open the question of whether U.S. affiliates of foreign corporations can also make unrestricted contributions to independent campaigns. When Barack Obama—a former professor of constitutional law—mentioned this possibility in his 2010 State of the Union Address, the TV cameras showed Judge Samuel Alito shaking his head. Alito and the court's conservative majority insisted that existing election regulations would prevent this.

It's true that a Federal Election Commission rule prohibited corporate executives who were *foreign* nationals from directly making the specific decisions about which candidate their U.S. affiliates should contribute their money to. But obviously, the *American* managers of an *American* subsidiary of Sony, Samsung, or Siemens understand where the parent corporation's interest lies in a U.S. election. Moreover, foreign nationals who have permanent resident visas in the United States already make direct contributions to U.S. political campaigns.

As Obama understood, if corporations have the same First Amendment right to free speech as individuals have, then even foreign corporations have the same free speech rights as foreign individuals. A foreign national, after all, is guaranteed the right to stand on a soapbox in a public park and criticize an American political figure. And he or she already has the right to hire lobbyists to influence U.S. public policy. So why wouldn't foreign corporations legally doing business in the United States have the same constitutionally protected right? Moreover, if they have the same right, and money is equated with speech, why wouldn't they exercise this right with the huge surplus of dollars they possess that has been generated by our trade deficit?

Citizens United has not ended the two-party system, but it will solidify the political requirement that ambitious young people drawn to the more socially liberal Democratic Party be credentialed by corporate donors. Corporate interests are not all the same, of course. On any given day, in legislative committees and in the offices of department assistant secretaries, hedge funds oppose banks, wheat growers oppose ranchers, nuclear power firms oppose oil companies, and so on. Thus, once certified as reliable in their positions on low taxes, deregulation, privatization, and globalization, Democrats will be free to finance their careers by becoming champions of one or more business sectors in the endless conflict over who gets what from Washington and the state governments.

Democrats will remain the party of compassion, the party that feels your pain, appealing particularly to minorities and single women, whose share of the electorate is growing, and the secular, socially liberal rich and professional classes. These constituencies will give the party something of political value to offer those who deal out the corporate money. We can expect the Democrats to win a share of elections as the political pendulum swings back and forth between the media-defined Left and Right. But they will have little incentive to address the simmering issues of economic stress, which will only grow worse in the coming era of austerity.

On October 30, three days before the 2010 election, TV comedians Jon Stewart and Steve Colbert held their Rally to Restore Sanity and/or Fear at the Washington Mall. An estimated two hundred thousand people came, and the overwhelming majority were liberal, well-educated Democrats. The crowd was as large or even a bit larger than the rally that right-wing talk show host Glenn Beck had organized in August. And it was much bigger than the rally organized by Democratic groups the week before in an effort to energize their activists for the election. It was billed as a protest against the nasty uncivil politics and the absence of rationality that is often presumed to be the source of America's problems.

It was a select crowd with a shared sense of moral superiority and insider irony. Writer Janet Malcolm noted that unless you were a regular watcher of the Stewart and Colbert TV shows, you wouldn't get many of the jokes and would have no idea why Colbert was jumping around in his comic book cape and jumpsuit. She called it a giant "preen in."[24]

There was virtually no discussion of the issues of joblessness, foreclosures, or falling wages. As one observer put it, "The comedians could tell you why the right wing was funny, but not why they were wrong."

This was the weekend before election day, and one wonders about the state of the liberal political consciousness—of both the hosts and their audience—that had them flying and driving to Washington to celebrate themselves on the Mall rather than knocking on doors and working the phone banks in their own neighborhoods to prevent the know-nothings for which they had such contempt from taking over Congress. There was little doubt that the Glenn Beck marchers, after resting from their own sojourn in August, were out on the street doing what they considered the Lord's work to elect Republicans.

Within a year the wistful political paralysis of the Jon Stewart rally gave way to the angry confrontations of Occupy Wall Street (OWS). In mid-September 2011, a loose network of largely young activists—inspired by the Arab Spring uprisings in the Middle East and the large protests against austerity in Europe—took over Zuccotti Park in lower Manhattan in the geographic heart of the financial plutocracy. Their slogan, "We are the 99 percent," referred to the doubling of the share of income going to the richest 1 percent of Americans since 1979.

From the encampment emerged daily demonstrations, teach-ins, and efforts to engage employees going to work at the banks and investment houses. The movement quickly spread to hundreds of other cities. The punditry had asked, Where was the outrage? Here it was. For some, OWS was an answer to the Tea Party. For others it was the transformative politics that Barack Obama had promised but had not delivered. For still others it was the start of the long awaited struggle over who gets what in the United States. "This is what revolution looks like," wrote columnist Chris Hedges. A former *New York Times* reporter who had covered two decades of turmoil in Africa, Latin American, and Asia, Hedges announced that for the Democratic and Republican parties OWS "was the beginning of the end."[25]

In most cities, local officials were at first generally tolerant, but then they turned on the occupiers. In November, New York City mayor Michael Bloomberg had the police evict the occupiers from Zuccotti Park; the police used tear gas and pepper spray on the occupiers and arrested hundreds of demonstrators. Police in Oakland, California, attacked demonstrators with tear gas, and at the University of California at Davis police systematically shot pepper spray in the faces of handcuffed students. Driven out of the occupied public spaces by the police and the encroaching winter, Occupy Wall Street disappeared from the prime time news.

The mainstream media complained that the occupiers didn't know what they wanted, disingenuously scoffing that the protesters had no program. But there was no lack of ideas associated with the movement. Plenty of proposals for creating jobs, investing in the future, reordering budget priorities, taxes, and financial reform were debated and discussed seriously at the various teach-ins in New York and elsewhere. Polls consistently showed that a majority of Americans agreed with the specifics of the OWS message.

The problem with OWS movement was not that it lacked a program. The problem was that thus far it had not been credible as a vehicle for political transformation. The public agreed with the OWS message, but a picture is worth a thousand words—and the OWS words were blurred by the TV news images of shaggy countercul-ture, of the cranks at the margins, of the sometimes sinister infiltra-tors (anarchists? police provocateurs?) looking for violence, and of what seemed to be paralyzing rules of consensus decision making.

Indeed, OWS made a point of not being an instrument for seizing political power. Unlike the Tea Party strategy of taking over the Repub-lican Party, the OWS spokespeople explicitly distanced themselves from the Democrats. And they seemed excessively concerned about being taken over by labor unions and other progressive political movements.

Ironically, having broken out of the laid-back indifference in which the country's young people were trapped, OWS remained within the political boundaries of a naive hope in the governing class's responsiveness. After Zuccotti Park was cleared, Kale Lash and Micah White of Adbusters wrote an op-ed in the *Washington Post* summarizing the experience so far and promising to return to the street come spring. The heart of their complaint was that the gov-erning class ignored them:

> Why didn't Bloomberg come down to talk to us? Or Gold-man Sachs chief executive Lloyd Blankfein? Why didn't Presi-dent Obama acknowledge the protesters—largely the people who elected him—and mingle in the open-air town halls? What a grand gesture that would have been. How come our political leaders are so isolated, our discourse so rigid? Why can't the American power elite engage with the nation's young?[26]

The occupiers' 99-percent-versus-the-1-percent formulation was appealing. But the visible confrontations were with the police whom most Americans see as workers doing their job of keeping order and with the clerks and lower middle managers walking to their jobs—not with the superrich, who are well protected from personal contact with even ordinary people and who were out of the reach of the OWS activists. What was important to the governing class—the financial markets—was unimpeded. After all, the money was not in bank vaults or safes in Wall Street offices, nor was it in offices in London or Zurich. It was in cyberspace.

9

Grand Bargain?
A Done Deal

That U.S. politics are "dysfunctional" has reached the status of a cliché. The government, goes the familiar story, is paralyzed because it is polarized with ideological divisions and personal animosities that prevent the two parties from making the decisions to support a "grand bargain" over the nation's priorities.

There is little doubt that over the last several decades the heavily subsidized expansion of the populist radical right wing on talk radio, on Fox News, and in the print media has increased the nastiness quotient in our mainstream public discourse. This in turn has pushed the Republican leadership into being more overtly partisan. Witness Senate leader Mitch McConnell's proud assertion after the 2010 midterm election that "the single most important thing we want to achieve is for President Obama to be a one-term president."[1] McConnell is not the first leader of the opposition party in our history to have had that goal, but few, if any, would have expressed it in public.

In their unabashed commitment to destroy Obama's presidency, Republicans held up appointments, refused to vote for programs they had previously supported, and demanded concessions in order to approve bills for the routine management of the government. They also drained some of the clubby atmosphere from the social life of the political class. Much to the consternation of the punditry, Democratic and Republican members of Congress don't have drinks and dinner together and fraternize at receptions the way they used to.

In actual policy terms, the ideological gap between the parties has widened largely on social issues. Republicans have become more outraged over abortion, women's and minority rights, and the separation of church and state, while Democrats have dug in their heels to defend the liberal position. In some cases, gay marriage being the most spectacular, Democrats have aggressively challenged what was assumed to be dangerous political taboo.

Economic questions are another story. There, the ideological gap has narrowed. The Republican Party leaders have moved further to the right. And so have the Democrats. So regarding the country's economic future, U.S. politics have been quite "functional"; they are producing outcomes that best serve the interests of those ultimately in charge—the rich and powerful.

The deal has been cut over the central question of which of the three great claimants on America's resources—Wall Street, the Pentagon, or the middle class—will be sacrificed so the other two might thrive. The middle class got the short straw.

This is not the result of some secret backroom cabal. It is the predictable outcome of the decisions already made on how to manage the economy and how to finance elections.

It is a safe bet that over the next decade or so, the banking and financial sector will continue to expand under the protection of the U.S. government. Even before the *Citizens United* decision (see chapter 8), Wall Street had demonstrated its enormous political power to escape the consequences of its own recklessness. With *Citizens United*, Wall Street now has more than sufficient political clout to kill tax or regulatory proposals that would reduce its ability to speculate, to funnel capital overseas, and to further expand its share of the nation's income, wealth, and political power.

Not everyone who works for a bank or a hedge fund is secure. Backroom—and, increasingly, front-room—functions will continue to be offshored and automated. The growth of U.S. jobs for securities analysts, lawyers, and accountants will diminish and at times shrink. Smaller undercapitalized firms that reach too far for yield will be allowed to go under. But the globalized financial sector as a whole will prosper and continue to suck capital and talent out of the U.S. economy.

The demonstrated inability of the Democrats to challenge Republican narrative on fiscal policy guarantees an extended era in which domestic budget cutting will dominate the economic debate. And the consequent Republican success in shifting the blame for the economic crisis from Wall Street to Washington has shut the door even tighter on closing the deficit gap by raising revenue. In the next decade, should the political pendulum put enough Democrats in Congress, some increased taxes on the rich may well be forthcoming. But given the ever growing dependence of both parties on corporate money, the increase will be marginal at best. In all probability it will come in the form of closing tax loopholes in exchange for lowering tax rates, with little net budget relief.

This means that virtually all of the pain will be felt on the government spending side. And inasmuch as "big government" remains the villain in the Republicans' morality play, they can be expected to pursue it ruthlessly.

In the spring of 2011, the Republicans revived the idea of a constitutional amendment to require that the federal government balance its budget every year. In 1997, a similar balanced budget amendment easily got the required two-thirds vote in the House, but it failed by one vote in the Senate. Had it passed, it would have then required ratification by three-quarters of the state legislatures.

The 2011 proposal also would mandate a 60 percent congressional supermajority to raise federal taxes; in addition, it capped federal spending for all time at 20 percent of the GDP. (Under Ronald Reagan, the average level of government spending had been 22.1 percent.) In a few months the bill had more than two hundred sponsors in the House. When liberal Democratic senator Mark Udall of Colorado announced his support, he said (echoing Obama, who had echoed the conservatives), "American families have to balance their own checkbooks—and, especially in these hard times, they're wondering why their federal government doesn't have to do the same."[2]

All that's needed to pass the bill is one election in which the Republicans gain both houses of Congress and the presidency. In that climate, the ratification by the necessary three-quarters of the states would seem very possible. Still, even with liberals like Udall clamoring on board, the balanced budget amendment may never become law. But the Republicans will keep pushing it, and the Democrats who oppose it will spend their time and energy defending themselves from the charge that they like to "tax and spend."

None of this means that the federal budget will ever actually be balanced or that it will even appreciably shrink in the next fifteen years. Continued slow growth will keep revenues depressed. What it means is that there will be little chance to expand the federal budget in order to pump more financial air into the shriveled cushion of the U.S. standard of living.

That leaves the defense budget as the major source of funds with which to relieve the financial stress of middle- and low-income Americans. But inasmuch as the vast majority of American politicians will continue to support the expansion of American military power in the world, there is virtually no chance that the military will not continue to remain a huge diversion for the resources needed to defend middle-class living standards.

Global military hegemony remains deeply embedded in the mindset of the governing circles of both parties. Andrew Bacevich, a military historian at Boston University whose son was killed in the Iraq War in 2007, wrote in 2011, "Presidents may not agree on exactly what we are trying to achieve in the Greater Middle East (Obama wouldn't be caught dead reciting lines from Bush's Freedom Agenda, for example), but for the past several decades, they have agreed on means: whatever it is we want done, military might holds the key to doing it."[3]

Twenty years after the end of the Cold War, the United States is spending almost as much on the military as the rest of the world combined and has seven hundred or more bases around the world. After the Cold War, military spending as a share of GDP dropped from about 5 to 6 percent in the 1970s and 1980s to about 3 percent ten years later. Post-9/11, George W. Bush took it back to 5.5 percent for the fiscal year 2009, where it remained for the next several years.

That the share of our economy allocated to the military used to be higher seems to many to prove that the country can afford it.

Of course, the perception of what the United States can "afford" is in the eye of the beholder. The same Washington policymakers who have declared Social Security, which runs 6 percent of GDP, an unacceptable burden on the economy maintain that spending roughly the same amount on the military is no problem.

Double standards aside, the issue here is the future financial condition of *Americans*, not America. In the three decades after World War II a robust economy was able to support both high Pentagon budgets and rising living standards. In the Reagan era, the military budget was financed the way we financed general prosperity—by borrowing. In the coming era of slow growth, fiscal austerity, and rising debt, the costs of empire will be paid in real time. And there is virtually no chance that reductions in military spending will provide anything like the resources needed for the investments and social programs required to stop the decline of middle-class living standards.

Elements from the left wing of the Democratic Party and the libertarian right of the Republican Party dissent, but the vast majority, and certainly the most influential, of the country's politicians and pundits are strong supporters of maintaining a large aggressive military presence around the world. When Barack Obama dismissed in his 2012 State of the Union Address anyone who believed the United States was "in decline," he was consciously echoing Robert Kagan, an unabashed champion of the United States as a global empire and whose writings the president was enthusiastically promoting. The "decline" Kagan is concerned with has nothing to do with the well-being of Americans, but everything to do with the projection of military power.[4]

There is little evidence that this will change. Indeed, with the continued economic weakness, the country's ability to project its "soft" (nonmilitary) power has faded. Money for foreign aid, cultural exchanges, and scholarships for foreign students—never popular with much of the public—is on the decline. And despite the new free-trade agreements, serving the U.S. consumer market and attracting U.S. investors is no longer the unique avenue to growth among less developed nations. With the United States blamed for the financial crisis, its attraction as an economic model—compared with China, for example—also lost its luster among the less developed nations.

Thus, "hard" (military) power remains the U.S. governing class's trump card in the global power game. U.S. diplomats are still accommodated, their e-mails and their phone calls are answered, and their words are listened to respectfully in conference rooms around the world because they represent the globe's most advanced, extensive, and dangerous armed forces. At sea, in the air, in cyberspace, and in its ability to deploy ground troops anywhere in the world rapidly, the U.S. military dominates. In 2011 the U.S. military budget was higher, adjusted for inflation, than at any time since the end of World War II.

In the agonizing wrangle over how to cut the budget, most Democrats and some Republicans insist that defense spending must share in the sacrifice. Accordingly, Obama and the congressional Republicans agreed that if the bipartisan supercommittee they established in the summer of 2011 could not agree on a long-range budget plan, defense spending would be included in the across-the-board budget cuts.

In January 2012, surrounded by the top military brass, the president called for an 8 percent reduction in the military budget over ten years. The Pentagon gave a listless salute to President Obama's request for cuts, but in the background briefings the military insisted that their support was conditioned on the understanding that the budget decisions were reversible, and their allies in Congress and the punditry immediately denounced the cuts as unacceptable.

Obama offered a new strategy to justify the smaller budget: a leaner and meaner armed forces would rely on high technology, such as smart weapons, robots drones, and armed satellites to replace troops. But the country had heard it before from previous presidents and secretaries of defense, including George W. Bush and Donald Rumsfeld. Anthony H. Cordesman, a prominent member of the U.S. foreign policy establishment, commented, "I have listened for decades to, 'This time we're going to be more efficient, this time we're going to use technology.'"[5]

As Andrew Bacevich points out, the end result is always the same. Thus, in Afghanistan and Iraq, "Whereas the architects of full spectrum dominance had expected the unprecedented lethality, range, accuracy, and responsiveness of high-tech striking power to perpetuate military domination, the veterans of Iraq and Afghanistan knew better. They remain committed to global dominance while believing that its pursuit will require not only advanced weaponry but also the ability to put boots on the ground and keep them there."[6] But finding enough boots is a problem. The great lesson the governing class learned from Vietnam was that they should avoid a draft at all costs. The U.S. middle classes are hawks in short-run theory and doves in long-run practice. As long as going to was "voluntary," there would be no mass protests from the young and no push back from their parents.

So in the absence of a draft, the military turned more and more to private contractors to deliver what used to be delivered by soldiers—food, clothing, ammunition, transportation, and intelligence—and done by soldiers—loading aircraft and guarding other soldiers. In 2009, 48 percent of the U.S. armed forced in Iraq and 57 percent in Afghanistan worked for private contractors. This further raised the cost of war. The typical employer of a military contractor pays four to five times what the government pays a soldier for doing the same job.[7]

One part of the ritual is that the defense budget projections do not include the cost of actual war. The media consistently reported Obama's proposed 2012 budget for the Department of Defense as $558 billion. But that number did not include the $118 billion cost of fighting the wars in Afghanistan and Iraq. Nor did it include the nuclear weapons program hidden in the Department of Energy budget, military aid to other countries, the Veterans Administration, or the CIA. When you add all of that in, the total is close to a trillion dollars.

The exact number is a secret, because the Department of Defense has never been audited. The Pentagon has repeatedly defied the Government Accountability Office's efforts to get accurate numbers on what the military actually spends. In his book *The Complex*, journalist Nick True reports on a few of the outrageous items that were uncovered in 2007: "$998,798 in transportation costs for shipping two 19-cent washers . . . $492,096 for shipping a $10.99 machine thread plug . . . a subsidiary of Halliburton that charged for 10,000 meals a day it never served."[8]

For decades, such examples of massive waste in military spending have been reported in the mainstream media, testified to in congressional hearings, and ridiculed throughout our culture. Occasionally a contractor is fined, a procurement officer is reprimanded, or an assistant secretary is embarrassed in front of a TV camera. But the Pentagon is impervious. In its 2011 final report to Congress after three years of study, the Commission on Wartime Contracting made a conservative estimate that the waste, fraud, and abuse in the Iraq and Afghanistan Wars might come to sixty billion dollars, but the commission didn't know for sure because it never could get a good accounting.

There is no stomach in the political parties for a knock-down, drag-out fight with the military-industrial complex. Defense contractors are important employers in every state and in a majority of congressional districts. They hire legions of lobbyists armed with generous campaign contributions.

The military reaches into virtually every nook and cranny of American consciousness. The Pentagon is a major financier of universities through research grants and scholarships. It is a major and visible sponsor of popular entertainment, from NASCAR racing to high school athletics. When it provides the facilities and logistics for war scenes on TV shows and in movies, it censors the scripts to make sure that Americans at war are presented in the most favorable light. Each military branch has a line of retail clothing, stuffed animals, and perfume aimed at advertising military culture with armed forces' emblems and slogans.

Moreover, in a high-unemployment economy, the armed forces are becoming one of the few opportunities for upward mobility for working-class kids who cannot afford to go to college otherwise. The drawn-out wars in Iraq and Afghanistan shrunk the pool of young people willing to join the military, so recruitment standards had to be lowered. But once the recession hit and the jobs dried up, joining the military became more attractive, despite the dangers, and recruitment standards have been raised.

Given the broad and deep base that the military has in American culture, there will be ample opportunity to rationalize a continuing high level of military spending as long as there is bipartisan support for the United States as global hegemon. So far, there is no *effective* political dissent from this agenda. Congress has willingly ceded to the president its constitutional authority to declare war. Congress impeached Bill Clinton, almost deposed him, and certainly ruined his second term over an artful fib concerning his trivial sexual peccadillo with a consenting adult, but it gave a free pass to George W. Bush, who lied to Congress and the public in order to justify initiating a war that sent some forty-five hundred Americans to die. This has not changed. Virtually everyone in Washington who deals with government budget projections knows that when a president decides to start another war, Congress and the media will fall in line and, no matter what the country's financial condition, the money will be borrowed and spent.

The champions of lavish military spending hold the patriot card, and it is a rare politician who dares to try to trump it. And actual war or no war, over the next decade there will be ample rationales for continuing, if not expanding, the military budget.

The U.S. governing class is now committed to the proposition that America's vital interests require us to fight an endless war on terrorism. As journalist Greg Jaffe observed in the *Washington Post* near the tenth anniversary of the 9/11 attacks, war is no longer an aberration, it is the norm. The very idea that such a war can be won—and therefore ended—has disappeared from the language of national security and foreign policy. The Defense Department's global security assessment tells us that we are in "a period of persistent conflict. . . . No one should harbor the illusion that the developed world can win this conflict in the near future."[9]

Global networker Anne-Marie Slaughter, after working as the State Department's chief policy planner, agrees: "In this world we will not 'win wars.' We will have an assortment of civilian and military tools to increase our chances of turning bad outcomes into good—or at least better—outcomes."[10]

Within that framework, there will be plenty of room for debate. Advocates of drone warfare will argue with those who think there is no substitute for boots on the ground. Strategists will argue over whether the terrorist bombs exploding in Yemen and Somalia are more of a threat than those being set off in Pakistan or Nigeria. Neoconservative and neoliberal policy intellectuals will debate ideas for winning hearts and minds in the latest theater of terrorist war. Secretaries of defense and presidents will continue to underestimate what each new major thrust against the ubiquitous enemy will cost.

Whether one believes that the war on terrorism is justified by a real threat to U.S. security or that it is a trumped-up excuse for maintaining the military-industrial complex, by its very nature it is sure to widen. The perceived physical threat—another 9/11-level attack on the United States—will continue to be reinforced by other geopolitical agendas. Given our intrusions into hostile and unstable societies, the chances of such another attack grow every day.

In the Middle East, there is the obvious objective of maintaining the flow of crude oil to U.S. refineries. Among others, Alan Greenspan wrote that the war in Iraq was "largely about oil."[11] How large a factor it was is still being debated, but it was undoubted very big, and it will continue to justify our ongoing military presence there. Even if we had a clear, widely supported, national commitment to our energy independence from the Middle East, the development of price-competitive and environmentally benign energy sources—and the restructuring of infrastructure and living patterns to accommodate them—will take decades to accomplish. As yet we do not even have such a commitment. Also in the Middle East, the defense of Israel, including indulging its current right-wing government's provocative territory expansion, remains a rock-bottom tenet of U.S. foreign policy.

In geopolitical terms, terror is a tactic or an act—not a specific enemy definable in space. In American politics it commonly recalls the horror of 9/11 and provides the government with justification for virtually any aggressive action against those who it labels "terrorists" with little immediate need to prove the case. Having its "war on terror" accepted by the public and acquiesced to by the courts, the governing class is now liberated from constitutional restraints on military action abroad—and to some extent violations of constitutional protections at home. There is after all, a war on. Moreover, the designation of who is a terrorist is more often than not in the eye of the beholder. One nation's terrorist is another nation's patriot. Thus, the potential for dragging the United States into civil wars and other nations' quarrels has increased dramatically.

Closer to home, the war on terrorism is very likely to demand more resources and attention to the developing struggle for influence south of the U.S. border. The United States, as an export market and a source of investment, no longer dominates South America as it used to. Brazil, Argentina, and Chile have entered the global market on their own. In 2009, China surpassed the United States as Brazil's largest trading partner. Venezuela, Ecuador, and Bolivia have rejected the traditional subservience to American interests.

Colombia is the most prominent contemporary model for the U.S. response to this trend. The U.S. government has poured six billion dollars' worth of military equipment, training, and advisers to prop up the Colombian government's fight against FARC, a leftist movement that is said to support itself by drug trafficking and that has been branded by the State Department as a terrorist organization. FARC is no doubt a threat to the State Department's influence and U.S. multinational investments in Colombia, but it is hardly a menace to the well-being of the average American; the price of coffee will be the same no matter who rules Colombia. The claim that the U.S. presence in Colombia is justified by the so-called war on drugs is mocked by the well-known support given by successive Colombia governments to right-wing paramilitary groups that are themselves deeply involved in the drug trade and that specialize in systematic violence against trade unions. After a decade of U.S. assistance to Colombia's "democracy," Colombia remains the most dangerous place in the world to be a trade unionist.

Unrest in Mexico is a different story. Through trade, immigration, and the sheer fact of the long U.S.-Mexican border, instability in Mexico *will* have a direct impact on Americans. And unstable it has become. In 2006, Mexican president Felipe Calderón launched a war on narcotrafficking, motivated at least in part by a cloud of suspicion that surrounded his election. The war was a colossal error, because Calderón lacked the means to win it. The government, the police, and even large parts of the army are themselves heavily involved in the drug trade. The result has been an explosion of violence. By the end of 2011, at least fifty thousand Mexicans had been murdered, and half of the country's thirty-one states could not provide effective protection for their citizens.

The governments of Mexico and the United States are replicating the Colombian model in Mexico. After decades of keeping the U.S. military at arm's length, Mexico is now receiving military equipment and training from the U.S. armed forces, the Drug Enforcement Agency, and the CIA.

With the economic slowdown in the United States, emigration no longer offers Mexico as much of a way to relieve its unemployment by sending workers across the border who will send their earnings to their families back home. The increasing joblessness among the young has made it easier for the drug cartels to recruit young men into their organizations, which produce twenty-five to thirty billion dollars a year that supports the Mexican economy. There is little chance of the U.S. market for illegal drugs shrinking; decriminalizing and regulating drug use is beyond the political pale and the twenty-year war on drugs has been a colossal failure. Nor, given the power of the American gun lobby, is it very likely that the U.S. government will stop the sale of arms to Mexican criminals. Therefore, the conditions that are supporting civil disorder in Mexico will continue.

Aside from the expenditures on the endless war on terrorism, there will be irresistible pressures for more military spending to counter the expansion of China's military ambitions. Thus, commenting on the internal discussions leading to the new leaner defense posture announced at the beginning of 2012, President Obama's national security adviser made it clear to the press that U.S. strategic priorities included "the need to expand its military influence in Asia." According to the *Washington Post* "Obama ruled out a proposal to cut an aircraft carrier group, arguing that reducing the number from eleven would undermine his ambitions in the Pacific and in the Persian Gulf."[12]

China's U.S. corporate partners have for years maintained that its emergence as a superpower will be benign as long as the United States accommodates its economic needs. A prosperous China would be a responsible power, it has been claimed. In the narrative of the Wall Street of Washington geopolitical analysts, the Chinese governing class will be happy to leave the policing of the world to the United States if we will just let the Chinese get as rich as they can.

But the governing class of China is no monolith. Indeed, in such a heavily centralized political system, the armed forces play an even bigger role than they do in the United States. And history does not record many instances of large successful economies that left their national security needs to their commercial rivals.

The budgetary issue is not whether the United States and China will start shooting at each other any time in the near future. It is whether the inevitable expansion of Chinese military power in its own backyard will provide a justification for more military spending or at least a resistance to any effort to shift substantial resources from the military to civilian uses in the United States. The answer is clearly yes.

Within the Chinese armed forces, there is a growing strident nationalism among the younger officers that will offer plenty of reasons to spread anxiety in Washington. "Chinese military men, from the soldiers and platoon captains all the way up to the army commanders," a China scholar in Singapore told the *New York Times*, "were always taught that America would be their enemy."[13]

"Why do you sell arms to Taiwan?" the Chinese government asks. "We don't sell arms to Hawaii." In 2011, a former adviser to the Chinese military told the international editor of the *Telegraph* of London that "the young officers are taking control of strategy, and it is like young officers in Japan in the 1930s. This is very dangerous. They are on a collision course with a US-dominated system."[14]

The conventional U.S. military wisdom had been that China was a landlocked power whose export-led growth made the country vulnerable to unprotected sea lanes. Thus, for example, by 2010 China had supplanted the United States as Saudi Arabia's principal oil customer, but this meant that China was even more dependent on tanker routes through narrow stretches of the Strait of Malacca and large expanses of the Indian Ocean. And the U.S. Navy rules the seas.

In 1996, when the Chinese tried to influence a Taiwanese election with threatening ballistic missile exercises, President Clinton sent two aircraft carriers to Taiwan, and the Chinese were silenced. After that experience, the Chinese government committed itself to the buildup of a world-class navy, adding new surface warships, nuclear launch submarines, and long-range coastal ballistic missile installations to cover the South China Sea. With no aircraft carriers the Chinese began reconditioning one that they bought from the Russians and started to build one of their own from scratch. In 2011, China launched its eighth navigation satellite and was planning twenty more.

The Chinese military budget is still a small fraction of U.S. military spending. China cannot seriously threaten the United States as a global military superpower in the foreseeable future. But it is getting strong enough that in a few years it could push back the U.S.

dominance of China's own neighborhood. And that is enough to ring alarm bells in Washington.

Already the Pentagon is reporting that the United States has lost its monopoly on "smart bombs" in the area. The Chinese are deploying precision-guided ballistic and cruise missiles that could reach the U.S. base on Okinawa and, according to one prominent military analyst, "overwhelm" U.S. aircraft carriers.[15] In 2010 the U.S.-China Economic and Security Review Commission reported that China's nonnuclear missiles have "the capability to attack" and close down five of the six major U.S. Air Force bases in South Korea and Japan.[16]

Regardless of whether you think that the various threats to U.S. interests around the world are real, imaginary, and/or unimportant, as long as the American governing class remains committed to waging a global war on terrorism, securing hegemony in Latin America, and maintaining military superiority in China's neighborhood, there is almost no possibility of shifting significant federal resources from the military to the civilian parts of the U.S. economy in the foreseeable future.

The full brunt of austerity will come down on domestic spending.

Much domestic spending by the federal government is channeled through the states. So the cutbacks resulting from the grand bargain in Washington have begun to squeeze state and local governments' budgets mercilessly, just as demand for help to a battered public is increasing. Moreover, as states become even more desperate for jobs, the bidding wars to attract business are getting more intense, further shrinking funds for schools, public safety, and social services.

A 2011 report by Good Jobs First estimates that states and localities are now spending some $70 billion a year to bribe companies to locate in their jurisdiction. These incentives include decade-long tax holidays, interest-free loans, and subsidies to pay for worker training that once was routinely paid for by the companies themselves.[17] For example, in North Carolina, the state paid the Dell Corporation $2 million to train workers for company-specific tasks. When Dell abruptly moved out, the state paid to retrain the laid-off workers. Then, as an incentive to locate in Winston-Salem, the state gave the Caterpillar Corporation $1 million for training, and a local community college provided the company with a training curriculum worth another $4.3 million.[18]

The net effect is a huge transfer of public funds to the business sector with no net gains for the country. Much of the local benefits are doubtful. Good Jobs First reports that less than 60 percent of the 238 state programs did not actually require that the subsidized business create jobs, and over 60 percent had no wage level requirement. Moreover, where conditions did exist they were generally not enforced.[19]

The result of these pressures on local and state budgets is that life for those who are tumbling toward the bottom of the income pyramid is becoming meaner and more brutish. In 2010, firefighters in a Tennessee community stood aside and watched as a home burned down because the family had not paid a seventy-five-dollar fee the local government had instituted for fire protection. A year later the same thing happened to another family in the same town. "There's no way to go to every fire and keep up the manpower, the equipment, and just the funding for the fire department," explained Mayor David Crocker.[20]

Forced to slash its budget, in October 2011 the city council of Topeka, Kansas, repealed its law against domestic violence so that it would no longer have to pay to enforce it. Domestic violence is still against state law, of course, so the idea was to force the state of Kansas to prosecute the crime instead of leaving it to the city to do so.[21] Perhaps the state will—this time.

A few months earlier, economist Jeffrey Keefe of Rutgers University reported on the impact of budget cuts on the police forces of five high-crime New Jersey cities. The cuts saved taxpayers $28,250,000. Based on an established statistical relationship between police protection and crime, the cuts were estimated to lead to the following level of increase in crime:

- 34 murders
- 9 forcible rapes
- 290 aggravated assaults
- 1,815 robberies, burglaries, larcenies, and auto thefts

The financial cost of this increase in crime came to $364,448,096, almost all of it absorbed by the victims.[22]

10

Flickering Hope: Schools, Trade Winds, and the Bubble's Return

Three economic arguments remain for convincing ourselves that the scenario of chapter 9 is too pessimistic. The first rests on faith in the power of the reform of our educational system. The second is the possibility that natural market forces might somehow turn global trends in America's favor. The third is hope for yet another credit boom to reflate the middle class cushion.

In March 2011, Barack Obama visited several U.S. high schools to demonstrate his commitment to education. During the tour, he pledged that by 2020, the United States would have the highest proportion of college graduates in the world. "That's our goal," he announced in a Miami high school auditorium. "That's how we'll out-educate other countries, that's how we'll out-compete other countries, that's how we'll win the future for the United States of America."[1]

Sharing the platform was former Florida Republican governor Jeb Bush, who also vigorously seconded the president's goal.

President Obama was obviously exaggerating. Neither improved education nor any other single program is the silver bullet with which the United States will "out-compete" the rest of the world. Nevertheless, even by itself, a dramatic improvement in the skills and intellectual capacity of U.S. workers could make a substantial contribution to our nation's competitiveness.

Bill Clinton, George W. Bush, and Barack Obama all proclaimed themselves "education presidents." Yet during their terms, U.S. students—except for those from the richest 10 percent of families— kept falling behind in virtually all of the international comparisons of student achievement.

When Obama announced his goal of making the United States the most college-educated economy, we ranked seventh among advanced nations in the share of its workforce with a two-year associate degree or better. Among younger workers, we ranked twelfth, at 40 percent. The leading nations—Russia, Canada, and Finland—were all at 55 percent. Not one state within the United States had reached that level.[2]

Compared with the education systems of these other nations, U.S. postsecondary education is largely financed by the students and their families themselves. After adjusting for student aid, the average annual cost of a public university for an in-state student is sixteen thousand dollars a year. A private university costs, on average, thirty thousand dollars per year. By 2011 the average student debt upon graduation was twenty-four thousand dollars, and the share of students who cannot afford college has been steadily growing. Thus, in a decade when family incomes will be further battered, closing the gap between ourselves and the Canadians, the Russians, and the Finns (even assuming that they remain at their current levels) will require a vast increase in public subsidies.

As Obama spoke in Miami, public universities and community colleges—which enroll more than 85 percent of all higher-education students—were shrinking departments and cutting programs. From 2008 to 2009 (the last year for which data is available), their per-pupil spending dropped as budget-strapped state and local governments cut back appropriations. Private universities and colleges—which already spend three and a half times as much per student as public universities—raised their per-pupil spending substantially.[3] Primary and secondary schools were being closed and merged all over the country. Teachers were laid off, and classrooms were packed with more students. In some places, the school week was cut to four days. In small towns and rural areas, schools were being further undermined by reenergized attacks from religious fundamentalists on the very idea of secular education.

The president's pledge, which he repeated throughout his tour, was for the United States to outdo the world in education at every age level. In its 2008 survey of the academic achievement of fifteen-year-olds in sixty-five countries, the United States ranked seventeenth overall, twenty-third in science, and thirty-first in math.[4]

During his tour, Obama called for an increase of 11 percent in federal education spending. Given the goals, and the fact that the federal contribution to school funding was only 8 percent of the total (the rest supplied by state and local governments), it was a modest commitment. Still, it was obviously a step in the right direction. The audience cheered. Jeb Bush stared into space. That winter, the Republicans, threatening to close down the federal government, forced further cutbacks in education in the budgets of both the federal government and the state governments they controlled.

Throughout the debates, the Republicans again had the ideological advantage; the Democratic Party elite had accepted their narrative that the core problem with U.S. education was not a lack of resources but the teachers' unions. The ultimate way to fix U.S. education, in this view, is to break the unions and privatize the schools.

The narrative is politically appealing to a significant number of people for several reasons. First, it allows politicians to champion both better education and tax cuts. Second, it simplifies the complex and controversial issues of exactly how to improve our highly decentralized education system. Third, it avoids the uncomfortable question of the contribution of poverty and parental inattention to the lack of student achievement. Fourth, blaming unions appeals to conservative corporate leaders who favor privatizing schools.

In the past decade a powerful, bipartisan school "reform" movement has emerged to attack the public school system. The movement is generously financed by a network of billionaires, including the Gates (Microsoft), Walton (Walmart), and Broad (SunAmerica) foundations. Also prominent is a group of wealthy hedge fund operators and investment bankers, who in 2005 started Democrats for Education Reform in order to convince Democrats to embrace the traditional Republican education agenda.

Echoing the management styles that have pervaded the U.S. corporate sector for the past twenty years, business-model reformers urge "disruptive innovation": schools that are not performing should be shut down, have their teachers replaced en masse, or be privatized. In response, states and cities deliberately hired education chancellors with no teaching experience and, in some cases, former corporate executives with no education experience at all. Education conferences and publications airily discuss the management philosophy inspired by former General Electric CEO Jack Welsh: regularly fire the 10 percent of employees that the supervisors consider the least productive.

Inasmuch as the reform movement's political appeal is its promise to deliver better education without spending more tax money, one objective of its supporters is to prove that class size doesn't matter. Arne Duncan, Obama's secretary of education—a prominent "reformer" who himself has no teaching experience—repeatedly says that he would rather have his children in a class of twenty-eight with a really fantastic teacher than in a class of twenty-three with a mediocre teacher.

Obviously, schools need all the fantastic teachers they can get, along with a classroom size in which the teacher can provide sufficient attention to each student. So on its own merits, the class size versus teacher issue makes little sense. Moreover, despite their best efforts, the reformers cannot come up with convincing evidence that class size doesn't matter.

Studies consistently show that roughly 60 percent of the determinants of a student's success come from outside and beyond the reach of the school. Prominent education analyst Richard Rothstein notes:

> If a child's parents are poorly educated themselves and don't read frequently to their young children, or don't use complex language in speaking to their children, or are under

such great economic stress that they can't provide a stable and secure home environment or proper preventive health care to their children, or are in poor health themselves and can't properly nurture their children . . . then children of such parents will be impeded in their ability to take advantage of teaching, no matter how high quality that teaching may be."[5]

It is not simply that poverty limits achievement. It also limits access for achievers. Students with high test scores from low-income families complete college at a slightly lower rate than students with low test scores from high-income families. At elite universities, where future leaders are trained, 74 percent of those who enter come from families in the top 25th percent income bracket. The middle 50 percent of families supply 23 percent of the entrants. Only 3 percent come from families in the bottom one-quarter.[6]

This point would seem so obvious that it is beyond debate. Yet it has been consistently sidelined in the mainstream discussion of school reform. It makes the financial elite uncomfortable, and it leaves the political elite—which has abandoned responsibility for poverty—with nothing to say.

The quality of teaching in the United States must certainly be improved. Unions do tend to make it harder, though not impossible, to fire poor teachers, but there is little evidence that this is a central issue. Indeed, long before Wall Street elbowed is way into education policy, teachers' union leaders had been sounding the alarm of an impending crisis in teacher quality, resulting from the retirement of an earlier generation of smart women and minorities whose opportunities in other fields had been blocked by discrimination. In 2003, Sandra Feldman, the president of the American Federation of Teachers, warned, "We're not getting in now the same kinds of people. It's disastrous."

Among the other facts smothered by the Wall Street–financed blitz against the unions is that the school systems around the world that do the best—starting at the top with Finland, South Korea, and Singapore—are completely unionized and run by the central government. Compared with U.S. teachers, the teachers in these countries are much better paid relative to other professionals in the society.

Teachers' salaries in South Korea, for example, are on par with what engineers and doctors earn. Teachers are chosen from the top one-third of college graduates, and their training and living expenses are paid for by the government. Although the curriculum is standardized, the teachers have more autonomy in how they teach than teachers do in the United States. In all countries in which students do better, the teachers have much higher social status.

President Obama knows this. "In South Korea," he said at one stop on his tour, "teachers are known as 'nation builders,' and I think it's time we treated our teachers with the same respect." A study of the costs of improving American education by the McKinsey management consultants concluded that for $30 billion a year, Americans could raise average K–12 teacher salaries from $39,000 to $65,000 with a cap at $150,000. Along with some other improvements, "it could lift the portion of teachers who came from the top third of their college class from 14 to 68 percent."[7]

Given the bipartisan grand bargain that will concentrate the burden of the federal deficit reductions on discretionary spending, which includes education, the chances of even this modest suggestion being adopted in the coming decades are nil.

The most important model for reform is the charter school, a publicly funded school that can be for-profit as well as nonprofit and that is independent from the normal personnel and curriculum rules. At congressional hearings and conferences, on TV and radio talk shows, in magazines, and at blue-ribbon commissions studded with business-oriented reformers, charter schools are celebrated as the savior of "public" education and as the vision of the educational future.

One product is the widely distributed documentary film *Waiting for Superman*, in which the heroes are virtuous charter school idealists who are fighting selfish teachers' unions. The film has been heavily promoted in major newspapers and magazines and on popular TV shows like Oprah Winfrey's.

But as education historian Diane Ravitch—herself a onetime supporter of charter schools as a way to experiment with improving teaching methods—pointed out in a devastating review, the film is a model of misleading propaganda. It dismisses poverty and the social

environment as a cause of student failure to achieve, despite the consensus of the serious research literature that student performance is
most affected by factors coming from outside the school. The film
neglects to mention that unlike public schools, charter schools are
highly selective in admitting students.

According to Ravitch, the film's hero, charter school organizer
Geoffrey Canada, "kicked out his entire first class of middle school
students when they didn't get good enough test scores to satisfy
his board of trustees." Nor does the film mention that the school's
board of wealthy philanthropists raised huge subsidies that were
unavailable to public schools or that Canada himself took an
annual salary of four hundred thousand dollars. For the film to
promote such lavishly funded charter schools while attacking the
public schools for spending too much money is, Ravitch wrote,
"bizarre."[8]

Most of all, the film glosses over the actual evidence on charter
school performance. The most definitive study available, directed by
the wife of a leading proponent of charters schools, found that 17
percent of charter school students performed better than public
school students, 46 percent no better, and 37 percent worse.[9]

Many reformers are undoubtedly sincere in their concern with
the quality of education in public schools and their belief that unions
are an obstacle to improvement. Others are clearly motivated by ideological hostility to unions and the public sector. But the school
reform movement has an even more powerfully motivated ally: corporations that see profit opportunities in the slow dismantling of the
public school system.

In the new era of austerity, school budgets have been relentlessly
squeezed relative to the educational needs of the students and
increasingly in absolute dollars. Desperate for revenue, schools have
rented out access to their students to commercial businesses in a
variety of ways, such as exclusive rights to market food; ads on bul-
letin boards, textbooks, buildings, and buses; corporate-provided
educational materials; and commercialized video news programs.

"Allowing for some peaks and valleys in individual categories,"
reported a professor of education at Arizona State University in
2005, "overall levels of school commercialism have relentlessly
increased over the past decade and a half."[10]

In 2010, more than eight million grade school students were exposed to *Channel One*, a twelve-minute TV program with news snippets, features, and commercials produced by a for-profit company. Children love the colorful, eye-catching visuals and the quick, clever programming—a dramatic contrast to the surrounding classroom with cracked walls, worn furniture, and unwashed windows. Teachers get relief from their workload, and the school budget gets some revenue.

The attack on public education has opened up even more profit potential in the growth of private vocational schools. As young people become more anxious about their future, for-profit trade schools have flourished. Since the financial crisis, enrollment has grown about 20 percent per year, most of it financed by the federal government and student debt.

Pell grants to students at these schools in the 2010–2011 school year are estimated at ten billion dollars, more than would go to students at equivalent public schools. One of the largest firms, the Career Education Corporation, reported revenues in 2009 of $1.84 billion, 80 percent of which came from the federal government.[11]

Deanne Loonin, a lawyer who defends debtors at the National Consumer Law Center, told the *New York Times* in April 2011, "About two-thirds of the people I see attended for-profits; most did not complete their program; and no one I have worked with has ever gotten a job in the field they were supposedly trained for. For them, the negative mark on their credit report is the No. 1 barrier to moving ahead in their lives. It doesn't just delay their ability to buy a house; it gets in the way of their employment prospects, their finding an apartment, almost anything they try to do."[12]

Peter Goodman of the *New York Times* reported, in a survey of the industry, that the schools thrive on high-pressure tactics and misleading promises that their courses in auto mechanics, computer technology, cooking, and other trades will lead to good jobs and upward movement on the career ladder. One of Goodman's examples was a twenty-one-year-old man who was working at a pet store for eight dollars an hour. Recruiters for a nine-month program in auto refinishing and upholstering told him that upon graduation, he'd be making fifty to seventy thousand dollars a year, so he agreed to pay thirty thousand dollars to enroll.

Fourteen months after completing the program, however, this young man has failed to find an automotive job. Instead, he is working for twelve dollars an hour weatherizing foreclosed houses. With loan payments of six hundred dollars a month, he puts in six- and seven-day weeks to keep up. "'I've got $30,000 in student loans, and I really don't have much to show for it,' he said."[13]

The private vocational school industry is politically well connected. The *Washington Post*, for example, owns the Kaplan test preparation service, and in 2000 it used Kaplan to buy into a chain of private vocational schools headquartered in Atlanta. The business skyrocketed, and by 2010 it accounted for more than 60 percent of the *Washington Post*'s revenue.[14]

Meanwhile, investigators from the U.S. Department of Education were reporting that Kaplan and other vocational school operators had been putting heavy pressure on low-income students to take out government loans—in some cases telling them not to worry about paying them back.

When the department began to tighten up on the rules for such loans, Donald Graham, the *Washington Post*'s CEO, led an intense campaign to protect his investment, hiring high-priced lobbyists and editorializing against the tighter rules in the paper. One result was that in the 2011 budget standoff between President Obama and Speaker of the House John Boehner, the president acquiesced to Boehner's demand that a District of Columbia's policy of refusing to provide local tax money for private school vouchers be overruled.[15]

Even more profit may lie in the reformers' ultimate goal of making charter schools the model for U.S. primary and secondary education. Charter schools are supposed to be community based, run by boards of parents and local residents and therefore more responsive to neighborhood needs than "faraway" city school boards. The notion that low-income parents who are struggling to survive economically have the time and capacity to adequately oversee the complicated task of educating children and managing a school was itself problematic. Predictably, it has been largely abandoned in favor of turning the schools over to "professional" school managers, some of whom are sponsored by foundation-supported nonprofits and some by private for-profit corporations.

Not only can the managers of charter schools hire and fire teachers as they see fit, they can rent, buy, and sell buildings; lease contracts for management consulting, accounting and legal services, food concessions, and transportation; and pay their managers far more than public school principals are paid. Moreover, they can do it all with public money. In states where charter schools are required to be nonprofit, profit-making companies can still set them up and then organize a board of neighborhood residents who will give them the right to manage the school with little or no interference.

The reality behind the "community-based" charter schools was revealed by the *St. Louis Post Dispatch*. Its journalists discovered an e-mail that Dennis Bakke, CEO of Imagine Schools, a private company that manages seventy-one schools in eleven states, had sent to the firm's senior staff in September 2008. This champion of school accountability reminded his managers not to give school boards the "misconception" that they were "responsible for making decisions about budget matters, school policies, hiring of the principal, and dozens of other matters." The memo suggested that the community board members be required to sign undated letters of resignation. "It is our school, our money, and our risk," he wrote, "not theirs."[16]

Some of the clients of Imagine Schools were paying 40 percent of their public revenue in rent to real estate firms owned by Imagine. The company netted $206 million in part by selling twenty-seven buildings to a huge movie theatre real estate corporation. The buildings were then leased back to Imagine, who subleased them back to the schools it operated. The *New York Times* reported that a school in the Bronx had paid Imagine ten thousand dollars a month more in rent than the building's owner was actually charging.[17]

One reason that charter schools are an attractive investment vehicle is the 39 percent tax credit for financing charter school construction enacted in the last year of the Clinton administration. Any good accountant can show how that could almost double an investor's money in seven years. At the beginning of the decade, JPMorgan Chase announced a $325 million fund—$275 million in loans—to establish its presence in the industry.[18]

According to Rupert Murdoch, the U.S. education industry represents a five-hundred-billion-dollar opportunity for investors. In 2010, he hired prominent reformer Joel Klein from his post as chancellor of the New York City Department of Education to run Murdoch's education technology company. A few months later the firm received a $2.7 million contract that had been negotiated while Klein was still education chancellor.[19]

The purpose of Rupert Murdoch and his empire, JPMorgan Chase, Imagine Schools, or the Washington Post Company is not to ensure that the United States can "out-educate" and "out-compete" the world. It is to make profits. The model, of course, assumes that presumably honest, high-minded bureaucrats like Joel Klein will carefully monitor their performances. But the cutbacks in staffing and the creeping coziness between those who get the contracts and those who approve them strongly indicates that profits will dominate. As the investment and ethos of the business corporation further infuses U.S. education, teachers will be treated less like professionals with a calling and more like the employees of other for-profit enterprises—that is, judged by their contribution to the bottom line.

There is no reason to believe that the Republicans and their center-right Democratic allies will not continue their attacks on teachers' unions and, by strong inference, on public schools. They will not have to win every political battle, but they will be on the offense, and teachers and other public workers will be on the defense.

Arne Duncan's notion that newly minted and highly motivated fantastic teachers would compensate for large class sizes will prove hollow. The new generation of teachers are neither higher paid nor more fantastic. We can fully expect the average class size to rise, from about twenty-five students in 2010 to perhaps thirty-five to forty. In response to the budget-cutting in California in 2011, some schools had sixty students per class that year.

Union membership among teachers will eventually shrink, just as union membership in the private sector saw declines within major industries once the Democrats became lukewarm to their traditional allies. Seniority protection, always a management complaint, will be chopped away, and so will the mentoring and group support that is essential to a well-functioning school faculty.

As the General Electric mentality spreads, individual teachers will start competing with one another. Problems with troublesome poor students, inadequate materials, hostile parents, and the emotional psyches of adolescents are unlikely to be shared with colleagues. Principals, hired for their ability to keep costs down and to spot profitable opportunities in real estate and vender contracts, will be of little help. The teacher who acknowledges the need for help—which might translate into added costs—will be perceived as a liability and not likely to have his or her contract renewed. The burnout rate will rise.

Despite its critics, teaching to the test will be further enshrined as the standard pedagogical method and become what teachers are trained to do. We can expect online technology to become the pedagogy of choice, driven by its lower cost. Despite the downward pressure on their pay, teachers will still be more expensive than shared software.

Online teaching is not new. Universities have been using it for years to supplement classroom and lecture hall instruction, to accommodate small numbers of students interested in esoteric subjects, and to spread opportunities to working adults who could not afford to study full-time on campus. But providing online teaching for mature, motivated college students is one thing. Expecting eight-, twelve-, or sixteen-year-olds to have the necessary discipline to learn while sitting in front of a computer is quite another.

A 2011 *New York Times* article about online teaching in a Memphis high school suggests the likely path to learning: "Mr. Hamilton, who had failed English 3 in a conventional classroom and was hoping to earn credit online to graduate, was asked a question about the meaning of social Darwinism. He pasted the question into Google and read a summary of a Wikipedia entry. He copied the language, spell-checked it, and e-mailed it to his teacher."[20]

With so much money at stake and corporate campaign spending so lavish, we would be naive to think that corporate lobbyists will not become a major influence on education policy. A glimpse of the future comes from Idaho, where the state school superintendent recently promoted a plan that would require every student to take at least four online courses with laptops purchased from funds that had been set aside for teachers' salaries. According to the director of the Idaho Educational Association, the superintendent's 2010 reelection campaign "had received more than $50,000 in contributions from online education companies like K–12 Inc., a Virginia-based operator of online charter schools that received $12.8 million from Idaho last year."[21]

The upper rungs of the income and wealth ladder will feel much less of the impact of school reform. Imagine Schools might be the answer for kids in Harlem and even in Queens, but not in Westchester. People in the richest enclaves in the United States will send their children to private schools or pay the necessary taxes to support healthy local public schools in which classroom size is small. Given the general deterioration of wages and working conditions, the supply of unhappy, first-rate, experienced teachers who want to teach in a more secure and comfortable environment will expand, giving richer school districts even more ability to choose from the best.

In the wealthy suburbs of New York, Chicago, Los Angeles, and other cities, high-quality teachers will instruct well-prepared students in an environment free from the assault of teenage marketing. Music, art, and cultural experiences will continue to be supported. Chinese, French, and Arabic will be taught by teachers who actually speak Chinese, French, and Arabic. Science will not be taught by the click of a keyboard, but by real teachers engaged in hands-on creative projects. Math instruction will be both challenging and imaginative. High school students will spend six months abroad.

Even in these highly social competitive circles, teaching students how to think, reason, and organize for group innovation will be more important than teaching to the test. Students at elite schools will dedicate more time exercising their bodies on the playing field and their minds in laboratories and through quiet reading. Watching TV will be strictly limited, and junk food will not be encouraged as a way to cover the deficit in the school budget.

These children will continue their educations at elite universities and make the connections that channel them into the transnational corporations and global networks celebrated by David Brooks and Anne-Marie Slaughter (see chapter 7). Meanwhile, the majority of America's young people will be trained beneath the cover of upbeat optimism to survive in a country that is being outsourced, outdone in competition, and outdone in education.

● ● ●

With no industrial policy, a commitment to unregulated trade, and a continuing inadequate investment in the nation's infrastructure and people, the U.S. governing class has neither a plan nor a strategy for halting our international competitiveness decline.

So what? According to the free-market optimists, sooner or later the market itself will adjust to these "global imbalances" (the euphemism they use for the U.S. trade deficit). They point to examples of "onshoring," the decision by some companies to move jobs back from Asia to the United States, as evidence that the trade winds may be blowing back in our direction. The media are sprinkled with stories of American businessmen complaining about rising shipping costs, quality problems with Chinese products, and the hassles of dealing with protectionist governments. So, argue the economic bright-siders, the market itself could enable Americans to rebalance their trade with the rest of the world with little pain.

It's true that higher fuel costs should slow down imports from overseas, but they will also slow down our exports. Given that imports are so much greater, the net effect on the trade balance should be positive. Slowing down imports will make more U.S. markets competitive for domestic suppliers. It is already happening for some large heavy items like furniture and big appliances.

But to make a substantial dent in the U.S. trade deficit, the price of fuel will have to climb a lot higher. In his 2009 book, *$20 per Gallon*, Christopher Steiner estimates that the tilting point for U.S. imports will occur when gas reaches roughly fourteen dollars per gallon and stays there. At that price, the fuel cost of sending a container ship from Shanghai to the U.S. East Coast will triple.[22] That fuel prices will raise over time is a good bet, but in the absence of a political cataclysm in the Middle East, it will certainly take more than a decade to reach that high a price. In any event, the damage that a fourteen-dollar-per-gallon gas price will do to the standard of living in an unprepared U.S. economy will dwarf whatever advantages it might bring to the trade balance.

Moreover, slowing down imports from Asia and Europe will not automatically translate into more jobs in the United States. The refusal of Barack Obama and Hillary Clinton to fulfill their promise of renegotiating NAFTA has, in effect, created a permanent continental economy in which low wages, government control over unions, and pliable business regulations will give Mexican locations for businesses a comparative advantage for decades.

NAFTA allows both U.S. and foreign producers to use Mexico to provide free access to the U.S. market. There is little reason to doubt that American companies coming back from Asia and looking for the lowest costs would rather land in Mexico. The same is true for Chinese, South Korean, and Taiwanese companies, which already import components for assembly in Mexico and then ship them duty-free to the United States.

The rising culture of violence in Mexico is a problem. In recent years, an increasing number of Mexican businessmen have been targeted for kidnapping and extortion. But the global corporations are safe, and their operations are untouched. Companies like GE, GM, Microsoft, and Citigroup have enough resources to cover the bribes, enough security measures, and enough overall political clout to protect their operations.

Moreover, in the next few years it is highly likely that in one way or another, law and order will be restored. The most likely scenario is a deal involving the army, the government, and the older established drug cartels. The deal would include a division of territory among the narcotraffickers, a government pledge not to interfere with a certain level of drug exports to the United States, and a joint effort to destroy the Zetas and other vicious criminal gangs. Given that the U.S. government has neither the will nor the capacity to curb Americans' drug consumption, the business of supplying drugs for the thirty-billion-dollar U.S. market will continue.

Like the rising cost of fuel, problems of quality control in places like China will also cause some second thoughts about offshoring. For example, after Chinese-made wallboard flooded the U.S. construction market, enough turned out to be of such poor quality that the U.S. construction industry turned back to North American sources.

The incidence of onshoring is small, however, and most of the cases discovered by the media are idiosyncratic. In different articles about onshoring, both *Fortune* magazine and *USA Today* have featured Sleek Audio, a family-owned U.S. business that manufactures high-end headphones and has decided to move most of its work from

China back to its factory in Florida. The firm's CEO complained that the Chinese connections were poorly soldered and sometimes arrived broken. Making the earphones in China was still cheaper overall, but for the small company, it was too much trouble. The founders' son had to make six two-week trips a year to China and handle phone calls at 11 p.m. Now that they are bringing the work home, he said, "My wife loves that." Just how many new jobs will this onshoring decision create? *USA Today* reports that Sleek Audio "has already hired five employees in its Florida plant and plans to add another 15."[23]

Unlike this small company, most multinationals that are offshoring their production have plenty of people to send to China to impose quality discipline on their contractors. Apple's iPhone is made in China from components from Japan, South Korea, and Taiwan and is the best of its kind. It adds roughly two billion dollars a year to the U.S. trade deficit.[24]

An indication of how thin are the prospects for onshoring back to the United States was a January 2012 White House conference on the subject that featured a company named Galaxe Solutions whose CEO proudly announced that it had hired 150 people as part of a program called "Insource Detroit." But a trip to Galaxe's website tells the viewer that the company's entire business model is in fact built around an offshoring business model that "provides the enterprise with a powerful technical delivery line through the transfer of primary development functions to its facility in Bangalore, India."[25]

A few decades ago, the Made in Japan tag on an item was considered a sign of poor quality. Now, like the Japanese then, the Chinese governing class is committed to moving as rapidly as possible up the global ladder of high value-added production. There is little doubt that it will succeed.

Most important for the question of the middle-class standard of living is that onshoring is almost always associated with substantial cuts in U.S. wages. Thus, GE has moved production of an energy-efficient water heater from Chinese contractors to a small factory in Louisville, Kentucky. The workers there used to make twenty-two dollars per hour; now they make thirteen.

The final claim for a benign American adjustment to the global market is that economic theory tells us that trade deficits cannot last forever, as long as a nation's currency circulates freely. This is because a country that consistently buys more than it sells will be putting more of its currency into the hands of its trading partners with whom it is running deficits. Since increasing the supply of anything relative to demand lowers the price, the value of the currency will fall. This raises the price—and reduces the demand for—imports, and it causes the opposite effect for exports. So, goes the argument, exports will rise faster than imports, and eventually trade balance will be restored.

The conventional wisdom is not wrong, but the case of the United States is different, in part because the U.S. dollar is still the most important reserve currency for the world's central banks and for writing contracts in oil and other globally traded goods. It is also seen as a safe political haven in times of turmoil and economic stress. Demand for the dollar is therefore somewhat independent of the U.S. trade balance.

In addition, the central banks of nations whose currency is not freely traded often manipulate the value of their currency to keep it low relative to the dollar and thus keep their exports more competitively priced. China is the obvious example.

Here is another example of the leaders of both political parties pursuing policies with eyes wide open that undercut the competitiveness of American workers. The phenomenon of exchange-rate protectionism was well known to the Republican and Democratic negotiators of the rules of the World Trade Organization and the other free-trade adjustments of the past twenty years. Nevertheless, pressured by their multinational "American" corporate financiers who were eager to partner with the Chinese, they deliberately excluded from the agreements any prohibition on currency manipulation.

This was no oversight. It was repeated in agreement after agreement. And like most political folly, the reason for it lies in the special interests of the rich and powerful. Both Wall Street and the Pentagon favor a highly valued dollar because it enables them to buy assets around the world more cheaply. In Wall Street's case, this means foreign business assets. In the Pentagon's, a higher valued dollar makes it less costly to maintain its bases, its foreign missions, and its wars.

Sooner or later, as the U.S. economy naturally shrinks in importance, the dollar will have to give way as the world reserve currency. Already, the leaders of the BRIC nations—Brazil, Russia, India, and China—have called for a new global credit system managed by the

International Monetary Fund (IMF) or a new institution and based on a basket of currencies, which would diminish the dollar's global importance. But this would be an enormously complex process that would take at least a decade of negotiation among the world's two hundred and some nations—starting with a commitment from the United States. Even in the most optimistic scenario of international cooperation, this is unimaginable.

Short of that, another possibility would be an agreement among U.S. trading partners to allow the dollar to fall substantially in order to rebalance our international books. This is imaginable. A similar agreement was actually struck in the mid-1980s in meetings in New York's Plaza Hotel among the United States, Western Europe, and the Japanese when the U.S. trade deficit threatened to spiral out of control. But this was in the context of the Cold War, when the United States was the protector of the capitalist world. Today, with virtually every nation trying to export its way back to prosperity, there is little political room for another Plaza Accord.

It is reasonable to assume that the dollar will fall in value, but given the forces that resist its decline, it will take a very long time before it reaches the level at which the United States can balance its trade. Moreover, for the dollar to perform its function of rebalancing trade, it not only has to fall, it has to stay down. It takes years to build factories, develop workforce skills, and set up new marketing channels. Investors in manufacturing need to be assured that government policy will keep the dollar down.

Although a fall in the dollar will improve the balance of payments, the effect of it too will be to lower the American standard of living. A lower dollar will raise the price of imports, starting with oil but extending to the roughly 30 percent of all the goods that Americans now buy. The price of clothing, shoes, toys, computers, cars, food, paper products, and virtually all of our electronics will rise substantially.

Having left our fate to the mercies of the global market, we will be subject to its laws. America's trading accounts with the rest of the world will be settled by some combination of the following:

- Severe sustained public budget austerity suppressing growth, reducing imports by reducing incomes

- A substantial drop in the value of the dollar, also reducing incomes
- Lower wages in the expanding sectors of tradable goods and services, which will spread to the rest of the economy, reducing incomes

There is one last imaginable scenario that could conceivably result in at least a temporary halt in the decline of middle-class incomes: one final binge of borrowing and consumption that would briefly re-create the credit boom that crashed in 2008—one last carefree romp in the sandpile of speculation and debt.

Let us make the assumption that the world's central banks can and will pump enough capital into the financial system to stop the spread of European sovereign debt defaults that erupted in 2011 as an aftershock to the crash three years earlier. If they cannot or will not, we will certainly fall into a 1930s-style depression.

But even if they do, we will still be left with a U.S. financial system in which the largest banks and investment firms are too big to fail, too global to monitor, and too powerful to regulate. And a political system in which the combination of Wall Street lobbying and right-wing populist budget cutting will ensure that the regulatory agencies will not have the resources to fulfill even the modest reforms of the Dodd-Frank Act.

We will also be left with large chunks of the financial system overhung with debt. Banks will still be carrying nonperforming loans and other assets on their books and surviving on cheap money from the Federal Reserve that will not last forever. Pension funds will be saddled with long-term obligations that they cannot meet.

The desperate search for higher yield through higher risk has already begun.

The North Carolina legislature has authorized its state pension fund to invest in junk bonds, real estate, and commodities. Wisconsin is moving pension funds into derivatives, swaps, and complicated repurchase agreements. The Texas teachers' pension put money into securities derived from Chicago parking fees. Pension boards that previously turned away hedge funds are now eager to do business with them.

"In effect," the former chairman of the Texas teachers' pension board told the *New York Times*, "they're going to Las Vegas. Double up and catch up."[26]

Many individual middle-class investors, faced with stagnant or declining wages, could also return to the stock market. With housing prices back down to earth, Medicare and Social Security steadily chipped away, and guaranteed pensions a thing of the past, getting lucky in the stock market will seem to be the only hope for a dignified retirement.

Wall Street is already on the prowl to find substitutes for the subprime mortgage get-rich-quick investment narrative. These next big stories might come from a number of places. For example:

- Global currency trades that annually total $3.2 trillion. Having been specifically excluded from the Dodd-Frank Act, they are completely unregulated.
- New U.S. high-tech firms with ties to Chinese manufacturing and marketing companies
- Urban real estate companies in dozens of spectacularly growing cities around the world, such as Ghaziabad in India, Beihai and Chongqing in China, Chittagong in Bangladesh, Lagos in Nigeria, and Santa Cruz in Bolivia
- Privatization of state and local government services, such as public safety, transportation, and education—including the opportunities in real estate generated by the for-profit private management of charter schools.

Securities traders, brokers, and bankers now have the capacity to use such get-rich-quick narratives to invent even more complex derivatives, and they have the technology to click them into the market at lightning speed. The overwhelmed regulators will be even more overmatched. As the *New York Times* reported in 2011, unregulated hedge funds are now acting as community banks, making high-interest loans to risky businesses and adding to their debt burden.[27]

A new financial bubble generated by these and similar market ploys will not have the economic lift of the subprime mortgage market, nor will it last as long. But it might last long enough to bring back "the confidence fairy." Rising prices for the stock of companies connected to one of the primary narratives promising future profits could spill over to the rest of the market, improving the value of the portfolios of investors. A punditry starved for good news would proclaim that finally the recovery is kicking in. Consumers, anticipating better times ahead, will take on more credit. Growth will accelerate, and the unemployment rate will fall. Political leaders will declare the miniboom as the just reward of the American people's patience, fortitude, and enterprising spirit.

The markets will overshoot, as they always do. With the experience of 2008–2009 not forgotten, the electronic financial herd will be operating on an even more sensitive hair trigger. On the slightest bit of disappointing news, money will roll out as fast as it rolled in. When faced with an impending market drop, hedge funds, whose business model is entirely short-term, will dump loans even faster than banks do; shares prices will fall, banks will demand that loans be repaid or more collateral put up, and we will have 2008 all over again.

But the next time Wall Street puts the economy through the ringer, it will be much harder for the Treasury Department and the Federal Reserve to clean up the mess. Another bank bailout will strain the already thin credibility of the dollar, and the global financial herd will have more places to store its money than in treasury notes that are once again bordering on default. Many fewer international contracts will have been written for dollars. The Federal Reserve will no longer be able to simply issue more credit without the global markets demanding a much higher interest rate premium for lending to the United States.

In another decade, China will be the world's largest economy, as well as the United States's largest creditor. Conventional Washington wisdom denies that this provides the Chinese with geopolitical leverage, brushing the threat aside with the hoary adage that if you owe the bank a hundred dollars it is your problem, but if you owe it a million it is the bank's problem. There is some truth to this—up to a point. In the end the creditors' threat to foreclose on the debtors typically trumps the debtors' threat to bankrupt them. History reinforces the point. Thus, for example, when the British and French invaded the Suez Canal in 1956, U.S. president Dwight Eisenhower forced the British into a humiliating retreat by a threat to sell off British bonds and undercut the pound sterling.[28]

So it is not hard to imagine that the next financial bubble might play out differently than the last.

The stock market tanks. Credit dries up. The unemployment rate spikes, and the plunging dollar drives up the price of oil and other imports. The media bring back the 1970s term *stagflation*: the deadly combination of prices and unemployment rising together.

The treasury secretary and the chairman of the Federal Reserve fly to Beijing and ask the Chinese to support the dollar with large purchases of treasury bonds. They are told that the U.S. president should make his case in person. The American media are outraged. But Wall Street tells the president that he has no choice. He and the Chinese leader meet at a secluded place in Asia. A joint communiqué indicates no deal, and the president flies back home.

A few days later the Chinese start buying a large quantity of treasury bills. When the market turmoil subsides, the U.S. administration quietly cuts off military sales to Taiwan, cancels plans to expand bases in the Philippines, and drops all complaints against China at the World Trade Organization.

To mollify a dangerously disgruntled military-industrial complex and the angry populist Right, the administration also substantially increases the defense budget, paying for it with further cuts in civilian spending.

This is not, of course, a prediction, and the details are illustrative. But it is a reasonable scenario of the way a future recovery will play out in a weakened U.S. economy that still rests on the Reagan-era foundation of sand—financial speculation, trade deficits, and consumer debt.

11

From Service to Servitude

Whether or not we get one more brief romp in the sandpile of debt and overconsumption, we are already locked into a substantial drop in the typical American worker's income. "Jobs, jobs, jobs" will remain the mantra of both parties, and the strategy will be "lower wages, lower wages, lower wages." Reaching this conclusion does not require us to assume anything other than an extension of our current economic trajectory. As this book has argued, neither the natural workings of the market nor the country's political leadership will change that trajectory. At this point, all avenues of escape from a substantial decline in middle-class living standards are blocked.

We can make reasonably optimistic assumptions about the next decade: there will be no new recession, Europe will recover from its crisis, the conflict over the federal budget policy will be resolved with a combination of budget cuts and taxes accepted by both parties, there will be no new war, there will be no run on the dollar, the next few presidents will avoid any further acts of economic folly. But the damage has already been done. By the mid-2020s we can expect about a 20 percent drop in the real wages of the average American who has to work for a low or moderate standard of living. Should future economic trends prove more negative, the drop will be steeper. Almost as many women as men now work outside the home, so expanding family participation in the workforce is largely an exhausted response to faltering wages. Thus, unlike the three previous decades of wage stagnation, this time family incomes as well as individual wages will decline.

A drop of 20 percent or so in hourly wages may understate the actual cut in take-home pay. Should the Obama health-care law survive its legal and political challenges, private insurance premiums will be taken out of more paychecks. If the law does not survive, and the modest efforts at controlling insurance costs are abandoned, even more money will be taken out. If Social Security is to be maintained as a stand-alone insurance system, the payroll tax holidays in 2010 and 2011 will have to be made up, cutting the paycheck even more.

The postcrash recession has already given us a glimpse of the future of American workers. To use a term coined by economist John Irons, the economic "scarring" of three years of high joblessness will drag down workers' earnings for years to come.[1] We already know that young people entering the job market during recessions never fully recover from their lost opportunities. Yale professor Lisa Kahn reports that every 1 percent increase in the unemployment rate drops the entry-level wage about 7 percent. Even after seventeen years, the earning gap continued. White males who graduated from college during the recession of 1981–1982 lost 25 percent. Kahn concluded that "the labor market consequences of graduating from college in a bad economy are large, negative, and persistent."[2]

After being unemployed six months or more, a worker's chances of regaining his or her previous wage drop sharply. Job applicants who've been out of work for a while become viewed as damaged goods: suspect and risky. Those who are unemployed for long stretches in their teens or early twenties have a greater probability of becoming heavy drinkers, depressed personalities, and physically disabled than those who worked steadily.[3]

The stress of prolonged unemployment on family life is enormous, especially in traditional marriages, where the husband's status is closely connected to his ability to earn a living. According to

British economist Andrew Oswald, being out of work for six months is the worst thing that can happen to a man's mental health, "equivalent to the death of a spouse."[4] The effect spreads throughout the family. A 2009 study by Ann Huff Stevens and Jessamyn Schaller of the University of California at Davis found that when a parent loses his or her job, it increases the chances of a child being held back a grade by 15 percent.[5]

Young people out of school and burdened with debt—many of whom move back in with their parents or share a crowded apartment while they hold down several jobs in their twenties—will find themselves, in their thirties, still stuck in low-paying jobs with few prospects. Without important connections, indulgent parents, or extraordinary talent the days of meandering from college to several years of "finding oneself" while driving cabs or waiting on tables to eventually jumping back on track to an upwardly mobile professional career are over. With not enough professional jobs to go around, large numbers of college-educated people will remain stuck in doing work for which their education was unnecessary.

Even so, they will have an advantage in the competition. Everything else being equal, employers would rather have a college graduate waiting on tables, grooming and walking dogs, and mowing lawns. As a result, the demand for the majority of workers who are not college graduates will decline even further. Wage depression—and the mental depression that often follows—will deepen among the U.S. professional classes as well. The incomes of engineers, program designers, attorneys, accountants, graphic and video artists, audiovisual specialists, data analysts, and those in similar occupations will suffer in pitiless competition with people all over the world who are just as smart and trained as they are but willing to live and work for much less.

Among nonprofessional corporate employees, the bottom tier of the two-tier wage system will expand. As older workers retire, the average compensation even in the dwindling number of unionized firms will gradually lower. Firms that had been paying workers eighteen to twenty-five dollars an hour will drop to an average of twelve to sixteen dollars.

But it will not stop there. The creation of two tiers is more than just a one-time response to temporary rough times; it is a strategic management method. Whatever wage the company is now paying will cease to be relevant when someone new is hired. The job of the personnel department will be to calculate the lowest wage an eligible candidate will accept. Two tiers will expand to three, or as many as the labor market full of desperate job-seekers will permit. Entry jobs that once paid twenty dollars an hour and are now going for sixteen dollars an hour will go for fourteen.

In the fourteen-dollar-an-hour world, labor markets are commonly connected across industries and occupations. For example, a September 2011 *New York Times* report on the unemployed featured a young Californian man who had just been laid off from a $14.34-an-hour job as a machine operator in a Georgia-Pacific box factory. "It is a very dangerous job," Terrance Myrick told the reporter. "There are operators in my plant who are missing fingers or missing legs. They're still working there, though." Before that, he was delivering pizzas. Before that, he'd been laid off from a job as assistant manager in a supermarket.[6]

When wages and benefits drop to the second or third tier in the largest corporations, it has a depressing effect on the rest of the economy. As wages drop, life becomes more precarious. In 2010, approximately 25 percent of workers were already making ten dollars an hour or less. Of these, two-thirds received no sick pay if they became ill. Two full-time working parents of two children who each made ten dollars an hour fell 5 percent short of the minimum needed to keep their family out of poverty. If either the mother or the father was sick for 3.5 days in one month, it was the equivalent of losing the family's entire monthly food budget. For a single parent of two children who made ten dollars an hour, the earnings were even less than what was necessary to keep a family from falling into poverty. A 3.5-day sickness is an economic disaster.[7]

A special analysis of income data run by the Census Bureau in the fall of 2011 at the request of the *New York Times* showed that some fifty-one million "near poor" Americans were struggling to survive on incomes less than 150 percent of the poverty line (forty-five thousand dollars for a family of four). Half are non-Hispanic whites who live in the suburbs and are married. Twenty-eight percent of the heads of household work full-time all year. Adding them to the category of officially poor gives a total of a hundred million people—roughly one third of the U.S. population—living in desperate or deteriorating circumstances. A woman who told the *Times* she was "living paycheck to paycheck" had a family income 29 percent above the poverty line. "One bad bill will wipe you out," she said.[8]

Both industrial workers and their unions have, however grudgingly, accepted the ratcheting down of wages in order to stay competitive in the global economy. In Louisville, Kentucky, where General Electric and Ford plants are now paying ten to fifteen dollars less than they used to, there is little trace of resistance. People feel lucky to have a job. Thirty-seven-year old Linda Thomas is angry that she is not being paid for doing the same work as older workers, "but," she told journalist Louis Uchitelle, she "keeps silent. Too many unemployed people," she explains, would clamor for her job and her wage if she were to protest. "'You don't want to rock the boat,' Ms. Thomas said. 'You take a chance on losing everything you have if you do.'"[9]

As Alan Blinder concluded, and the Bureau of Labor Statistics has predicted (see chapter 4), the vast majority of new jobs created in the next decade will be in services that cannot easily be exported.

When the rich get richer, they tend to spend more on personal comforts: maids, nannies, governesses, tutors, companions for the elderly, gardeners, handymen, personal assistants, cooks, security guards, trainers, therapists, sports and fitness coaches, chauffeurs, and masseuses. As the higher-paying, more secure jobs connected to the global economy are outsourced, the supply of educated workers with personal skills who are willing to work for less will expand.

Blinder tried to soften the grim implications of his calculations by suggesting that there were still niches in the economy where personal services might provide higher-wage opportunities. But his prominent examples, teachers and health-care workers, are, he notes, "quasi-public" occupations that are supported by government spending. So, he observes, "Government policy can influence wages and working conditions directly by upgrading the structure and pay of such jobs—developing more professional early childhood teachers and fewer casual childcare workers, for example, *as long as the tax-payer is willing to foot the bill.*"[10]

Clearly, the taxpayer is not willing. So, throughout the public and "quasi-public" sector, the squeeze on revenues is pushing wages and salaries in the other direction. The health-care system has not accommodated the growth in demand for registered nurses with an upgrade in their professional status and compensation, but rather has demanded a speedup in which nurses are pushed to work twelve-hour shifts and do their paperwork at home. And instead of suffi-ciently expanding nursing school opportunities for Americans, we are importing nurses from abroad who are willing to work for less money as well as sending patients overseas to be treated even more cheaply.

The drive to cut health-care costs has just begun. Diagnosing, patient monitoring, and other traditional one-to-one processes will increasingly be done more remotely, undercutting staffing needs. The care will probably not be as good. The practice of prescribing drugs as a quick substitute for time-consuming, customized hands-on treatment will certainly expand. But the lesson of the last twenty years of efforts to reform the system is that the privileged position of the health insurance and pharmaceutical companies trumps concern for the quality of health care. The priority will continue to be cutting costs in both the doctor's office and the hospital.

With the political door still tightly shut against any form of socialized single-payer insurance system, cost-cutting pressures will expand the practice of shipping the whole patient overseas. Already some private insurance companies are sending patients in need of expensive surgery and treatment to cheap facilities in Mexico, India, and Thailand, where the cost of treatment is low enough to justify the cost of transportation. Bills to permit Medicare to do the same have been introduced in Congress. U.S. hospitals and doctors will oppose this, just as U.S. auto and steel unions opposed free-trade agreements. But as Medicare premiums rise, the age of eligibility lengthens, and more U.S. doctors opt out of the system, budgeting pressure will erode the assumption that sick Americans will be treated at home, in their own country.

● ● ●

Reliance on personal services for growth implies a low productivity and, therefore low-wage, economy. High worker productivity does not guarantee high wages when the bargaining power of labor is weak, but, without it, rising living standards cannot be sustained. In a growing balanced economy wages in the high productivity manufacturing industries can rise while prices for manufactured products remain stable or fall. In low-productivity services sectors, prices have to rise in order to pay higher wages.

The classic 1966 study by William J. Baumol and William G. Bowen pointed out that while output-per-worker in manufacturing had grown spectacularly, the efficiency of a symphony orchestra playing Mozart had not improved in over two centuries. Therefore, for musician's wages to increase along with the wages of industrial workers, the price of a symphony ticket has to rise much faster than prices in the industrial sector.[11] Similarly, the public sector, which is also labor intensive, will naturally require higher prices (in the form of taxes) to maintain the quality of its services.

In a full-employment economy with a healthy industrial sector, workers whose wages are rising can afford to pay high prices for services and pay rising taxes. But with the offshoring of the high-productivity sectors, the source of rising wages shrinks. Add the ideological resistance to tax increases and the undercutting of the bargaining position of labor, and you have a formula for wage stagnation. Add in economic policies that favor price stability over full employment and you have a formula for wage decline.

Still, Pollyanna will not be suppressed. Like Alan Blinder, the few pundits who have looked toward the personal service future tell us to cheer up. "The people of the future will be richer than the people of today," writes Matthew Yglesias. And as rich people, they will be able to pay for people to do things for them. "Nicer restaurants are more labor-intensive than cheap ones, and the further up the scale you go, the more specialized skills (think sommelier) come into play." Yoga instructors, personal trainers, artisanal cheese makers, personal shoppers, and interior decorators will thrive.[12]

Walter Mead is even more hopeful. The personal-service jobs of the future, he writes, will usher us into "the land of milk and honey." The Internet and the two-earner professional family have created "a substantial group of families that are money rich and time poor."

This, he argues, opens up opportunities for the "value-added inter-mediation": the job of doing things for people that they do not want to do themselves. Travel agents are a dying breed, he notes, but there's money in being a "vacation counselor." Private college coun-selors will thrive. People will have their own children's birthday party planner, their own electronic gadget adviser, and a relocation consul-tant to help them deal with real estate brokers. A full-service financial adviser will help them with the agonizing decision of which car insur-ance policy they should buy. The reason all this will be possible, Mead explains, is that "the Internet and the knowledge revolution will allow these new professionals to acquire knowledge cheaply on the net."[13]

The jobs described by Yglesias and Mead already exist. The coun-try is awash with personal consultants, mostly as a result of the loss of well-paying steady jobs with benefits. In the credit boom era, many made a decent, if precarious, living. In an age of austerity, the claim that the demand for new personal-service intermediaries and other types of personal services can reverse the slide in income for the vast majority of workers is wishful thinking.

Given the more than 150 million Americans in the labor force, it would require a very large number of "value-added intermediaries" to make this the driving force to a high-wage future. It would also require a large and growing number of people rich enough to hire an army of such personal consultants—and probably to hire a full-time personal secretary to manage them.

Yglesias and Mead assume that the demand will come from an expanding class of highly paid two-earner professional families. But this is precisely the class that is now poised to be devastated by the next wave of offshoring.

The very rich—those at the top of the rentier class, which lives on its worldwide investments—will, of course, always be with us. So will their personal lawyers, accountants, and brokers. A slice of the globally networked professional class celebrated by David Brooks and Anne-Marie Slaughter will also prosper. They will hire people to take care of their large homes and to tutor their children in Chinese, tennis, and sophisticated strategies for getting into the best private schools and universities. They will hire personal assistants to shop, pay their bills, and run their errands. Coaches will come to their homes to instruct them in physical fitness, mental relaxation, and spiritual transcendence. They will need maids, cooks, and gardeners.

But the percentage of Americans rich enough to keep large numbers of personal servants in a middle-class lifestyle will surely shrink. The prospective trend of the distribution of income and wealth tells us that the rich may well get richer, not that there will be proportionally more of them.

Upper-middle-class professionals, competing even more for their jobs, will still want help with their stressed-out personal lives. But they will not be willing to pay middle-class wages, and with a chronic surplus of labor, they will not have to.

Blinder, Yglesias, and other analysts, like Arne Kalleberg of the University of North Carolina, suggest that the education system could focus more on upgrading the skills associated with the personal-service sector. But the skills required to provide high-quality service in most of the fast-growing occupations do not require a lot of formal education. In his book, *Good Jobs, Bad Jobs*, Kalleberg describes the education required for the ten occupations with the largest projected job growth from 2006 to 2016. Only registered nurses and college professors require college educations. Nurse aides require some formal post–high school training. Customer-service representatives require moderate on-the-job training. The rest—restaurant workers, retail salespeople, office clerks, janitors, home health care aides, and personal aides—require only short-term training on the job.[14]

"Perhaps, contrary to what we have come to believe in recent years," Blinder writes, "people skills will become more valuable than computer skills. The geeks may not inherit the earth after all."[15] This comment is a bombshell; it explodes everything that Americans have been taught for at least the last half a century about the financial value of higher education.

Blinder's logic is compelling. If personal services dominate the job market of the future, why are we telling our children that they must excel in math, science, and computer skills to succeed? If the job forecasts are near accurate, it is too late for most Americans to maintain, much less raise, their living standards in the global job market. The best they can do is to service those few at the top who have successfully joined the global elite.

And just what are the "people" skills that are required for the personal-service future? They do not require a degree in communication science or psychology. They are not the skills of marketing or salesmanship that enable you to persuade customers that your product fits their needs. In a high-unemployment, personal-service economy, *you* are the product, and you must make yourself attractive, accommodating, and pleasing. These are the skills of *ingratiation*.

The boss always has the upper hand, of course. But in a mine, a factory, an office, or a hospital there is a generally recognized line between doing a good job and having to satisfy the boss's personal whims. It was no accident that the union movement began in the sectors that mined, made, or transported tangible goods rather than among the maids, cooks, and tutors employed to provide personal services to the rich. When the work product can be evaluated objectively (as in the production of a car or a shirt, or a record of phone calls made per hour) there is some psychological space between employer and employee within which a union can challenge abuses of power. Indeed, the personal independence that comes from collective bargaining power is disturbing enough to the governing class that union workers have often been labeled "labor aristocrats."

But *personal* service, by definition, is largely about satisfying the boss's *personal* whims. So in a society in which you have no right to the job, in which no unique skills or connections are required, and in which there are many people outside the door ready to take your place at a moment's notice, the workplace will become even more of a daily challenge to your self-esteem.

The servant economy will not quite replicate the "upstairs-downstairs" world of Edwardian Britain. At the top of the wealth pyramid—a fraction of the top 1 percent—some personal staff will continue to be live in. But further down the income distribution, a portion of the personal-service sector will be organized by labor contractors who will provide regular services like housecleaning, gardening, and home repair. The labor contractor is one of Mead's value-added intermediaries; he or she will relieve the client of the messy problem of directly employing servants, which so often fatigued the lady of the house in Victorian England. These intermediaries also relieve the client of the legal obligation to pay payroll taxes, respect labor laws, and otherwise have any personal obligation to their servants.

The widening use of labor contractors throughout the economy will, on the one hand, help to stabilize work and in some cases will avoid the risks to the worker of being cheated and abused. On the other hand, it may make it harder to enforce the laws that protect workers on the job. It will certainly make it more difficult for workers to identify who, in fact, is the employer. Is it the person whose house you cleaned, or was it the contractor who sent you to clean the house?

Labor contractors have always been difficult for unions to organize because they obscure the identity and location of the boss. Unlike jobs in a factory or a restaurant, such work provides no central site to picket. With perseverance and luck, it can be done. But it is hugely expensive and time-consuming just when union treasuries will be shrinking and budget austerity will effectively reduce federal and state governments' ability to enforce minimum standards for wages, hours, and working conditions. Even child labor and workplace safety laws will be increasingly violated as corporate lobbyists pressure politicians to cut budgets for the agencies that protect workers.

The lives of labor contractors themselves will be almost as precarious as the lives of their workers. With the labor supply large in markets that generally do not require much start-up capital to enter, the pressure to satisfy client demands for both quality and low prices will be relentless. The failure rate of small business has always been high; in the personal services economy it will be even higher. There will undoubtedly be efforts to control local markets—in some places by large corporations, in others by mobsters. But in a low-productivity economy that is generating fewer large incomes, paper-thin profit margins will keep wages low. The employer's inability to provide job security will in turn generate high turnover, low morale, and weak loyalty on the part of the employees.

For many young people with no special connections, the military will be an increasingly attractive option. The pay is low, but there are good benefits and opportunities for free education and training. It will provide a career ladder that with a little luck may lead to higher-paying work opportunities with military contractors.

The accelerated and celebrated use of drones and other computerized advanced weapons will allow recruiters to argue to prospects that technology has diminished their chances of ending up as a foot soldier or as a casualty. With a larger pool of recruits for the Pentagon to draw from, the trend toward lowering the physical and mental standards that were adopted during the Iraq and Afghanistan Wars will be reversed. The military will be unable and unwilling to take all who apply.

The New Deal and the union ethos that it spawned did not only protect wages, ensure workplace safety, and eventually protect individuals from discrimination, it established a social rule that humans were not to be treated as commodities or beasts of burden. Without those protections on the job, the demands of the bottom line can and will become instruments of personal abuse.

Thus, the social casualties of slow growth and rising inequality will not just show up in the paycheck, they will also show up in the spirit. Trade union safety nets provide American workers with protection from the relentless assault of supply and demand on their personal dignity. A union contract, or the threat that they might demand one, gives workers a voice in the small things that make up a person's self-esteem: the right to go to the bathroom, a clean workplace, a vacation, and a sense of community with one's coworkers. Seniority means that older and younger workers are not in mortal combat for daily survival on the job and that older workers will not be laid off just because younger workers can be hired to replace them for lower pay.

Among the benefits of the union movement that have never been widely appreciated is the way in which it has ameliorated the natural tendency for workplace conflict between generations. Before unions, older workers were under constant threat of being replaced by those who were younger, stronger, and more educated, so they were notoriously unwilling to share the information and on-the-job skills that they had accumulated over time. Asked by this writer in the 1970s what differences the union had made after the mills were organized in the 1930s, a retired steelworker told of having been hit on the head with a shovel when as a young man he had tried to watch an older worker test a sample of steel for tensile strength. After the union came, with seniority and solidarity, elderly workers were happy to share their skills with the next generation. As unions disappear and lose their power, the war between generations will return to the shop floor.

The New Deal expanded the bargaining power of all workers, unionized or not, by reducing the terror of losing your job. Unemployment compensation gave a worker time to look for a new job after leaving an abusive boss without having to sleep on a park bench. Social Security allowed the elderly to face their last years without having to beg in the streets.

With these protections gone or greatly diminished, the humiliations of daily working life under raw capitalism will return. Bosses will be more arrogant and demanding. Overworked bureaucrats at shrunken government agencies will be less responsive. The community of mutual support among working people will be strained. As both unions and regulations become slowly crushed in a time of forced austerity, the divisions will return between the old and the young, whites and nonwhites, women and men, and immigrants and the native-born.

The divisions will extend to politics as well. For years, conservatives have unsuccessfully tried to incite the young against the old around Social Security and Medicare. Yet younger people, even those who believed that they would not get these benefits when they themselves retired, have generally opposed reducing benefits for Grandma and Grandpa. But as more young people are stuck on the lower rungs of the career ladder and saddled with student-loan debt, their frustrations will become easier for corporate propaganda to exploit. Already the programs have been made ideologically vulnerable by the Democrats' acceptance of the label "entitlement," suggesting something unearned and undeserved. Moreover, as retirement drifts out of reach for more older people, they will try to stay in their jobs longer, further increasing competition between young and old.

• • •

No serious pundit argues that Social Security has anything to do with the deficit. In fact, it's just the opposite: the program's annual surplus has been financing the federal government. Despite this, cutting Social Security benefits is a priority among deficit hawks in both parties.

President Obama and the Democrats insist that they will defend Social Security to the last drop of their political blood. Yet Obama appointed two well-known advocates for cutting benefits to head his deficit-reduction commission, thus legitimizing the notion that Social Security must be sacrificed to keep the nation solvent. And in 2010, he championed deep "temporary" cuts in the payroll tax, which funds the program, as a substitute for more stimulus spending. At some point, the payroll tax will have to be raised back to where it was (and perhaps higher to make up for the lost revenue) and/or benefits will have to be cut.

Within the governing class there is already a majority for increasing the age of eligibility for Social Security retirement. The public opposes it, but the public also opposed raising the full retirement age from 65 to 67 when Reagan's bipartisan commission slid that into the law in 1982. Because it only affected people born in 1938 or later, many Americans were completely unaware that they would have to wait longer to get their benefits. That change is estimated to have dropped the average share of income replaced by Social Security from 41 percent in 2002 to 36 percent by 2030.[16] The governing class did it once, and they can do it again.

As benefits are eroded and doubts about Social Security's promised pay-off grow, Wall Street's campaign for Social Security privatization will be revived in the op-eds, blogs, and talk shows. The 2008–2009 stock market crash made it harder to sell the notion that individuals could do better by picking their own stocks and bonds. But having successfully lobbied for further cuts in benefits, privatization promoters will argue that the government can't be trusted to deliver what it promised, so even small returns from the stock market would be better than none.

The willingness of Democrats to let pass without much challenge the Republican mantra that Social Security is unsustainable, and therefore will not be there for young people when they retire, will set the table for Wall Street's feast. Sometime in the next decade, the Social

Security Act is likely to be amended to allow contributors to divert a portion of their payroll taxes to a private 401(k) plan. Grateful banks, brokerages, and hedge funds will no doubt honor Pete Peterson, the billionaire who has bankrolled their campaigns to dismantle Social Security, with events in the major cities of the global money market.

Medicare is even more likely to go on the block. The direct assault on the program by the radical Right after the congressional elections of 2010 was rebuffed. (Many Republican candidates had actually campaigned on a pledge to protect the program from cuts that Obama had agreed to under pressure from the Republicans themselves.) So instead of a radical and visible effort at privatization, the Republicans, aided by the usual cadre of Blue Dog Democrats, will campaign to slice benefits and increase costs in ways that rarely make headlines.

The list of treatments and procedures that Medicare will pay for, and the amount that they will pay for them, will shrink. Medicare's administrative expenses—already far lower than those of private health insurance companies—will also be squeezed, creating long delays in reimbursements, breakdowns in the system of verifying who is eligible, and backlogs of frustrated citizens trying to resolve their individual cases. Reimbursement for psychiatric care will be slashed and the rate at which new cures and innovative treatments are recognized—even those that could save money—will slow to a crawl. More doctors will opt out of the system, and the shift within the profession toward more specialization aimed at a high-income clientele will accelerate.

Medicare costs have risen substantially less than costs for private insurers over the last four decades. So privatizing Medicare will accelerate health care spending and increase the pressure to cut services. The "death panels" that Sarah Palin falsely charged, in 2009, were in Obama's health-care proposal might actually appear under a Republican administration in the guise of informal rules to deny reimbursement for a large number of procedures for patients over eighty-five.

The civilian public sector throughout most of the United States will be smaller, demoralized, and increasingly dysfunctional. The effect on the economy will be multiplied because much federal spending is spread throughout the states in ways that leverage other dollars. Federal money is often the essential extra funding needed to pay for building a bridge, keeping a preschool open, supporting a rural clinic or an urban food bank, or opening a community college adult education program. Combined with the austerity that slower growth will force on the states, the result will be a dramatic reduction in public investment and a further shredding of the safety net for relieving the financial stress of a high-unemployment society.

The gap will grow between what the economy spends and what it needs to spend on education and training to keep American workers from falling further behind in the global contest for good jobs. Federal spending on education will decline. Class sizes will rise and impose new demands on teachers. Education programs for the poor, such as Head Start, Pell grants, training, and remedial education, will shrink.

Aid to community colleges for job training and vocational retraining not directly related to business needs will decline. Universities will increasingly depend on foreign students who can pay the full fare and will expand the number of spaces for them.

The $2.2 trillion gap in infrastructure spending will certainly widen and the dream of a national high-speed interurban train system will be dead. State infrastructure investments will increasingly be packaged with business location subsidies that serve the needs of individual businesses with the most political influence rather than projects that service the broader community's economic development.

We can expect that more bridges, tunnels, and highways will be closed, and at times they will fall or break down. Dramatic disasters will make headlines and set off temporary public demands for more spending on safety and modernization. But in an age of austerity, budget realities will ultimately prevail. Even at the height of the economic boom in 2007, the collapse of a Minnesota bridge that plunged a hundred cars into the Mississippi River, killing 13 and injuring 145, was not enough to motivate the kind of spending commitment necessary to rebuild the nation's transportation infrastructure.

Unlike during the Great Depression of the 1930s, the prices of the basic necessities of middle-class life in the era of austerity are likely to rise. Americans will be competing with the rest of the world in the market for U.S. corn and wheat, beef and fish, and oil and gas. Moreover, the financial markets based on these commodities, out of the effective range of regulation by national governments, will become subject to sudden speculative episodes. This will generate swings in prices that will make life even harder for people surviving on meager paychecks.

The energy problem for the United States in the near future is not that we or the world will run out of oil. It is that we will pay a higher and higher price for it, in both cash and the quality of the environment. The combination of slowly sinking incomes and rising oil prices will reduce airline travel and cut service to hundreds of middle-sized cities. Author Christopher Steiner writes that when gasoline reaches eight dollars a gallon, old venerable airlines with high overhead and legacy costs will go out of business. The remaining profitable routes could be bought up by stripped-down start-up companies, and service to even medium-sized cities—such as Grand Rapids, Michigan; Worcester, Massachusetts; Durham, North Carolina; and Glendale, Arizona—could be abandoned. Steiner writes, "The days of swinging out to the West Coast to see Aunt Jolene and Uncle Freddy, or flying home for Thanksgiving because it feels good, will be over, except for those with cash to burn."[17]

The federal capacity to respond to disasters will also weaken. In the wake of hurricane damage in the late summer of 2011, the Republican members of Congress demanded that before any new spending was authorized, offsetting cuts had to be made in the federal budget. At a time when the nation's televisions were showing flooded middle-class homes and people trapped and drowned in their automobiles, such a level of penny-pinching was out of the question. But the budgets for emergency preparedness will certainly be on the chopping block, even as weather patterns become more erratic and savage.

Reductions may be expected in the regulation of health and safety standards in the workplace; of meat, dairy, fruit, and vegetables, and other foods; of air and water pollution controls; of medicines; of children's toys and clothing; of air and truck transportation safety; and even of police and fire protection. Medicaid and federal health care for poor children will be cut. The number of hospital emergency rooms will shrink, so more poor people who are sick and in pain will simply not be treated. Some who are turned away will go home and die.

A United States that does not redevelop will become more underdeveloped. Begging by families on the street will increase. Buses and railroad cars will age and become threadbare. Graffiti will be left on walls. The public landscape—parks, roadsides, vacant spaces—will look shabbier, overgrown, and unkempt. More trash will litter the streets and more garbage will float in our rivers. Clean-up will be left to volunteers. Water pipes will leak, undermining streets; sewers will back up more frequently. What comes out of the faucet will, in a growing number of communities, look murky and, in some, it will smell. More motels and hotels will advise against drinking the water from the bathroom tap.

Access to national parks and wilderness areas will be restricted. Small national parks will close. In many areas, the National Park Service will shrink to skeleton crews. Fewer park rangers will patrol to protect the environment and the visiting public. Entrance fees will have to rise substantially, pricing families out of camping vacations. We can expect that little by little, the parks themselves will be dismembered as land is sold off to compensate for dried-up public funding. Cheap amusement parks will be built at the park entrances, and logging and mining will expand in the interiors.

Government employees will make do, subsidizing equipment out of their own pockets when they can. More teachers in poor school districts will be forced to buy their own supplies and books in order to do their job. Untrained volunteers will staff more public programs, including people to work in police departments on administrative and routine patrol functions. At first, volunteers will tend to be former police officers and middle-class retirees. As the need expands, the selection criteria may eventually have to be loosened, opening the door to volunteers with criminal records. Given the unlikelihood that the National Rifle Association will lose its grip, there will be places in America where the law is expected to be enforced by armed volunteers.

Bad economic times will be good for the drug trade. The cutbacks in police departments, especially in the smaller towns and cities, and in the federal anti-drug agencies, will make it easier for the expansion of Mexican drug cartels into the United States. Loaded with cash and easy access to weapons in the United States, the experienced and better organized Mexican groups will muscle out or buy out the existing haphazard and small-scale illegal drug distribution systems in U.S. cities. In a few years' time, mutilated bodies may appear in highway ditches, behind bushes in city parks, and washed up along riverbanks. As in Mexico, undermanned police departments in U.S. cities will begin to struggle against cartels who are armed with sophisticated communications equipment, computerized logistics, the latest weaponry, and enough money to bribe police officers who are struggling to pay their bills like other workers.

Some cushion will remain. The United States will not suddenly become a third-world country. Assuming that there is no new economic calamity over the next two decades, most Americans are likely to experience the downshifting of their living standards in gradual steps. People will ratchet down their lifestyles a notch, and then another notch. The near-poor will live a little more like the poor. People with nonsupervisory jobs will live more like the near-poor. Middle-level managers in the 2020s will live more like their employees did a decade prior. Professionals will forgo vacations, high-end cars, and other status symbols they had once assumed were rightfully theirs.

Most people of working age will be employed, just as most people were during the Great Depression. But because of the increasing instability of employment, at any given time, many if not most will have experienced being out of work sometime in the previous year. On the wage side, real incomes will fall when people are laid off and can only find a job that pays less, when their health insurance premiums are raised or discontinued, or when the supervisor starts telling them they are now expected to work more hours without more pay.

On the cost-of-living side, the down-shifting will come as a sudden realization that the monthly bills for food, utilities, and other necessities are relentlessly rising faster than incomes. Or it will come when the bill from the dentist or the furnace repair cannot be paid. Or the moment when it's clear that you can no longer afford the second car or the first or the occasional restaurant meal, concert, ball game ticket, or family vacation. Or to send the kids to camp or to college.

The nightmare of juggling work and child care, well known to half the country that is poor or near-poor, will drift up the social ladder. As the steady full-time job with benefits gives way to having to fashion an income out of several temporary, part-time jobs, day labor, competing for consultant contracts, piecework, selling on commission, and other tenuous employment, the treadmill of work and family life will move faster and faster, and the quality of life lived by most Americans will deteriorate.

Technological progress will soften, or at least obscure, the drop in living standards. Even in the Depression, products such as radios, phonographs, and autos improved from 1930 to 1939. So we can expect continued improvements in the quality and innovation of the imported electronic gadgets and the cascade of software applications to entertain those who can still afford them.

Giant TV screens and pocket-sized monitors integrated with a variety of new satellite links will deliver more entertainment options for Americans sitting on their sofas and make communications simpler and faster. Cell phone apps will open keyless front doors, turn on the oven, and stream surveillance photos of your home when you are away. Virtual imaging will allow matchmaking services to use avatars to simulate dates. Voice-activated computers will replace the keyboard and mouse.

The forced changes will not seem all that bad. For some, despite the low pay, the solitude, and the instability, piece work—another term for professional freelancing—will seem a blessing. Parents can save on the cost of babysitting and be with their young children all day. Others will relish the freedom and flexibility of not having to punch a clock. In a time of austerity, divorce will be more expensive, forcing some couples to keep the family together. And as individual automobile transportation becomes less affordable, more people will enjoy bicycling to work or to the store on a pleasant day.

But, as people in the third world know, bicycling in the rain and sleet is not so pleasant. Forcing unhappy parents to stay together is not necessarily best for the children. And freelancing can sour quickly when it turns into dog-eat-dog competition with younger people who can work harder and faster, and when it becomes clear that there will never be enough savings to live on when you're sick, old, and exhausted.

For some, it will mean cutting back on luxuries, like eating out, going on vacations, or buying this year's style in clothes and electronics. For others, it will mean more meals without meat or fish and patches sewn onto threadbare winter jackets. For still others, it will mean selling the house and squeezing into a small rented apartment. For others, a homeless shelter will become home.

Psycholgically, the shift to a servant economy will generally be harder on men. Whether socially determined or otherwise, women as a group are generally more comfortable with and are better at jobs involving the care of others, and they are often willing to work for less. As personal-service employment grows, the wage gap between the sexes will continue to narrow—not because women are earning more, but because men are earning less.

For all of the progress in sexual equality, the male self-image is still more closely tied to the position of breadwinner. Men are bombarded with macho cultural icons: the athletes, the swaggering Wall Street speculators, and the gunslingers of interactive electronic games. Men have to earn a living, so most will work at whatever they have to, but by and large they will not like it.

The surrounding culture will relentlessly push back the shame and ache of falling living standards back on the individual. The pronouncements from TVs, classrooms, and pulpits will continue to hammer home the message that people are responsible for their own fate. Self-help books, videos, and guest lecturers will promise that you can beat the odds if only you submit to the Seven Principles, the Five Steps, or the Ten Tenets of Success. People will be told that they should smile when what they really want to do is cry or hit someone, or they'll be advised to ignore the abusive boss and swallow their pride.

The culture will bombard Americans, especially the young, with mind-numbing contradictory advice. The politicians will tell them to go to school, and their parents will tell them to go to work. The popular-advice media will tell them to save their money, but the ubiquitous advertising, with the most alluring images, will demand that they spend their money.

Some will find solace in a closer family life. Others will walk out the door, abandoning children and spouses. Others will go to church or another spiritual refuge more frequently. Many will drink more alcohol, take more pills, and smoke more dope.

In his 2009 book, *Methland: The Death and Life of an American Small Town*, Nick Reding describes how young people in a north Iowa town take to selling homemade crystal methamphetamine as an alternative to working in a hellhole of a poultry factory for long shifts under conditions that numb body and mind. "The argument I make in the book is very simple," Reding told an interviewer. "The harder it is for people to make money honestly, the easier it will be for an increasingly large portion to choose to make it dishonestly"[18]

But most Americans—including the college educated and technically trained—will suck it up and do what they must to survive. As their youth turns to a middle age while they still juggle several low-wage servant jobs in order to scratch together a living, their dreams will shrink to fit that reality. Barbara Ehrenreich, in her book *Nickel and Dimed* wrote of her experience working at several of these jobs in the still prosperous late 1990s. She described her surprise that her intrinsic "special" persona as an educated intellectual was never noted by her fellow workers or supervisors. Then she realized why. "There's no way, for example, to pretend to be a waitress: the food either gets to the table or not. People knew me as a waitress, a cleaning person, a nursing home aide, or a retail clerk not because I acted like one, but that's what I was. . . . In every job, in every place I lived, the work absorbed all my energy and much of my intellect. I wasn't kidding around."[19]

Not only do you become your job, over time you tend to see the economic world through the lens of the work you do. Your personal experience of how the economy works will be different if you spend your working life as one of Yglesias's or Mead's sommeliers or birthday party consultants, as opposed to being a factory worker, a miner, or a carpenter. Working to make things teaches you that, however weak your bargaining position might be, you are essential for the creation of wealth. Working as a servant teaches you that the source of wealth is the wealthy. You may despise them in your heart and get back at them in hidden ways, but your survival trickles down from their largesse. It biases the mind toward a conservative politics. People in an economy dominated by personal servant jobs are likely to perceive the unequal distribution of income, wealth, and power as the natural order of things; it is what creates their jobs.

It does not have to be this way. Yglesias suggests that the future personal-service economy would also need an expanded welfare state and stronger unions. In other words, if the United States adopted the sociopolitical institutions of Sweden, it might not be so bad. People can wait on tables, massage backs, and clean houses with dignity. Just so, but a Scandinavian-style social democracy is hardly where the United States is now headed.

12

Hope, from the Ashes of No Hope

The U.S. governing class does not lack access to ideas and proposals that can stop the decline in average incomes. Rather, it lacks the will to pursue them. The current economic model is obviously not working perfectly, but for the privileged and powerful it is working well enough. If anything, the extraordinary display of Wall Street's political muscle in the wake of the financial crash and the Supreme Court's *Citizens United* decision will further weaken our political leaders' capacity to change our economic trajectory.

Yet even within the confines of this plutocracy, it does matter who becomes president and who runs Congress. More economic stress is on the way. Under Democrats, it will come at a slower pace and hurt the working classes less than under Republicans. Under Democrats, there will be less shredding of social safety nets than under Republicans. Under Democrats labor unions will be tolerated; under Republicans they will be assaulted. Under Democrats, Supreme Court appointees will tend to be economic centrists; under Republicans they will tend to be economic reactionaries. These distinctions are not unimportant. For people who struggle every day to pay the rent or mortgage, to buy food and clothes for their kids, to squeeze out a health insurance premium, there is a world of difference between having a smaller Social Security or unemployment compensation check and not having one, between having access to a threadbare Medicare program and having no program at all, between having to piece together a living with several low-paying part-time jobs and being completely without work.

So the difference between the parties is significant, but just electing Democrats will not stop the fall in the standard of living.

As chapter 9 argues, the basic grand bargain has been agreed to. Thus, aside from promoting the political soap opera that is delivered around the clock by the news media, the business and political establishment has little to say to Americans about their economic prospects other than that they should not give up hope. This is the United States of America, after all. A prominent economist, Robert Hall, succinctly summarizes the catechism: "We're not Japan. In America, the bet is still that we will somehow find ways to get people spending and investing again."[1]

"Somehow" something will come up. Some unpredictable black swan will appear to lead us back to the old-time prosperity. Some deus ex machina will descend from above the stage to rescue the middle class from the script described in chapter 11 without discomforting the rich and powerful. Perhaps we will invent another Internet, the Chinese will self-destruct, or the magical tax cut will bring back full employment.

"I'll go home," says Scarlett O'Hara at the end of *Gone with the Wind*. "And I'll think of some way to get him back. After all, tomorrow is another day."

Sequels were written to concoct happier endings. But at the close of the original, we know that Scarlett will never get Rhett back. We also know that we Americans will never get back to the good times of rising wages from 1947 to 1973 or to the string of credit bubbles that compensated for wage stagnation from 1979 to 2008. The world in which both of those eras played out has disappeared.

Moreover, the ecological limits to growth are starting to impinge upon us. No serious observer believes that the world's natural resources can sustain the growth of consumption necessary to bring the standard of living of the rest of the world up to the level of the major advanced nations. By 2050, we can expect the global population to have grown by another 2.5 billion, to more than 9 billion people, most of them in the poor and developing regions. That U.S. consumers, representing less than 5 percent of the world's current population, can continue to use 25 percent of the world's fossil-fuel resources is not credible. Moreover, although we don't know how long it will take for the full force of climate change to arrive, we can see it coming.

In the wake of our recent financial disasters, to imagine that these resource and environmental pressures can in any way be resolved by the price mechanisms of unregulated markets is preposterous. Yet, no serious observer believes that our current political institutions are capable of dealing with that reality. A governing class that will not bring itself to rescue the sinking incomes of the majority of its voters in the next election is hardly going to lead the world to stop a projected rise in the sea level decades in the future. And neither is it likely that a public, suddenly finding itself under more financial stress, will force its governing class to pay more attention to the fate of the planet. Indeed, since the financial crash of 2008, sentiment is moving the other way, The Harris Poll reports that the share of Americans who believe that burning fossil fuels is leading to climate change fell from 71 percent in 2007 to 51 percent in 2009 to 44 percent in 2011.[2] Somehow, we'll think of something—tomorrow. We hope.

It is already too late to stop the decline in the middle-class standard of living for the next few years. It may even be too late to stop it from declining for the next twenty years. But if it is not, reversing the slide will require more than modest changes in economic policy. It will require, in Marshall Ganz's useful terminology (see chapter 8), a transformational politics capable of halting the U.S. governing class's march into a future that may work for it but that certainly will not work for the rest of us. It will require reaching back to the question that Americans were starting to ask when we were faced with the oil price shocks of the 1970s: "What kind of a country do we want to build?" The question assumes an intention to shape tomorrow, not simply to guess at it.

But we remain trapped in the age of Reagan. The proposition that we have a collective, national obligation to shape our future, much less the planet's, is today beyond the ideological reach of U.S. politics.

To bring a different future within our grasp, we must first abandon hope that our current political system will deliver it. We must face the reality—not just the easy "plague on both their houses" attitude that is so often an excuse for refusing the obligations of citizenship—that no established party (Democratic, Republican, or even third-way centrist) that is dependent on money from the reactionary rich and the globalizing corporations will act to alter our economic trajectory. From the point of view of the governing class, if the American people are willing to suffer an official unemployment rate above 9 percent for three years, they will probably—if maintaining elite privileges so requires—accept it for three more years, or six, or more.

Thus far, the political consequences have favored the Right. Flush with funding from the conservative and libertarian wealthy, the Tea Party coalitions have successfully exploited that part of the U.S. materialist, me-first culture that can become mean-spirited and nihilistic when pushed to the wall.

The motivations of Tea Party members and sympathizers are mixed. The organized groups include libertarians, Christian fundamentalists, antitax small-business owners, anti-immigrant activists, and National Rifle Association members. But a large part of the membership comes from the angry, previously unaffiliated. They tend to be older and a bit above average in income, and many of them are now seeing their hard-earned retirement nest eggs shrinking from the policy of the Federal Reserve (a favorite target) to keep interest rates low. They have bought into the simple but easy-to-understand explanation that the crisis is the fault of liberal government, even though some of them are as angry at Wall Street as they are at Washington.

There has always been a right-wing fringe in U.S. politics that rears its head from time to time and threatens to destabilize the centrist establishment. But eventually the Establishment always slaps them down; this was the case with the McCarthyism movement in the 1950s, the John Birch Society in the 1960s, and the Southern backlash against racial integration in the 1970s. After the election of Reagan, enough of the extreme Right was co-opted by the corporate wing of the Republican Party to make it almost irrelevant as an independent force.

And so it may be again. To their corporate backers, the Tea Party members are useful idiots. But in a remarkably short amount of time, the Tea Party was able to force the leadership of the congressional Republicans to toe its line—to the point of jeopardizing the party's chances of unseating President Obama. Their ability to push the Republican Party to the brink of making the United States default on its debt for the first time in history, which would have been a disaster for U.S. banks in debt to foreigners, suggests that their multinational backers may be playing with fire.

Sarah Palin is one bellwether. Her understanding of economics may be (to put it charitably) confused, and her political maneuverings may be baffling, but she knows her constituency. It is worth pondering that some of her February 2010 national Tea Party convention speech could have been delivered by any self-respecting populist of the Left:

> While people on Main Street look for jobs, people on Wall Street, they're collecting billions and billions in your bailout bonuses. Among the top 17 companies that received your bailout money, 92 percent of the senior officers and directors, they still have their good jobs, and every day Americans are wondering, where are the consequences for they—helping to get us into this worst economic situation since the Great Depression? Where are the consequences?[3]

Should the Tea Party, or whatever may emerge as the next step in the evolution of right-wing populism, continue to be the repository of angry citizens' responses to the abuses of the governing class, it would not be the first time in history that a movement of the far right, financed with corporate money establishment conservatives, took power as a fraudulent champion of ordinary people.

That Americans would vote into power a political movement whose agenda would so undercut what is left of middle-class economic security seems like a long shot. But the Tea Party's war chest and its Fox News–led propaganda machine has no match on the Left. As the election of Ronald Reagan showed, if the alternative to a conservative is an ineffective centrist Democrat, all bets are off.

The potential damage is not just to the economy. Political analyst John Nichols notes that the Tea Party's contempt for big government does not extend to the brazen centralizing of power by the candidates they have elected to state government. In Ohio, Wisconsin, and Michigan, Republican governors have overridden local towns and city governments to prevent them from resisting business interests. In Wisconsin, when Democrats successfully won recall elections against two Republican senators, Republicans moved to change the constitution in order to limit such elections.[4] The success of the brazen theft of the 2000 election by the Republican majority on the Supreme Court has clearly emboldened the Right to reach for power using whatever tactics it thinks it can get away with.

In the context of an extended economic crisis and an endless war on terrorism, there are now even more instruments of political oppression available to any Federal Administration with a weak loyalty to democracy and an intolerance for dissent. The curbing of civil liberties under George Bush has largely been validated by Barack Obama. This includes the power to impose indefinite detention without a trial, to abduct and send suspects to other countries for torture, to restrict habeas corpus, to prosecute guilt by association, to engineer the legal disappearance of people in custody, to loosen constraints on FBI surveillance of people not charged with a crime, and even to kill U.S. citizens without due process of law. Candidate Obama pledged not to permit torture in his administration, but as Professor Mark Danner notes, Obama's decision not to prosecute anyone in the Bush administration for torture has simply transformed the procedure from a criminal act to a policy option.[5]

Chris Hedges, a former *New York Times* reporter who shared a Pulitzer Prize, writes that a fascist future is in the cards. When it arrives, "The goal will no longer be the possibility of reforming the system but of protecting truth, civility, and culture from mass contamination. . . . The goal will become the ability to endure.[6]

The evidence does not yet nearly suggest Hedges's nightmare scenario. Still, there is little doubt that democracy becomes more vulnerable during hard times. One recent study of how people in various countries respond to the statement that "having a strong leader who does not have to bother with Parliament or elections" is good, showed that in the United States being unemployed increases the favorable response from 27 to 38 percent.[7]

The American Right has proved itself tougher, more strategic, and bolder than the Left. If that continues, no one can be sure where it will lead.

The organized movements of the political mainstream Left—the labor unions, the environmental movement, and women's and minority organizations—have thus far been unable to capitalize on the crisis. Ideologically, they are caught in a catch-22:

- Reversing middle-class decline requires that the government intervene in the economy.
- The influence of money in politics ensures that the government will intervene on behalf of corporate interests, not the middle class.
- Therefore, the middle class will distrust the government and will not support its intervention in the economy.

As a result, the Left has not come up with a unifying and appealing challenge to the Right's simple answer for the economic crisis: lower taxes and smaller government. The liberal blogs and op-eds lament the relentless stream of statistics that show worsening inequality. The public seems to agree that this is a problem, yet they remain wary of government efforts to change it. A June 2010 Gallup poll reported that Americans, by 57 percent to 35 percent, thought that income should be more equally distributed, but they rejected (49 percent to 47 percent) the idea that government should tax the rich to do it.[8] This disparity reflects the widely held suspicion that policies to redistribute income will eventually end up sparing the rich and redistributing income from people further down the social ladder to those even further down. One result of their inability to break out of liberalism's catch-22 is that the major institutions of the Left are stuck seeking protection from the Democratic Party, despite the fact that the party has been so compromised by its enemies.

Again, it is not that the Left doesn't see it. Labor union leaders, for example, fully understand that the Democratic Party takes them for granted. Richard Trumka, the most dynamic leader the AFL-CIO has had since its inception in 1955, has complained bitterly about the Obama administration's broken promises to labor. Contempt for labor was routinely expressed by the Wall Street and young Wall Street wannabes who worked for both Presidents Clinton and Obama. When Rahm Emanuel, who was chief of staff to both, told negotiators on the auto bailout to "fuck the UAW," it was nothing the people in the White House had not heard before. Nor was he publicly (or apparently privately) rebuked by President Obama, who could not have been elected, nor could he be reelected, without union support.

But having been systematically weakened by Reagan era policies, union leaders are more dependent than ever on Democrats to shield them from the Republican Right that is out to destroy them. So, on the one hand, the blogs and newsletters of unions and other liberal groups criticize the Democrats as being too beholden to Wall Street. On the other hand, they urge their members to mobilize for the Democrats at election time in the quixotic belief that this will some-how "put pressure" on them. Election day for Democratic constituencies are now mostly efforts to shore their crumbling defenses. Hope implicitly rests on the dangerous premise that some outside catalyst—perhaps the next, even greater economic catastrophe—might force the needed political change.

This represents a fundamental failure of our democracy. Within the two-party system the way out of this trap would be for the progressive party—the Democrats—to explain the economic reality to the electorate: for the middle class to prosper, the government must intervene to reignite growth, to guide that growth into a sustainable future, and to subordinate the dreams of Wall Street and the military industrial complex to the well-being of the middle class.

But the dependence of the majority of Democratic Party leaders on corporate largesse for their careers and for their personal wealth blocks that escape. Like Clinton, Obama turns populist at election time. And, as with Clinton, once elected Barack Obama refused to exploit the educable moment. It was no accident. As journalist Thomas Edsall observes, the pollsters and consultants who guide the Party and who themselves are connected to the money that supports the governing class, continue to promote the Democrats' long-term trend away from economic class issues that have the potential to unite their constituencies and toward the politics of social identity that fractures. This obsession with social niche marketing feeds into the right wing portrait of the Democrats as affluent liberals, single career women, and racial minorities.

This vision is an aggregation of special interests. The suburban liberal elite want environmental protection, good schools, freedom for individual lifestyles, and a lid on taxes. Their fellow Democrats on the other end of the wealth continuum want food stamps, health and child-care subsidies, and a generally stronger and more expensive safety net.

In times of rising prosperity, reconciling these different agendas is hard enough. But in a prolonged period of pressure on living standards at the middle and the bottom of the income and wealth pyramid, it is a formula for division. It is after all, the minority poor and single mothers who bear the brunt of a politics of austerity.

One outcome of the emphasis on social liberalism, notes Edsall, "could be exacerbated intra-party conflict between whites, blacks and Hispanics—populations frequently marked by diverging material interests. Black versus brown struggles are already emerging in contests over the distribution of political power, especially during a current redistricting of city council, state legislative and congressional seats in cities like Los Angeles and Chicago."[9]

The political professionals argue that the white working class is now lost to the Democrats (for example, polls show that the majority of independent voters in household with incomes below one hundred thousand dollars have disapproved of Obama's performance while those with incomes above that figure approved), and the share of minorities is growing. "Calculations based on exit poll and Census data," notes Edsall, " suggest that the Democratic Party will become 'majority minority' shortly after 2020."[10] But although the Democrats' demographically defined constituencies may be growing faster than the Republicans' are, non-Hispanic whites will remain a majority of the population for the next thirty years and a majority of the electorate beyond that.

Looking ahead to 2016, there is little reason to think that the potential candidates in the Democratic pipeline represent anything close to transformational leadership the country needs. Hillary Clinton and Rahm Emanuel are loyal products of the current system. As is Andrew Cuomo, who in his first year as governor of New York slashed public spending for the poor and lowered taxes for the rich.[11] None of the others in the early betting, such as ex-Virginia governor Mark Warner, Illinois senator Richard Durbin, and several small state governors, have shown a willingness to bite Wall Street or the military-industrial complex from whose financial hands they will have to feed.

The Democratic political consultants argue that given a polarized electorate, the politics of group identity is the only realistic way for the party to keep competitive in close races. In some cases they are surely right. But it is not a strategy for fashioning a large coalition unified by common economic interests. Occupy Wall Street's "99 percent" slogan may exaggerate the potential majority on economic issues, but the Democratic Party's "50 percent plus one" strategy abandons it.

So, is it hopeless?

To expect the American governing class at the top to change the direction of the economy that has brought its members prosperity—yes. To expect a confused and divided citizenry to agree on a common economic agenda and impose it on the governing class—yes.

There is simply not enough space now in our political discourse for the governing class to consider policy solutions that reach to the level of the problems that it is are supposed to solve. Serious regulation of Wall Street is off the table. Abandoning the role of world policeman is off the table. In the debate over health care, a single-payer health care system like Canada's is off the table. Industrial policies and trade policies are off the table. Strengthening the bargaining position of workers is off the table. Government planning to build a sustainable economy by moving off the sandpile of consumption and debt is well off the table.

These ideas are judged as impractical by the corporate media, which defines political reality for the electorate. Why? Not because we don't know how to make them work. It is because they are not consistent with the interests of the rich and powerful. Inasmuch as politics is defined as the art of the possible, credible reform must, by definition, be confined to a range of possibilities that do not conflict with the basic interests of the rich and powerful.

What then is the citizen to do? Wait until the next economic catastrophe? Perhaps if, next time, instead of just twelve trillion dollars, the markets lose twenty-five trillion dollars, and instead of reaching 10 percent, the unemployment rate goes to 20 percent, perhaps then our governing class will act for the good of the country. Or perhaps then the people will rise up.

Perhaps. But we could wait a long time for such a revolution in America. After eight years of depression, the unemployment rate rose back to 20 percent in mid-1938 and still there was no political insurrection. And, if there had been, it could as easily have come from the right as the left.

Acknowledging that it is hopeless to expect the governing class as presently constituted to change our economic trajectory does not signal the end to politics. Rather it could allow the citizen to concentrate on attacking the central obstacle to the reshaping of our collective future.

In just ten minutes of serious political discussion with other Americans about what is wrong with our country, you will most likely get to the bottom-line answer: the pervasive corruption of our politics by money. The vast majority of Americans believe that money corrupts and prevents the government from serving the public's needs. After the Supreme Court handed down its *Citizens United* decision, a *Washington Post*–ABC poll reported that at least 80 percent of Americans disagreed with it, including 76 percent of Republicans.[12] No matter; neither party's leadership is about to change this system.

Campaign financing is not the only way in which money corrupts government. Bribery has many faces: the hint of a future job, an invitation to meet important people, the sharing of an insider investment tip, the hiring of a relative or a friend, the connection that gets your child into a prestigious school, the purchase of twenty thousand copies of your ghostwritten autobiography. But nothing comes close to raising large amounts of money to get you reelected.

The consultants and political experts will tell you that voters have little interest in campaign finance reform. It's a "goo-goo" (good government) issue of interest only to high-minded liberals. It comes across to most voters as abstract and naive.

There's a good reason for this. The conventional liberal remedy is the voluntary public financing of campaigns, in which taxpayers finance political campaigns in exchange for agreeing on a spending limit. Thus, in the wake of the Watergate scandal, Democrats forced passage of the 1974 amendments to the Federal Elections Campaign Act, which provided for presidential candidates to receive funds from a three-dollar contribution checked off on the income tax form; in return, the candidates would give up the right to accept private contributions. A dozen or so states also provide public financing in some form for statewide elections.

The experience with public financing tells us that it is not the answer. First, most successful politicians would rather raise their own money because they can raise more of it themselves. That's what makes them successful. One vivid example is Barack Obama, who in the 2008 and 2012 presidential campaign refused to participate in the public financing system.

Second, the argument that we should use tax money to pay for the campaigns of politicians because they are so corruptible is a hard sell in the best of times. It is even harder when the public is told there is not enough public tax revenue to maintain Social Security and Medicare or pay teachers, police officers, and keep hospital emergency rooms open. One measure of how far the idea of public financing is from political reality is that more than 90 percent of U.S. taxpayers decline to allocate three dollars of their already paid taxes—*when it is made clear that it will be at no additional cost to them*—to the fund to finance presidential campaigns.[13]

Third, public financing will do nothing to stop the exploding use of election financing by the huge and growing political action committees claiming to be independent of the candidates they are promoting. This is now generating a tsunami of campaign donations from corporations and the rich, and it drives up the cost of the fixed amount of television time available for political advertising.

It will get worse. In June 2011, the Supreme Court followed the earlier *Citizens United* case by declaring unconstitutional the key provision of Arizona's public financing law, which provided that the candidates who opted for public financing could receive enough money to match spending by a privately financed opponent. As chapter 8 explains, it has also set a precedent for the legalization of foreign corporation contributions to U.S. election campaigns.

The Republican leadership was, of course, ecstatic about the *Citizens United* ruling. Democrats, including President Obama, were critical. But as in the case of the financial crash, neither Obama nor the congressional Democrats could muster the will to defend what was left of their independence from Wall Street. Their tepid response was to try to require public disclosure of the names of super-PAC donors. But even that modest bandage on the hemorrhaging of democracy could not pass in the Democratic-controlled Senate.

The root problem is the way the court has interpreted the Constitution, and this is not just the case with the Roberts court. Since at least 1886, the Supreme Court has been providing corporations with the rights of individual human beings that were neither contemplated by the Founding Fathers nor supported by the majority of Americans.

The solution, therefore, is a constitutional amendment establishing once and for all that corporations do not have the political rights of, in the language of the Court, "persons" and mandating hard limits on campaign spending.[14] Unlike the efforts of the radical Right to amend the Constitution over issues that are irrelevant to the process of governance such as abortion, flag burning, gay marriage, or prayer in the schools, regulating the money in politics is truly an important constitutional question.

A massive mobilization of citizens for a constitutional amendment has the potential for loosening the death grip of the nihilist antitax, antigovernment ideology on U.S. politics in the following ways:

- It gets to the easily understood heart of the matter: money.
- The overwhelming majority of the country agrees with it, crossing party and ideological lines. It is one of the only issues on which the majority of Wall Street Occupiers and Tea Party followers can agree.
- It breaks out of the stalemated and confused "government versus business" argument and focuses the anger on the

fundamental problem of the corruption of the government by big money.

- It has the potential for exposing the gap between the interests of the globalized governing class and the interests of the American middle class.

Amending the Constitution is obviously not easy. It requires approval by a two-thirds vote in each house of Congress and ratification by three-fourths of the states. An alternative—approval by two-thirds of the states to establish a constitutional convention to decide on an amendment—has never been used. But the Constitution has been amended eighteen times (once to add the Bill of Rights and seventeen more times to add individual amendments). And in other cases, when an attempt failed to add an amendment (such as the Equal Rights Amendment), the effort nevertheless played an important role in mobilizing support for the issue (such as sexual equality).

The conventional political wisdom is that trying to amend the Constitution is hopeless; the governing class will never allow it. But given the power over America's future of financial networks divorced from and uninterested in the well-being of the people, even more hopeless is the illusion that Americans can effectively deal with the long economic twilight of empire that lies in front of them without radically reducing the dominance of money over our democracy. Our democracy has not yet disappeared. Even today, a truly aroused majority of citizens can impose its will on the governing class. But the political catch-22 tells us that the citizenry will not be aroused by a laundry list of ideas, no matter how good. Too many citizens simply do not trust the government to deliver on them in the public interest.

If the conventional wisdom is right, it is not because the governing class and its corporate and military-industrial supporters are too powerful to challenge under any circumstance. It is because the opposition—Wall Street Occupiers, trade unionists, and progressive middle-class Americans—cannot unite around a simple message that gets to the root cause of our national inability to talk about, much less plan, an alternative to the future toward which we are hurtling.

• • •

A farmer, goes an old story, saw that at feeding time his big pigs would lie down in the trough to eat, preventing the little pigs from getting any food. He asked his college-educated conservative son for advice, and the son told his father that survival of the fittest was the law of nature, so he should just let the little pigs die.

Reluctant to lose his investment in the little pigs, the farmer asked his college-educated liberal son what to do. This son told him to double the feed, so that at least some food would spill over to the smaller pigs. That, the farmer knew, would be too expensive.

So he asked the advice of his daughter, who had not gone to college. She replied, "Get the pigs out of the trough."

If you are an American, your future depends on us doing just that.

Acknowledgments

Thanks to all who helped me along this book's journey, especially:

To my editor, Eric Nelson, for his patience and guidance.

To Larry Mishel and the staff of the Economic Policy Institute for their support and help, especially Ross Eisenbrey, Heidi Shierholz, Rob Scott, Josh Bivens, and Stephanie Scott.

To Mark Levinson, Ron Blackwell, Rich Trumka, Leo Girard, Doug McCarron, John Schmitt, Thea Lee, Tom Palley, Jared Bernstein, Mark Simon, Ron Hira, Barbara Somson, Dean Baker, David Smith, Ruy Teixeira, Lori Wallach, and Mike Wessel.

Notes

1. The Politics of Hope

1. Paul Kennedy, *The Rise and Fall of the Great Powers* (New York: Vintage Press), 1989.

2. Chapter 3 of my book *The Global Class War* (Hoboken, NJ: John Wiley & Sons, 2006) defines the governing class as the pool of top management talent from which both parties draw. The common characteristic of those in the pool is their connection to wealth. The common source of that wealth is the business corporation. Individual corporations compete against one another in the marketplace and often lobby on different sides of tax, subsidy, and regulatory issues, but on the fundamental questions of the nature of economic growth and the distribution of its benefits, corporate interests are united and dominant. *The Global Class War* estimated the superrich as comprising about 1 to 2 percent of the American people, with the total population of the economically privileged at about 20 percent.

When given three choices—rich, middle class, and poor—some 80 to 90 percent of Americans regularly self-identify as middle class. This book assumes that rough estimate. It does, of course, represent a wide range of income; the top and bottom edges of the middle 80 percent of Americans are separated by more than $100,000 per year. When an opinion survey offers a fourth choice, such as working class, the middle class splits in two, generally on the basis of educational attainment. Not surprisingly, the financial crash of 2008–2009 and the Great Recession have made people more aware of a shared economic vulnerability among the vast majority who must work for a living. The Occupy Wall Street formula of the "one percent versus the ninety-nine percent" somewhat understates the size of the governing class, but the inequality of wealth and economic power in the United States remains very lopsided by any reasonable measure.

3. Simone de Beauvoir, *America Day by Day* (Berkeley: University of California Press, 1999), 23.

4. Michael B. Sauter, Charles B. Stockdale, and Douglas A. McIntyre, "The Happiest Countries in the World," *24/7 Wall St.*, June 1, 2011, http://247wallst.com/2011/06/01/the-happiest-countries-in-the-world; the United States did not make the top 10 among thirty-four advanced nations (tactfully the Organization of American States did not reveal exact rankings of the laggards). For other surveys, see Diane Swanbrow, "Happiness Is Rising around the World: U-M Study," press release, University of Michigan News Service, July 1, 2008, http://ns.umich.edu/new/releases/6629 (United States ranked sixteenth out of fifty-two) and "New Year Poll 'On Happiness'" press release, Leger Marketing, December 30, 2011, http://www.legermarketing.com/admin/upload/publi_pdf/Press_Release_Global_Barometer_on_Happiness_for_2011-ENG.pdf (United States ranked thirty-third out of fifty-eight).

5. Karen Cerulo, *Never Saw It Coming: Cultural Challenges to Envisioning the Worst* (Chicago: University of Chicago Press, 2006), Kindle edition, chapter 1.

6. Benjamin Kunkel, "Dystopia and the End of Politics," *Dissent*, Fall 2008.

7. Barbara Ehrenreich, *Bright-Sided: How Positive Thinking Is Undermining America* (New York: Metropolitan Books, 2009).

8. Thomas Friedman, "How Did the Robot End Up with My Job?," *New York Times*, October 1, 2011.

9. JasonDeParle, "Harder for Americans to Rise from Lower Rungs," *New York Times*, January 4, 2012; Paul Krugman, "America's Unlevel Playing Field," *New York Times*, January 8, 2012.

10. Pew Research Center, *"How the Great Recession Has Changed Life in America,"* June 30, 2010, http://www.pewsocialtrends.org/2010/06/30/how-the-great-recession-has-changed-life-in-america/6/#vi-short-term-optimism-long-term-uncertainty; "Americans Hopeful about Financial Future: Poll," Reuters, June 30, 2011, http://www.reuters.com/article/2011/04/29/us-finances-future-survey-idUSTRE73S4KM20110429; Michael Cooper and Allison Kopicki, "Facing Hardship, Jobless Still Say They Have Hope," *New York Times*, October 26, 2011; Ronnie Crocker, "Boomers Have High Expectations for Retirement," *Houston Chronicle*, July 13, 2011.

11. Barbara Tuchman, *The March of Folly: From Troy to Vietnam* (New York: Alfred A. Knopf, 1984), 7.

12. Max H. Bazerman and Michael D. Watkins, *Predictable Surprises: The Disasters You Should Have Seen Coming, and How to Prevent Them* (Cambridge, MA: Harvard Business Press, 2004), 93.

13. Pew Research Center, "The American-Western European Values Gap," November 12, 2011, http://www.pewglobal.org/2011/11/17/the-american-western-european-values-gap.

14. Tuchman, *The March of Folly*, 287.

15. George Orwell, *1984* (London: Secker and Warburg, 1949), chapter 3.

16. John Podohetz, "The Case for Optimism," *Commentary*, November, 2011.

17. Quentin Hardy, "The Future Is Not What It Used to Be," *Forbes*, October 15, 2007.

18. Dwight D. Eisenhower, "In Case of Failure" message, Pre-Presidential Papers, Butcher Diary, 28 June 1944–14 July 1944, Dwight D. Eisenhower Library, Abilene, KS.

19. Tuchman, *The March of Folly*, 19.

20. Ibid.

2. A Brief History of America's Cushion

1. Jeff Madrick, *Why Economies Grow:The Forces That Shape Prosperity and How We Can Get Them Working Again* (New York: Basic Books, 2002), 9.

2. Benjamin Franklin, "Observations concerning the Peopling of Countries, Philadelphia, 1751," cited in Joseph Schaefer, *"Was the West a Safety Valve for Labor?" Mississippi Historical Review* 24, no. 3 (December 1937): 299–314.

3. Quoted in Schaefer, "Was the West a Safety Valve for Labor?," 311.

4. Howard Zinn, *A People's History of the United States*, rev. ed. (New York: HarperPerennial, 1995), 213.

5. Ibid., 222.

6. Quoted in ibid., 276.

7. Stuart Bruchey, *Enterprise: The Dynamic Economy of a Free People* (Cambridge, MA: Harvard University Press, 1990), 270.

8. Mario Cuomo, Keynote Address to the Democratic Convention, San Francisco, CA, July 16, 1984, http://www.americanrhetoric.com/speeches/mariocuomo1984dnc.htm.

9. Zinn, *A People's History*, 254.

10. Quoted in ibid., 292.

11. Quoted in ibid., 290.

12. Quoted in ibid., 292. The ellipsis is in the original.

13. "Annual Wages in the United States: Unskilled Labor and Manufacturing Workers, 1774–Present," MeasuringWorth.com, http://www.measuringworth.com/uswage.

14. Daniel Yergin, *The Prize: The Epic Quest for Oil, Money, and Power* (New York: Simon and Schuster, 1991), 178.

15. Bruchey, *Enterprise*, 427.

16. Quoted in ibid., 426.

17. Steve H. Hanke, "We Were All Keynesians—Then," Forbes.com, February 22, 1999, http://www.forbes.com/global/1999/0222/0204077a.html.

18. Daniel Bell, *The Cultural Contradictions of Capitalism* (New York: Basic Books, 1976), 251.

19. Paul H. Nitze, *NSC-68: Forging The Strategy of Containment, with Analyses by Paul H. Nitze*, ed. S. Nelson Drew (Washington, DC: National Defense University, 1994), 90.

20. Meritt Roe Smith, *Military Enterprise and Technological Change: Perspectives on the American Experience* (Cambridge, MA: MIT Press, 1985), 4; John Gertner, "True Innovation," *Washington Post*, February 20, 2012; Fred Block, "Innovation and the Invisible Hand of Government," in *State of Information: The U.S. Government's Role in Technology Development*, ed. Fred Black and Matthew R. Keller (Boulder, CO: Paradigm Publishers, 2011), 5–10.

21. Robert Whaples, "Hours of Work in U.S. History," Economic History Association, February 1, 2010, http://eh.net/encyclopedia/article/whaples.cork.hours.us.

22. John Maynard Keynes, "Economic Possibilities for Our Grandchildren," *Essays in Persuasion* (New York: W. W. Norton, 1963).

3. The Cushion Deflates

1. Robert R. Frank, "Gauging the Pain of the Middle Class," *New York Times*, April 2, 2011.

2. Heather Bouchey, "Family Time and the Middle Class," *American Prospect*, March 2011.

3. Barry Bluestone, "The Inequality Express," *American Prospect*, December 1, 1994.

4. David Halberstam, *The Best and the Brightest* (New York: Ballantine Books, 1992), 178–179.

5. Doris Kearns Goodwin, *Lyndon Johnson and the American Dream* (New York: St. Martin's Griffin, 1991), 296.

6. Martin Luther King Jr., speech given at the National Conference for New Politics, Chicago, August 31, 1967.

7. Martin Luther King Jr., "Declaration of Independence from War in Vietnam," speech given at the Riverside Church, New York, April 4, 1967.

8. Charles P. Kindleberger, *World Economic Primacy, 1500–1990* (New York: Oxford University Press, 1996), 174.

9. Garry Wills, *Nixon Agonistes: The Crisis of the Self-made Man* (New York: Houghton Mifflin Harcourt, 1979), chapter 6.

10. Robert F. Lanzilotti et al., *Phase II in Review: The Price Commission Experience* (Washington, DC: Brookings Institution, 1975).

11. Daniel Yergin, *The Prize: The Epic Quest for Oil, Money and Power* (New York: Simon and Schuster, 1991), 595.

12. W. Carl Biven, *Jimmy Carter's Economy: Policy in an Age of Limits* (Chapel Hill: University of North Carolina Press, 2002), 218.

13. "Stuart Eizenstat Exit Interview," Oral Histories at the Jimmy Carter Library, Jimmy Carter Library and Museum, http://www.jimmycarterlibrary.gov/library/exitInt/Eizenstat.pdf.

14. The three quotations in this paragraph come from Gar Alperovitz and Jeff Faux, *Rebuilding America* (New York: Pantheon, 1984), 52.

15. Quoted in Otis L. Graham, Jr., *Losing Time: The Industrial Policy Debate* (New York: Twentieth Century Fund, 1992), 54.

4. The Age of Reagan

1. Sidney Blumenthal, "The Sorcerer's Apprentice," *New Yorker*, July 19, 1995.

2. Richard B. Freeman, "Do Workers Still Want Unions? More than Ever," Economic Policy Institute Briefing Paper 182, February 2007, http://www.gpn.org/bp182.html.

3. Gordon Lafer, *Neither Free nor Fair: The Subversion of Democracy under NLRB Elections*, American Rights at Work, July 2007, http://www.americanrightsatwork.org/publications/general/neither-free-nor-fair.html.

4. Pat Choate, *Dangerous Business: The Risks of Globalization* (New York: Alfred A. Knopf, 2008), 140.

5. Paul Samuelson, "Where Ricardo and Mill Rebut and Confirm Arguments of Mainstream Economists Supportive of Globalization," *Journal of Economic Perspectives* 18, no. 3 (Summer 2004): 135–146.

6. Heidi Shierholz, Jared Bernstein, and Lawrence Mishel, *The State of Working America, 2008/2009* (Washington, DC: Economic Policy Institute, 2008).

7. "Outsourcing Innovation," *Bloomberg Businessweek*, March 21, 2005.

8. Ron Hira, "The H-1BL-1 Visa Programs: Out of Control," Economic Policy Institute, October 14, 2010, http://www.epi.org/publication/bp280.

9. Ron Hira, e-mail message to author, January 8, 2012.

10. Richard McCormack, "Indian Outsourcing Firms Use H-1B to Displace U.S. High-Tech Workforce," *Manufacturing and Technology News* 18, no. 1 (January 19, 2011), http://www.manufacturingnews.com.

11. "Meeting the Challenge of the Global Economy: Trade, Economic Security and Effective Government," A Hamilton Project Forum, Brookings Institution, July 25, 2006, http://www.brookings.edu/events/2006/0725 global-economics.aspx.

12. Alan S. Blinder, "Offshoring: The Next Industrial Revolution?," *Foreign Affairs*, March/April 2006.

13. Troy Smith and Jan W. Rivkin, *"A Replication Study of Alan Blinder's 'How Many U.S. Jobs Might Be Offshorable?,'"* Harvard Business School working paper, 2008, http://www.hbs.edu/research/pdf/08-104.pdf.

14. Alan S. Blinder, "Offshoring: Big Deal or Business As Usual?" in *Offshoring of American Jobs: What Response from U.S. Economic Policy?*, ed. Jagdish Bhagwati and Alan S. Blinder (Cambridge, MA: MIT Press, 2009), 49.

15. "The Impact of Free Trade on American Workers," *The Diane Rehm Show*, NPR, March 29, 2007.

16. Gordon Kent Sorey, *The Foreign Policy of a Multinational Enterprise: An Analysis of the Policy Interactions of Dow Chemical Company and the United States* (North Stratford, NH: Ayer, 1980), 54.

17. Clyde Prestowitz, *The Betrayal of American Prosperity: Free Market Delusion* (New York: Free Press, 2010), 213.

18. Reed Hundt, *In China's Shadow: The Crisis of American Entrepreneurship* (New Haven, CT: Yale University Press, 2006), 41.

19. David Rothkopf, *Superclass: The Global Power Elite and the World They Are Making* (New York: Farrar, Straus & Giroux, 2008), 116. Bracketed text is my addition.

20. Ralph Gomory, "China and the Future of Globalization," testimony before the U.S.-China Economic and Security Review Commission, Washington, DC, May 19–20, 2005.

21. Jeffrey Garten, "The High-Tech Threat from China: America Inc. Is Rushing Beijing Ahead by Sharing R&D Treasures," *BloombergBusinessweek*, January 31, 2005.

22. Rothkopf, *Superclass*, 117.

23. "Alan Greenspan," Mind Contagion, http:// www.mindcontagion .org/people/alangreenspan.html (accessed on January 5, 2011).

24. John Cassidy, "What Good Is Wall Street?," *New Yorker*, November 29, 2010.

Part II

The epigraph to this part is from Juan Forero, "Leaving the Wild and Rather Liking It," *New York Times*, May 11, 2006.

5. Who Knew? They Knew

1. Kara Scannell and Sudeep Reddy, "Greenspan Admits Errors to Hostile House Panel," *Wall Street Journal*, October 24, 2008.

2. Ken Brown and David Enrich, "Rubin, under Fire, Defends His Role at Citi," *Wall Street Journal*, November 29, 2008.

3. Devin Leonard, "Recession, You Look Familiar," *New York Times*, October 3, 2009.

4. Charles Duhigg, "Pressured to Take More Risk, Fannie Reached Tipping Point," *New York Times*, October 5, 2008.

5. "Sub-Prime Mortgage Crisis Has Spilled Over Into Home Equity Loans and Lines," *Common Sense Forecaster* (blog), January 17, 2008, http://commonsenseforecaster.blogspot.com/2008/01/sub-prime-mortgage-crisis-has-spilled.html.

6. William Cohan, "A Tsunami of Excuses," *New York Times*, March 11, 2009.

7. Quoted in Kevin Phillips, *Bad Money: Reckless Finance, Failed Politics, and the Global Crisis of American Capitalism* (New York: Viking, 2008), 180.

8. Thomas L. Friedman, "Palin's Kind of Patriotism," *New York Times*, October 7, 2008.

9. David Brooks, "Greed and Stupidity," *New York Times*, April 2, 2009.

10. Bill Marsh, "A History of Home Values," *New York Times*, August 26, 2006, http://graphics8.nytimes.com/images/2006/08/26/weekinreview/27leon_graph2.large.gif.

11. Joe Nocera, "The Big Lie," *New York Times*, December 23, 2011. Italics mine.

12. Duhigg, "Pressured to Take More Risk."

13. Jo Becker, Sheryl Gay Stolberg, and Stephen Labaton, "White House Philosophy Stoked Mortgage Bonfire," *New York Times*, December 21, 2008.

14. Editorial, "Don't Blame the New Deal," *New York Times*, September 28, 2008.

15. Phil Angelides, *"Fannie, Freddie and the Financial Crisis,"Bloomberg View*, August 3, 2011, http://www.bloomberg.com/news/2011-08-04/fannie-freddie-role-in-the-financial-crisis-commentary-by-phil-angelides.html.

16. The critical work was done by Fischer Black, Myron Scholes, and, later, Robert Merton. Scholes and Merton shared the Nobel Prize in Economics for 1997.

17. Gretchen Morgenson, "Was There a Loan It Didn't Like?," *New York Times*, November 11, 2008.

18. Michael Lewis, "The End," Portfolio.com, November 11, 2008, http://www.portfolio.com/news-markets/national-news/portfolio/2008/11/11/The-End-of-Wall-Streets-Boom.

19. Roger Altman, "Recent Financial Market Disruptions: Implications for the Economy and American Families," Brookings Institution, September 26, 2007, www.brookings.edu/projects/hamiltonprojectevents.

20. Alan Greenspan, testimony before the Senate Committee on Banking, Housing and Urban Affairs, Washington, DC, July 16, 2002, http://www.federalreserve.gov/boarddocs.

21. Dean Baker, *Plunder and Blunder: The Rise and Fall of the Bubble Economy* (San Francisco: Berrett-Kochler, 2009), 75.

22. Robert Shiller. *Irrational Exuberance* (New York: Crown, 2006), xiii.

23. Edmund L. Andrews, "Greenspan Concedes Error on Regulation," *New York Times*, October 23, 2008.

24. Alan Greenspan, *Age of Turbulence: Adventures in a New World* (New York: Penguin Press, 2002), 508.

25. Alan Greenspan, "The Challenge of Central Banking in a Democratic Society," speech to American Enterprise Institute, December 5, 1996.

26. Robert Rubin, *In an Uncertain World: Tough Choices from Wall Street to Washington* (New York: Random House, 2003), 257–258.

27. Lewis, "The End."

28. Robert Shiller, "Challenging the World in Whispers, Not Shouts," *New York Times*, November 2, 2008.

29. Gretchen Morgenson, "Seeing versus Doing," *New York Times*, September 26, 2010.

30. Gretchen Morgenson, "Raters Ignored Proof of Unsafe Loans, Panel Is Told," *New York Times*, September 26, 2010.

31. Binyamin Appelbaum, "Inside the Fed in 2006: A Coming Crisis, and Banter," *Washington Post*, January 12, 2012.

32. Robert O'Harrow Jr. and Jeff Gerth, "As Crisis Loomed, Geithner Pressed but Fell Short," *Washington Post*, April 3, 2009.

33. Jo Becker and Gretchen Morgenson, "Geithner, Member and Overseer of Finance Club," *New York Times*, April 26, 2009.

34. Anthony Faiola, Ellen Nakashima, and Jill Drew, "What Went Wrong," *Washington Post*, October 15, 2008.

35. Peter S. Goodman, "Taking Hard New Look at Greenspan Legacy," *Washington Post*, October 8, 2008.

36. Nelson D. Schwartz and Eric Dash, "Where Was the Wise Man?," *New York Times*, April 27, 2008.

37. Michlyo Nakamoto and David Wighton,"Citigroup Chief Stays Bullish on Buyouts," *Financial Times*, July 9, 2007.

38. Jo Becker and Gretchen Morgenson, "Geithner, Member and Overseer of Finance Club."

39. Gregg Easterbrook, "The Business of Politics," *Atlantic Monthly*, October 1986.

40. Ben Bernanke and Mark Gertler, "Monetary Policy and Asset Price Volatility," National Bureau of Economic Research working paper, February 2000; originally presented at the Federal Reserve Bank of Kansas City conference on "New Challenges for Monetary Policy," Jackson Hole, WY, August 26–28, 1999, https:www.nber.org/papers/w7559.

6. Obama

1. Barack Obama, Inaugural Address, January 20, 2009, http://www.whitehouse.gov/blog/inaugural-address.

2. David Corn, "Thank You, Wall Street. May We Have Another?," *Mother Jones*, January/February 2010.

3. Obama, Inaugural Address.

4. "Obama on 'Renewing the Economy,'" transcript of speech, *New York Times*, March 27, 2008.

5. Barack Obama, "House upon a Rock," speech at Georgetown University, April 14, 2009, http://www.whitehouse.gov/blog/09/04/14/The-House-Upon-a-Rock.

6. Gerald F. Seib, "In Crisis, Opportunity for Obama," *Wall Street Journal*, November 21, 2008.

7. Paul Krugman, "Falling into the Chasm," *New York Times*, October 24, 2010.

8. Martin Wolf, "Why Obama's Plan Is Still Inadequate and Incomplete," *Financial Times*, January 13, 2009.

9. "Larry Summers and Michael Steele," *This Week with Christiane Amanpour*, ABC News, February 8, 2009.

10. CNN Politics, Election Center, November 24, 2010, http://www.cnn.com/ELECTION/2010/results/polls.main.

11. Andrew Gelman, "Unsurprisingly, More People Are Worried about the Economy and Jobs Than about Deficit," *Statistical Modeling, Causal Interference, and Social Science*, June 19, 2010, http://www.stat.columbia

.edu/~cook/movabletype/archives/2010/06/unsurprisingly.html; Ryan Grim, "Mayberry Machiavellis: Obama Political Team Handcuffing Recovery," *Huffington Post*, July 6, 2010, http://www.huffingtonpost .com/2010/07/06/mayberry-machiavellis-oba_n_636770.html.

12. Grim, "Mayberry Machiavellis."

13. Ryan Lizza, "The Obama Memos," *New Yorker*, January 30, 2012.

14. Michael Luo, "In Banking, Rahm Emanuel Made Money and Connection," *New York Times*, December 3, 2008.

15. Nicholas Kristof, "Did We Drop the Ball on Unemployment?," *New York Times*, August 28, 2011.

16. Benjamin Applebaum and Helene Cooper, "White House Debates Fight Economy," *New York Times*, August 14, 2011.

17. Alan Simpson, "Social Security Is Like a Milk Cow with 310 Million Tits," CBS News, August 25, 2010.

18. Megan Carpenter, "Fiscal Commission Co-Chairs Simpson and Bowles Release Eye-Popping Recommendation," *Talking Points Memo*, November 10, 2010.

19. "Fed Downgrades Economic Forecast, Bernanke Vows to Do Everything,"ABC News, February 18, 2009.

20. Bob Ivry, Bradley Keoun, and Phil Kuntz, "Secret Fed Loans Gave Banks $13 Billion Undisclosed to Congress,"*Bloomberg Markets*, November 27, 2011, http://www.bloomberg.com/news/2011-11-28/secret-fed-loans-undisclosed-to-congress-gave-banks-13-billion-in-income.html.

21. Thomas M. Hoeing, "Too Big to Succeed," *New York Times*, December 1, 2010.

22. Eric Dash, "The Lucrative Fall from Grace," *New York Times*, September 30, 2011.

23. Susann Craig and Kevin Roose, "Wallets Out, Wall Street Dares to Indulge,"*New York Times*, November 23, 2010.

24. Phil Angelides, "Will Wall Street Ever Face Justice?," *New York Times*, March 2, 2012.

25. Gretchen Morgenson, "It Has a Fancy Name, But Will It Get Tough?," *New York Times*, January 28, 2012.

26. Gretchen Morgenson and Louise Story, "As Wall St. Polices Itself, Prosecutors Use Softer Approach," *New York Times*, July 7, 2011.

27. Peter Boone and Simon Johnson, "Will the U.S. Become the Next Ireland?," *New York Times*, March 18, 2010.

28. Sarah Murray and Douglas Belkin, "Americans Sour on Trade," *Wall Street Journal*, October 2, 2010.

29. Pew Research Center, "Public's Priorities for 2010: Economy, Jobs, Terrorism," January 25, 2010, http://www.people-press.org/2010/01/25/ publics-priorities-for-2010-economy-jobs-terrorism.

30. Ernest Hollings, "Against Jobs: Economy in Crisis," Economy in Crisis, January 7, 2010, http://www.economyincrisis.org.

31. "Reporters' Memo: "Bush's *NAFTA-Style Korea Free Trade Agreement Would Undermine Obama's Campaign Trade Reform Commitments*," *Public Citizen*, November 9, 2010, http://www.citizen.org/documents/g20-korea-obama-comparison-memo.pdf.

32. Robert E. Scott, "Free Trade Agreement with Korea Will Cost U.S. Jobs," Economic Policy Institute, July 1, 2010, http://www.epi.org/publication/free_trade_agreement_with_korea_will_cost_u-s-_jobs.

33. Russell Gold, "Overrun by Chinese Rivals, US Solar Company Falters," *Wall Street Journal*, August 17, 2011.

34. David Barboza, "Bridge Comes to San Francisco with a Made in China Label," *New York Times*, June 25, 2011.

35. Ariana Eunjung Cha, "A King Statue 'Made in China?,'" *Washington Post*, August 15, 2007.

7. The Shaky Case for Optimism

1. The full text of the 2011 State of the Union address can be found online at http://www.whitehouse.gov/state-of-the-union-2011.

2. Barack Obama, State of the Union Address, January 24, 2012, http://www.whitehouse.gov/state-of-the-union-2012.

3. E. J. Dionne Jr., "Off-Message, Biden Recasts the Obama Agenda," *Washington Post*, February 4, 2010. Italics in original.

4. Quoted in Geoffrey Wheatcroft, "The Voice of Unconventional Wisdom," *New York Review*, November 11, 2010.

5. Fareed Zakaria, *The Post-American World* (New York: W.W. Norton, 2008), 15.

6. Ibid, 205.

7. David Brooks, "Relax, We'll Be Fine," *New York Times*, April 5, 2010.

8. John Schmitt, "How Well Have Americans Been Doing," *Challenge*, September-October 2010.

9. Stephen Rose, *Rebound: Why America Will Emerge Stronger from the Financial Crisis* (New York: St. Martin's Press, 2010), 223.

10. Ibid, 177.

11. Joel Kotkin, *The Next Hundred Million: America in 2050* (New York: Penguin Press, 2010), 13.

12. Anne-Marie Slaughter, "America's Edge," *Foreign Affairs*, January/February 2009), http://www.foreignaffairs.com/articles/63722/anne-marie-slaughter/americas-edge.

13. Ibid.

14. Ibid.

15. Charles Duhigg and Keith Bradsher, "How U.S. Lost Out on iPhone Work," *New York Times*, January 21, 2012.

16. Ibid.

17. Ibid.

18. Ibid.

19. Ibid.

20. Ibid.

21. Janine Wedel, *Shadow Elite: How the World's New Power Brokers Undermine Democracy, Government, and the Free Market* (New York: Basic Books, 2009), Kindle edition, preface.

22. George Friedman, *The Next Hundred Years: Forecast for the 21st Century* (New York: Doubleday, 2009), Kindle edition, chapter 5.

23. Martin Jacques, *When China Rules the World* (New York: Penguin Press, 2009), Kindle edition, chapter 1.

24. Ibid.

25. Paul Starobin, *After America: Narratives for the Next Global Age* (New York: Viking Penguin, 2009).

26. Tom Tancredo, 2007 Republican Debate in South Carolina, May 15, 2007, www.ontheissues.org/house/Tom_Tancredo_Homeland_Security.htm.

27. Starobin, *After America*, chapter 7.

28. Ibid., chapter 12.

29. PRNewswire press release, April 8, 2007, www.prnewswire.com/news-releases/newsweek-cover-save-the-planet—or-else-57933962.html.

30. Starobin, *After America*, chapter 12.

31. David Brooks, "The Talent Magnet," *New York Times*, January 24, 2011.

32. Starobin, *After America*, chapter 12.

33. Brooks, "The Talent Magnet."

34. James Quinn, "California Is a Greater Risk Than Greece, Warns JP Morgan Chief," *The (UK) Telegraph*, February 26, 2010.

8. The Politics of Austerity

1. Paul Krugman, "The New Voodoo," *New York Times*, December 30, 2010.

2. *Economic Report of the President*, 2011, http://www.gpoaccess.gov/eop/download.html.

3. A. Gary Shilling, *The Age of Deleveraging: Investment Strategies for a Decade of Slow Growth and Deflation* (Hoboken, NJ: John Wiley & Sons, 2011), Kindle edition, chapter 9.

4. Fareed Zakaria, "How to Restore the American Dream," *Time*, October 21, 2010.

5. Ari Berman, "The Austerity Class," *Nation*, November 7, 2011.

6. Patrick Gavin, "Carville: Obama Needs a Pair," *Politico Click*, November 18, 2010, http://www.politico.com/click/stories/1011/carville_obama_needs_some_balls.html.

7. Mark Lilla, "The President and the Passions," *New York Times*, December 17, 2010.

8. Dana Milbank, "Obama Lost in Thought," *Washington Post*, April 26, 2001.

9. Marshall Ganz, "How Obama Lost His Voice and How He Can Get It Back," *Los Angeles Times*, November 10, 2010.

10. Eric Alterman, "Kabuki Democracy: Why a Progressive Presidency Is Impossible, for Now," *Nation*, July 7, 2010.

11. Gar Alperovitz and Jeff Faux, *Rebuilding America: A Blueprint For The New Economy* (New York: Pantheon Books, 1984), 177–178.

12. In December 2010, Rattner and the state agreed to a $10 million fine and a five-year ban on participating in any pension-fund business. The *New York Times* reported that Rattner's personal net worth was somewhere between $188 and $608 million.

13. Steven Rattner, *Overhaul: An Insider's Account of the Obama Administration's Emergency Rescue of the Auto Industry* (New York: Houghton Mifflin Harcourt, 2010), Kindle edition, chapter 4.

14. Office of the Special Inspector General for the Troubled Asset Relief Program, *"Factors Affecting the Decisions of General Motors and Chrysler to Reduce Their Dealership Networks,"* Washington, DC, July 19, 2010, http://www.sigtarp.gov/reports/audit/2010.

15. Rattner, *Overhaul*, Kindle edition, chapter 5.

16. Louis Uchitelle, "G.M. Seeks More Imports from Low-Wage Regions," *New York Times*, May 17, 2009.

17. Rattner, *Overhaul*, Kindle edition, chapter 9.

18. *Citizens United v. Federal Election Commission*, 558 U.S. 08-205 (2010).

19. Peter H. Stone, "Democrats and Republicans Alike Are Exploiting New Fundraising Loopholes," Center for Public Integrity, July 27, 2011, http://www.iwatchnews.org/2011/07/27/5409/democrats-and-republicans-alike-are-exploiting-new-fundraising-loophole.

20. Bill McKibben, "The U.S. Chamber of Commerce Darkens the Skies," *America Revealed*, March 31, 2011, http://www.spaulforrest.com/2011/03/us-chamber-of-commerce-darkens-skies.html.

21. Sarah Frier, "Insurers Profit Health Law They Fought Against," Bloomberg, January 5, 2012, http://www.bloomberg.com/news/2012-01-05/health-insurer-profit-rises-as-obama-s-health-law-supplies-revenue-boost.html.

22. Dan Eggen and T. W. Farnam, "Election 2010: Spending in Midterm Campaigns Could Affect 2012 Race," *Washington Post*, November 2, 2010.

23. Fredreka Schouten and Gregory Korte, "Conservatives Outspent Liberals 2–1 in Elections," *USA Today*, November 4, 2010.

24. Janet Malcolm, "Comedy Central on the Mall," *New York Review of Books*, December 9, 2010.

25. Chris Hedges, "This Is What Revolution Looks Like," *Truthdig*, November 15, 2011, http://www.truthdig.com/report/item/this_is_what_revolution_looks_like_20111115.

26. Kalle Lash and Micah White, "Why Occupy Wall Street Will Keep Up the Fight," *Washington Post*, November 17, 2011.

9. Grand Bargain? A Done Deal

1. "Mitch McConnell: Top Priority, Make Obama a One Term President," December 7, 2010, video clip, http://www.youtube.com/watch?v=W-A09a_gHJc.

2. "Udall Co-Sponsors Balanced Budget Amendment: Requiring a Balanced Federal Budget Is One Important Tool to Restore Fiscal Responsibility," Mark Udall, United States Senator for Colorado, February 1, 2011, http://markudall.senate.gov/?p=press_release&id=893.

3. Andrew J. Bacevich, "To the Shores of (and Skies above) Tripoli," *Tomdispatch* (blog), April, 12, 2011, http://www.tomdispatch.com/archive/175378.

4. James Mann, review of *The World America Made*, by Robert Kagan, *Washington Post*, March 8, 2012.

5. Elisabeth Bumiller and Thom Shanker, "Obama Puts His Stamp on Strategy for a Leaner Military," *New York Times*, January 5, 2012.

6. Andrew Bacevich, *The Limits of Power* (New York: Metropolitan Books, 2008), 135.

7. Progress in Action, "Legislation Introduced to Remove Private Military Contractors from Wars," January 23, 2010, http://www.progressinaction.com/afghanistan/legislation-introduced-to-remove-private-military-contractors-from-wars/.

8. Nick True, *The Complex: How the Military Invades Our Everyday Lives* (New York: Metropolitan Books, 2008), 87.

9. Greg Jaffe, "A Decade after the 9/11 Attacks, Americans Live in an Era of Endless War," *Washington Post*, September 4, 2011.

10. Anne-Marie Slaughter, "The End of Twentieth-Century Warfare," Royal United Services Institute, September 2, 2011, http://www.rusi .org/analysis/commentary/ref:C4e60f5608d2f5.

11. Alan Greenspan, *The Age of Turbulence* (New York: Penguin, 2007), 463.

12. Scott Wilson and Greg Jaffe, "In Creating New Defense Strategy, Obama Attempts to Outflank Congress," *Washington Post*, January 7, 2012.

13. Michael Wines, "U.S. Alarmed by Harsh Tone of China's Military," *New York Times*, October 11, 2010.

14. Ambrose Evans-Pritchard, "Appeasement Is the Proper Policy towards Confucian China," *Telegraph (UK)*, January 23, 2011.

15. Andrew Krepinevich, "Panetta's Challenge," *Washington Post*, July 15, 2011.

16. Viola Gienger and Tony Capaccio, "China's Carrier Poses Mostly Symbolic Threat, U.S. Admiral Says," Bloomberg, April 12, 2011, http://www.bloomberg.com/news/2011-04-12/china-s-soviet-era-carrier-poses-mostly-symbolic-threat-u-s-admiral-says.html.

17. Philip Mattera, Thomas Cafcas, Leigh McIlvaine, Andrew Seifter, and Kasia Tarczynska, "Money for Something: Job Creation and Job Quality Standards in State Economic Development Subsidy Programs," Good Jobs First, December 2011, http://www.goodjobsfirst.org/sites/default/files/docs/pdf/moneyforsomethingexecsum.pdf.

18. Motoko Rich, "Private Sector Gets Job Skills; Public Gets Bill," *New York Times*, January 7, 2012.

19. Mattera, Cafcas, McIlvaine, Seifter, and Tarczynska, "Money for Something."

20. Zaid Jilani, "Tennessee Firefighters Let Family's Home Burn Down Because They Didn't Pay Subscription Fee," *Think Progress* (blog), December 6, 2011, http://thinkprogress.org/special/2011/12/06/383580/tennesee-fire-fighters-family-home-burn/?mobile=nc.

21. A. G. Sulzberger, "Facing Cuts, a City Repeals Its Domestic Violence Law," *New York Times*, October 11, 2011.

22. Jeffrey H. Keefe, "False Savings: How Cutting Police Budgets and Laying off Cops in High-Crime Cities Lacks Economic, Social, and Common Sense," Economic Policy Institute, June 21, 2011, http://www.epi .org/publication/false_savings. Crime rates in the short run are affected by factors aside from economic stress, including how they are reported. One effect of cutbacks in police department personnel is that many crimes will simply not be reported, which in some areas is already a device for lowering the public's perception of its safety. See Al Baker and Joseph Goldstein, "Police Tactic: Keeping Crime Reports off the Books," *New York Times*, December 30, 2011.

10. Flickering Hope

1. Sheryl Gay Stolberg, "Obama and Jeb Bush Visit a Miami School," *New York Times*, March 4, 2011.

2. John Michael Lee Jr. and Anita Rawls, "The College Completion Agenda: 2010 Progress Report," College Board Advocacy and Policy Center, 2010, http://completionagenda.collegeboard.org/sites/default/files/reports_pdf/Progress_Executive_Summary.pdf.

3. Delta Project on Postsecondary Education Costs, "Trends in College Spending, 1999–2009," September 2011, http://www.deltacostproject.org/resources/pdf/Trends2011_Final_090711.pdf.

4. Organisation for Economic Co-operation and Development, Programme for International Student Assessment, 2009 database. "Figure 1: What Students Know and Can Do: Student Performance in Reading, Mathematics and Science," http://www.oecd.org/dataoecd/54/12/46643496.pdf.

5. Richard Rothstein, "How to Fix Our Schools," Economic Policy Institute, October 14, 2010, http://www.epi.org/publication/ib286.

6. Elise Gould, "High-Scoring Low-Income Students No More Likely to Complete College Than Low-scoring Rich Students," Economic Policy Institute, March 9, 2012, http://www.epi.org/blog/college-graduation-scores-income-levels/.

7. Matt Miller, "Obama's Rhetoric-Reality Gap on School," *Washington Post*, March 16, 2011.

8. Diane Ravitch, "The Myth of Charter Schools: The Inconvenient Truth behind 'Waiting for Superman,'" *New York Review of Books*, November 11, 2010.

9. Ibid.

10. Alex Molnar, "Tracking Commercialization Activities in America's Schools," Campaign for a Commercial-Free Childhood, http://www.commercialfreechildhood.org/articles/5thsummit/molnar.htm (accessed January 15, 2012).

11. Peter Goodman, "In Hard Times, Lured into Trade School and Debt," *New York Times*, March 13, 2010.

12. Tamar Lewin, "Burden of College Loans on Graduates Grows," *New York Times*, April 11, 2011.

13. Goodman, "In Hard Times."

14. Steven Mufson, "TV Stations, Kaplan Unit Boost Washington Post Co. Earnings," *Washington Post*, November 6, 2010.

15. Steven Mufson and Jia Lynn Yang, "The Trials of Kaplan Higher Ed and the Education of the Washington Post Co.," *Washington Post*, April 9, 2011.

16. Stephanie Strom, "For Charter School Company, Issues of Money and Control," *New York Times*, April 23, 2010.

17. Ibid.

18. JPMorgan Chase. "JPMorgan Chase Creates $325 Million Funding Initiative for High-Performing Charter Schools," press release, May 4, 2010, http://investor.shareholder.com/jpmorganchase/releasedetail.cfm?releaseid=466384.

19. Joy Resmovits, "Murdoch Education Affiliate's $2.7 Million Consulting Contract Approved by New York City," Huffington Post, July 15, 2011, http://www.huffingtonpost.com/2011/07/15/murdoch-education-affiliate-contract-approved_n_900379.html.

20. Trip Gabriel, "More Pupils Are Learning Online, Fueling Debate on Quality," *New York Times*, April 5, 2011.

21. Ibid.

22. Christopher Steiner, *$20 per Gallon: How the Inevitable Rise in the Price of Gasoline Will Change Our Lives for the Better* (New York: Grand Central, 2009), 158.

23. Paul Davidson, "Some Manufacturing Heads Back to USA," *USA Today*, August 6, 2010.

24. Yuqing Zing and Neal Detert, "How iPhone Widens the US Trade Deficits with PRC," National Graduate Institute for Policy Studies, November 2010, http://www3.grips.ac.jp/~pinc/data/10-21.pdf.

25. GalaxE.Solutions website, http://www.galaxesolutions.com/html/about/index.html (accessed January 11, 2012).

26. Mary Williams Walsh, "Pension Funds Are Adding Risk to Raise Returns," *New York Times*, March 3, 2010.

27. Azam Ahmed, "Bank Said No? Hedge Funds Fill a Void in Lending," *New York Times*, June 8, 2011.

28. Thomas I. Palley, "The Economic and Geo-Political Implications of China-Centric Globalization," The New America Foundation, February 2012, http://newamerica.net/publications/policy/the_economic_and_geo_political_implications_of_china_centric_globalization_0.

11. From Service to Servitude

1. John Irons, "Economic Scarring: The Long-Term Impacts of the Recession," Economic Policy Institute, September 30, 2009, http://www.epi.org/publication/bp243.

2. Lisa B. Kahn, "The Long-Term Labor Market Consequences of Graduating from College in a Bad Economy" (master's thesis, Yale University,

2009), http://mba.yale.edu/faculty/pdf/kahn_longtermlabor.pdf; see also Till von Wachter, Jae Song, and Joyce Manchester, "Long-Term Earning Losses Due to Mass Layoffs during the 1982 Recession: An Analysis Using U.S. Administrative Data from 1974 to 2004," Columbia University, April 2009, http://www.columbia.edu/~vw2112/papers/mass_layoffs_1982.pdf.

3. Don Peck, "How a New Joblessness Era Will Transform America," *Atlantic*, March 2011.

4. Ibid.

5. Suzy Khimm, "How Unemployment Hurts Children and Suppresses Academic Achievement," *Washington Post*, September 1, 2011.

6. Catherine Rampell, "Worry about a Wave of Layoffs," *New York Times*, September 20, 2011.

7. Elise Gould, Kai Filion, and Andrew Green, "The Need for Paid Sick Days," Economic Policy Institute, June 29, 2011, http://www.epi.org/publication/the_need_for_paid_sick_days.

8. Jason Deparle, Robert Gebeloff, and Sabrina Tavernise, "Older, Suburban and Struggling, 'Near Poor' Startle the Census," *New York Times*, November 18, 2011.

9. Louis Uchitelle, "Factory Jobs Gain, But Wages Retreat," *New York Times*, December 19, 2011.

10. Alan S. Blinder, "Preparing America's Workforce: Are We Looking in the Rear-View Mirror?" Working Paper No. 135, Center for Economic Policy Studies, Princeton University, October 2006, http://www.princeton.edu/~blinder/papers/pdf. Italics mine.

11. William J. Baumol and William G. Bowen.*Performing Arts: The Economic Dilemma* (New York: Twentieth Century Fund, 1966).

12. Matthew Yglesias, "The Yoga Instructor Economy," *ThinkProgress* (blog), March 7, 2011, http://thinkprogress.org/yglesias/2011/03/07/200135/the-yoga-instructor-economy.

13. Walter Russell Mead, "Where Are the Jobs?" *Via Meadia* (blog), American Interest, July 29, 2011, http://blogs.the-american-interest.com/wrm/2011/07/29/where-are-the-jobs.

14. Arne Kalleberg, *Good Jobs, Bad Jobs: The Rise of Polarized and Precarious Employment Systems in the United States, 1970s–2000s* (New York: Russell Sage Foundation, 2011).

15. Blinder, "Fear of Offshoring."

16. "Social Security Replacing Smaller Portions of Workers' Income," Economic Policy Institute, January 20, 2011, http://www.epi.org/economic_snapshots/entry/social_security_replacing_smaller_portions_of_workers_income.

17. Christopher Steiner, *$20 Per Gallon: How the Inevitable Rise in the Price of Gasoline Will Change Our Lives for the Better* (New York: Grand Central Publishing, 2009), 57.

18. Jeff Deeney, "Why Small-Town America Is Drowning in Drugs," AlterNet, February 21, 2012, http://www.alternet.org/story/154219/why_small-town_america_is_drowning_in_drugs.

19. Barbara Ehrenreich, *Nickel and Dimed* (New York: Metropolitan Books, 2001), 9.

12. Hope, from the Ashes of No Hope

1. Martin Fackler, "Japan Goes from Dynamic to Disheartened," *New York Times*, October 17, 2010.

2. Naomi Klein, "Capitalism vs. the Climate," *Nation*, November 28, 2011.

3. "Bank Bailouts Supporter Palin Criticizes TARP as 'Crony Capitalism,' 'Slush Fund . . . Just As We Had Been Warned About,' " Media Matters, February 6, 2010, http://mediamatters.org/mmtv/201002060024.

4. John Nichols, "Rick Perry's Attack on Democracy," *Nation*, October 10, 2011, http://www.thenation.com/article/163548/rick-perrys-attack-democracy.

5. Mark Danner, "State of Exception," *New York Review of Books*, October 13, 2011.

6. Chris Hedges, "American Psychosis," Share the World's Resources, June 24, 2010, http://www.stwr.org/united-states-of-america/american-psychosis.html.

7. Duha Tore Altindag and Naci H. Mocan, "Joblessness and Perceptions about the Effectiveness of Democracy," NBER Working Paper No. 15994, National Bureau of Economic Research, May 2010. Cited in Robert J. Shiller, "The Fire Bell of Unemployment," *New York Times*, November 26, 2011.

8. Lydia Saad, "Americans Divided on Taxing the Rich to Redistribute Wealth," Gallup.com, June 2, 2011, http://www.gallup.com/poll/147881/americans-divided-taxing-rich-redistribute-wealth.aspx.

9. Thomas Edsall, "The Future of the Obama Coalition," *New York Times*, November 27, 2011.

10. Ibid.

11. Eric Alterman, "Governor Cuomo Is Still Governor One Percent," *Nation*, December 21, 2011.

12. Dan Eggen, "Poll: Large Majority Opposes Supreme Court's Decision on Campaign Financing," *Washington Post*, February 17, 2010.

13. Tom Cole, "Barack Obama's $745 Million 2008 Campaign Ended Public Financing," *U.S. News & World Report*, April 11, 2011.

14. Several different bills have been introduced to Congress. For a comparative list, see Greg Colvin, "How to Choose? So Many Constitutional Amendments . . . ," Campaign for America's Future (blog), December 19, 2011, http://www.ourfuture.org/blog-entry/2011125119/how-choose-so-many-constitutional-amendments.

Index